AIRCREW
UNLIMITED

By the same author
The Big Drop
The Day of the Typhoon
Hurricanes Over Murmansk
Whittle—the true story
...So Few
Freedom to Forget (play)

Patrick Stephens Limited, a member of the Haynes Publishing Group, has published authoritative, quality books for enthusiasts for a quarter of a century. During that time the company has established a reputation as one of the world's leading publishers of books on aviation, maritime, military, model-making, motor cycling, motoring, motor racing, railway and railway modelling subjects. Readers or authors with suggestions for books they would like to see published are invited to write to: The Editorial Director, Patrick Stephens Limited, Sparkford, Nr. Yeovil, Somerset BA22 7JJ.

AIRCREW
UNLIMITED

The Commonwealth Air Training Plan during World War 2

JOHN GOLLEY
FOREWORD BY LORD BARBER

Patrick Stephens Limited

First published in 1993

British Library Cataloguing-in-Publication Data
A catalogue record for this book is available from the British Library

ISBN 1 85260 243 0

Library of Congress catalog card number 93-78064

Typeset by BPCC Techset, Exeter
Printed and bound in Great Britain by
Butler & Tanner Ltd, Frome and London

Contents

Foreword

WHEN JOHN GOLLEY first mentioned this book to me, I have to admit that my immediate thought was of ploughing through a rather dreary, specialist account of flying training during the Second World War. Instead, as I became immersed in it, I found it a truly fascinating story—a mixture of hard facts and personal reminiscences.

At one point the author quotes from a Top Secret and Personal message from Churchill to selected Commonwealth Prime Ministers, in which he explains why there was a requirement for 'not less than 20,000 pilots and 30,000 personnel of aircrews *annually*'. So much for high strategy, but what of the individuals involved? The great merit of this book is that it is not concerned only with politics, administration and statistics. Throughout the book the story is interspersed with the intimate recollections of those who trained overseas. We feel the elation of the pilot on being told that he had got his wings and we share the dismay of the one who was washed out.

This book fills a gap in the history of the RAF—and it is also a 'good read'!

The Rt-Hon. Lord Barber PC TD DL

Acknowledgements

I WORKED IN association with Francis Butcher CBE AFC, an ex-regular RAF and Colonial officer with a lively legal mind and a vast experience in flying training. He had spent six years researching and writing a document entitled 'Vital Command', putting into perspective the importance of flying training in the Royal Air Force, and its vital contribution to achieving command of the air during the Second World War. Generously, he handed this over to me and we co-operated in using his material for the basis of this book.

Likewise Hugh Morgan, who spent five years investigating the experiences of those who had volunteered for pilot training in the RAF and were sent overseas. Hugh is a graduate of both Cardiff and Warwick Universities and an aviation enthusiast. His father was a World War Two pilot who trained in Ponca City, Oklahoma, USA, and his uncle was an observer. Hugh very kindly gave me access to his many files, and helped with photographs and other material. Photographs were also kindly provided by Jack Bains, Adolf Galland, Francis Butcher, Derek Wilkins, John Gibson, Tony Millard, 'Sheep' Milne, Richard Riding, Norman Bate, Marion Stevens, John Evans, Ken Rimmell and Phil Murton.

I should also like to thank Generalleutnant Adolf Galland and Wolfgang Falck for their contributions to Luftwaffe training. Special mention must also be made of Michael Pierce for his splendid silhouettes which are so evocative. Finally, my thanks to my great friend Bill Gunston for providing research material, editing, and his renowned expertise.

John Golley

Glossary

ACDC	Aircrew Despatch Centre
ACHU	Aircrew Holding Unit
ACH GD	Aircraft Hand General Duties
ACRC	Aircrew Reception Centre
AFC	Air Force Cross
AFU	Advanced Flying Unit
AG	Air Gunner
ANS	Air Navigation School
AOC	Air Officer Commanding
AS	Air School
ATA	Air Transport Auxiliary
BAT	Beam Approach Training
BFTS	British Flying Training School
C-in-C	Commander-in-Chief
CATP	Commonwealth Air Training Plan
CFI	Chief Flying Instructor
CFS	Central Flying School
CO	Commanding Officer
CPR	Canadian Pacific Railway
DFC	Distinguished Flying Cross
DFM	Distinguished Flying Medal
DHSS	Department of Health and Social Security
DRO	Daily Routine Orders
DSC	Distinguished Service Cross
DSO	Distinguished Service Order
EATS	Empire Air Training Scheme
EFTS	Elementary Flying Training School
ETPS	Empire Test Pilot School
FAA	Fleet Air Arm
FIS	Flying Instructor School
Flt. Lt.	Flight Lieutenant
Flt. Sgt.	Flight Sergeant
FO	Flying Officer
FTC	Flying Training Command

FTS	Flying Training School
GCA	Ground Control Approach
GD	General Duties Pilot
Gosport tube	Direct voice communication tube between instructor and pupil
GR	General Reconnaissance
GTS	Glider Training School
HQ	Headquarters
IFTC	Imperial Forces Transit Camp
ITW	Initial Training Wing
JATP	Joint Air Training Plan (South Africa, 1941–6)
KDs	Khaki Drill
LAC	Leading Aircraftman
Lend-Lease	A scheme whereby the US Government lent equipment and resources (including aeroplanes) to the UK on a lease basis, these to be returned at the end of hostilities
Lt.-Col.	Lieutenant-Colonel
Lt.-Cdr	Lieutenant-Commander
MOD	Ministry of Defence
OC	Officer Commanding
OCTU	Officer Cadet Training Unit
OTU	Operational Training Unit
PDC	Personnel Despatch Centre
PO	Pilot Officer
QDM	Directional marker
RAAF	Royal Australian Air Force
RAF	Royal Air Force
RAFVR	Royal Air Force Volunteer Reserve
RATG	Rhodesian Air Training Group
RATW	Rhodesian Air Training Wing
RCAF	Royal Canadian Air Force
RFC	Royal Flying Corps
RN	Royal Navy
RNAS	Royal Naval Air Service
R/T	Radio Telephone
SAAF	South African Air Force
SBA	Standard Beam Approach
SFTS	Service Flying Training School
Sqn/Ldr	Squadron Leader
SRAF	Southern Rhodesian Air Force
SRATG	Southern Rhodesia Air Training Group
USAAC	United States Army Air Corps
USAAF	United States Army Air Force
u/t	under training
VC	Victoria Cross
Wg/Cdr	Wing Commander
WOP	Wireless Operator
WOP/AG	Wireless Operator/Air Gunner

Prologue

IT WAS A warm, fine summer afternoon in mid-August 1940. Bob Stanford glanced at his watch and checked it with the clock on the wall, stifling a yawn. Another 15 minutes and he would be able to leave the financial department of the Surrey County Council. He made a pretence of checking the green Sundry Recoverable Accounts invoices on his desk, but his mind was elsewhere. His boss, Leonard Morling, had given him permission to leave work an hour early to collect his tennis kit from his home in Raynes Park, as he was playing for the County Council that evening. His tennis was not all that brilliant, but he had a date after the match with a girlfriend who was in a class of her own.

The long, rather narrow room housed 16 clerical officers, both male and female. He found them pleasant but rather dull, like his job of checking invoices for the princely sum of 17s 6d a week. Casual conversation was frowned upon, and his only escape from the interminable monotony was when he went upstairs to fetch tea and biscuits for the department, or slipped out for a pee.

At lunchtimes he would usually join Flexman from Audit, and Rowlands from Public Health. If it wasn't raining, the three of them would go down to the bank of the River Thames, eat sandwiches and study any female talent in the vicinity. Their common bond and mainspring in life was that all three had volunteered for pilot/navigator training in the RAFVR. Slaving away in County Hall was simply regarded as a way of filling in time until the RAF sent the anxiously awaited papers.

Dead on 3.45 pm Stanford, having stashed away his invoices and lit his pipe, got up from his desk and walked out, thanking his boss as he did so. Morling, bent over an enormous sheet of figures, merely nodded, wiping his mouth with his handkerchief. Stanford was always glad to get out of that stuffy old place, and he felt free strolling along Penryn Road towards Kingston station in the bright sunlight.

Threading his way through the narrow streets, with the strong smell from the tannery in his nostrils, he called in at the tobacconist's on the corner. Pulling out a ten-bob note, he bought an ounce of Bondman in a round red tin, and carefully checked his change. He had enough money for the evening, and for the Saturday-night flick with Jean, the sister of a sergeant pilot who was flying Hampden bombers.

The picturesque market place of Kingston-upon-Thames was busy with weekend shoppers as he made his way across the cobbles. He always enjoyed the bubbly atmosphere of that market with its Tudor trimmings and church spire in the background. Probably because he was a sentimentalist, he thought. Sometimes he wondered how he would get on in the RAF, being a sensitive and highly tuned person. But the mere thought of becoming a fighter pilot overrode any doubts.

Both he and Rowlands were of the same mind. They had talked about it often enough. Both considered themselves to be individualists, and fighters would give them more scope. The flying VCs of the First World War such as Captain Albert Ball, Billy Bishop, McCudden and the like, had become their heroes. They had an advantage over Flexman, who had never been airborne in his life, because they had both experienced a five-bob flip with Sir Alan Cobham's circus when they were boys. Stanford had been eight at the time, and he had been mad about flying ever since.

Flexman, being slightly older and more staid, thought that multi-engined aircraft would be more his style. They ribbed him about it, telling him that he didn't know what he was talking about, as he had never been up in the air. He took it philosophically as he was that sort of chap, a more placid character who never got ruffled, not even when both Stanford and Rowlands argued that flying was the only thing that mattered to them, and that the only reason Flexman had volunteered was to get his arse out of County Hall.

Stanford was catching an earlier train than usual, and there were few people about as he walked up the slope on to the platform. Most times they would be pouring out of the Hawker Aircraft factory just around the corner. He had often wondered why the Luftwaffe hadn't had a go at it, especially as Hurricane fighters were playing such a big part in the battle. The station Tannoy suddenly crackled, and he hurried down the platform, seeing the train slowly emerging from the bend like some green snake. The last two coaches were more convenient for him because of the exit at Raynes Park.

The compartment was empty, and he opened windows on both sides. The air was warm as he lit his pipe and settled down. Just as the train was about to leave, the door opened and a pretty girl asked him if it was going to Wimbledon. Always the gentleman and admirer of talent, he said, 'I hope so, because I'm getting out at Raynes Park.' Closing the door for her, he sat himself down in the far corner and fumbled for his matches. Usually it took two or three, and these he upturned and replaced in the box. One of his standard remarks was that he smoked matches because they were cheaper than tobacco.

The train whined its way towards Norbiton, and Stanford took a furtive glance at the girl when he thought she wasn't looking in his direction. She was wearing a primrose yellow summer dress, had red hair, slim ankles, and her face had small, delicate features with large eyes and a wide mouth. She opened her handbag as the train entered Norbiton station and looked at herself in a pocket mirror, moistening her lips as she did so.

A few doors slammed shut, and the train recharged its air brake system before gathering speed, which it did rather quickly. Stanford was using up some more matches trying to get his pipe alight in the draught from the open window, when the train slowed down before coming to a stop outside New Malden station. Stanford was engrossed with his pipe when he heard the sound of an aeroplane, and immediately looked out of the window.

Much to his astonishment, he saw a twin-engined aircraft circling round, flying at about 500 ft abeam of the train, and there was no doubt about its origin. The black cross on its fuselage was clearly visible, and he recognized it as a Dornier bomber. He had studied aircraft recognition, and there was no doubt in his mind. Its pencil shape and twin tail fins convinced him. For a few fleeting seconds he was fascinated, mesmerized by the sight of this German bomber flying so low, swanning around of its own free will. He wondered what the hell it was up to, and why our fighters hadn't dropped on it. He could see the crew inside quite clearly before it slowly banked, turning towards the railway line.

The German pilot opened up his throttles, and the vroom, vroom, desynchronized sound from his Bramo nine-cylinder air-cooled engines got much louder. Stanford, still in a semi-trance, suddenly realized that the German was going to have a go at the train. Then he saw stabbing lights flashing from the forward gun positions of the bomber, and yelled at the girl to get down on the floor.

She sat there rigid, and Stanford grabbed her and pulled her down on the floor. The staccato sound of machine-gun fire from the Dornier's nose and front cockpit was broken by screams, and the crunch of fragmented glass. As the Dornier roared overhead there were several crumps as bombs hit the ground.

Stanford had his arms above his head, and his shoulders across the girl. It had all happened so quickly that she hadn't had time to react, and he kept telling her to keep still. As the sound of the bomber started to fade, the bombs exploded one after another. A great wind swept through the open windows of the compartment and the coach rocked and jumped on the rails. Stanford and the girl were lifted up and dropped on the floor and she began to sob uncontrollably and shake. For a fleeting second there was an awful silence.

The air inside the compartment was filled with dust, and there were screams and cries for help as Stanford gingerly got up from the floor. He worked his jaw to clear his ears from the blast, but the girl was his main concern. Her face was white, and she was rigid with shock. Leaning out of the window he saw people scrambling out of the carriages on to the embankment. The impatient jangle of ambulance bells and the wail of police sirens added to the noise and confusion following the attack.

Gently he managed to lift the girl on to the seat. Her teeth were chattering and she had a vacant stare as if she was frozen stiff and incapable of any form of reaction. Taking off his jacket, he placed it around her shoulders. There was little he could do except rub her hands, put on an air of cheerfulness, and tell her not to worry because it was all over.

Stanford had no idea at the time that this affair was destined to go full circle as far as he was concerned. Certainly it made an impression on him. He had actually seen the crew of a Dornier bomber as it circled to attack, and the twinkling flashes from its nose guns as it dived on the train. Feeling no fear during those pulsating seconds had done a lot to boost his self-confidence. Perhaps being close to the girl and having to put on an act had had something to do with it. He didn't really know, but he was pleased with the way he had handled the situation. The event had created quite a stir in his part of the world, and he wasn't slow to give his chums at County Hall a somewhat exaggerated account of the action. Naturally, the girl featured prominently in the event!

He had to wait for several months before his RAFVR papers dropped through the letter box, and life in County Hall receded into obscurity. After a few hours' tuition in a Magister at 15 EFTS Kingstown, outside Carlisle, he was sent solo. The remainder of his EFTS and SFTS flying training was done in Canada, flying Canadian Tiger Moths and Harvard IIs. It took him a little over a year to win his wings, by courtesy of the Empire Air Training Plan (Canada adopted the title of the British Commonwealth Air Training Plan in June 1942).

While the New World had given him his wings, he achieved his great ambition to become a fighter pilot in the old, flying Hurricanes and then converting on to Typhoons, Stanford took part in offensive operations in northern Europe. It was on one particular day in the spring of 1943 when the wheel turned full circle.

The target was a château nestling behind the crossroads at Tilly, south of a line between Bayeux and Caen in Normandy. A German conference was scheduled for that particular day, and Group gave them permission to do a low-level attack. Cloud was forecast to be down to about 800 ft across the Channel and in the target area. This would provide cover if they ran into trouble. There were just two of them, Flying Officer Ramsey 'Sheep' Milne, a Canadian, and Stanford, who was then a sergeant pilot.

The two Typhoons took off from Westhampnett, a satellite of Tangmere, and set course for the French coast, flying at wave-top height in open formation. Cruising at over 300 miles an hour across the white horses of the Channel always thrilled Stanford. The sheer sensation of speed, and flying alongside a chum, made him feel good. Securely strapped into his cockpit, breathing oxygen, surrounded by armour plating, controlling the power of his mighty Sabre engine with one hand while handling the aircraft with the other, uplifted his ego. Yet it required his total concentration to keep station abreast of Sheep, flying slightly above him.

In mid-Channel a strong wind was blowing spray off the tops of the breakers, leaving salt trails on the windscreen. He caught a glimpse of the heaving deep-green sea in the troughs, bubbling with white froth like some devilish cauldron. As the big, bulbous-nosed Typhoons hurtled their way towards France, stabs of sunlight poked their way through the cloud, and he hoped like hell that the weather wasn't going to break up, leaving them exposed to the Luftwaffe. The fact that this show was going to be a swift in-and-out job—Tilly was only a few miles inland—was a comforting thought.

The coast of France, ornamented with clusters of little seaside towns, rushed towards them, and as they flashed over the beaches he spotted Arromanches over to his right. Good old Sheep's navigation had put them right on course and they were over the first hurdle. He adjusted his reflector gunsight automatically, and rotated his safety catch to the FIRE position. Both were maintaining strict R/T silence as they roared inland, heading south.

Whenever Stanford approached a target he became keyed-up, but he was usually too preoccupied to let it bother him. On this occasion, however, his hands felt clammy inside his gloves, and he could feel the sweat soaking his back. Subconsciously, he was aware that there were only two of them instead of a full squadron on this particular operation, and flying at low level made them particularly vulnerable to enemy flak. He found himself anxiously looking around, expecting to see the golden streaks of tracer coming at them like express trains. He was relieved to find Sheep taking full advantage of natural cover from the contours of the countryside, flying only a few feet above the pastoral scene.

Instant pictures of mushroom-shaped water towers, yellow fields of mustard, rich brown soil, tree-lined roads, lush green woods and ancient churches in grey granite villages all rushed past Stanford's windscreen as Sheep weaved his way towards their target. They were following a river when Stanford's earphones registered a sharp click, and he heard the Canadian say, 'Okay, Blue Two. Target dead ahead. Line abreast, go. Stand by to pull up. Am pulling up now.'

Now flying at about 400 ft, Sheep circled the château, which was half hidden in the woods but exposed by its drive-in and gateway edifice. No vehicles were parked, and there was no sign of life. Again he flew round, taking careful note of the château's position relative to the crossroads, and then called Stanford, 'That's it alright, Blue Two. Not even a sign of a pig's arse. Must be duff gen. No sense in hanging around here. Let's go and find ourselves some trade.'

The cloud base was lifting, and shafts of sunlight began brightening up the Normandy countryside. Sheep had turned west and Stanford could see a strip of blue sky ahead. The weather was coming in from the Atlantic, and he knew that their cloud cover would soon be blown away. He was catching glimpses of people waving to them when suddenly his R/T crackled into life. 'Blue Two. Army trucks at twelve o'clock. I'm going down. Cover me, over.' Instantly, Stanford flicked his transmission switch: 'Wilco, Blue One—out.'

Stanford circled, screwing his head round looking out for bandits, stealing odd glances at Sheep's Typhoon as he did so. The Krauts were sitting ducks as Sheep hurtled straight down on them, firing his four 20-mm cannons. Lorries swerved off the road into the wooded banks as the road became obliterated with black smoke and orange flashes. It was all over in seconds, and as Sheep joined up with Stanford an arc of tracer from the roadside curled its way lazily up in their direction. Sheep gave Stanford the thumbs-up and called, 'Okay, Blue Two. Let's go find something for you.'

The train was puffing its way along from Bayeux to Carentan, and they spotted it as they crossed the Forêt de Cerisy. 'It's all yours, Blue Two. You lucky bastard. You know the form. Go for the engine. I'll cover you, over.' Stanford came back, 'Roger, Blue One, out.'

Checking his gunsight and firing button, Stanford broke away from Sheep and commenced a shallow dive towards the train. He was lucky because the train had lost the cover of the woods, and was steaming along out in the open. As he lined his Typhoon up, positioning himself to make a quarter attack, the shooting started. The bloody tracer came up slowly at first, then whizzed past over his canopy. He had the engine firmly in his sights and, opening his throttle wide, he pressed his gun button, firing a long burst before breaking away in a steep, climbing turn. Looking back, he could see that the train had stopped, and steam was pumping out of the engine in all directions.

Suddenly Sheep appeared out of nowhere and he could see him alongside, with his oxygen mask dangling, grinning like a Cheshire cat. 'You got yourself a loco, Blue One. Jesus, did I give that gun crew the shits. Lit a fire under their arses. Right, let's get out of here.'

When they had returned to base and been debriefed, Stanford told Sheep that he had been on the receiving end of a Dornier bomber while sitting in a train. 'I was mesmerized by that damn bomber,' he said, 'seeing the crew inside the greenhouse as it banked. It wasn't until I saw flashes from its guns that I took my finger out and got cracking.' 'Yeah,' said Sheep, lighting up a Sweet Caporal. 'All I can say is that you've now got your own back for that one. Sure as hell you filled that bloody engine full of holes. When I saw the bastards shooting at you I gave 'em a dose of my medicine. Didn't want to lose my number two did I?'

Stanford had been flying a high-performance machine, the fastest fighter at low altitudes in the business at that time. Suffice it to say that his initial and Service training, which he completed some 6,000 miles from the UK in Canada in Indian territory, had been of a high standard. Subsequently, he took part in air-to-ground attack operations through-out the invasion of Europe, when his Typhoon IB was equipped with rocket projectiles.

Stanford and his associates were able to do their training undisturbed by enemy action, and in conducive climates. He was only one cadet among some 140,000 who received their wings and flying badges in the Dominions and America. They were products of a 'vital command', which mass-produced aircrews to feed the expansion of the RAF and

Dominion Air Forces. Most cadets, including pilots, navigators, bomb aimers, wireless operator/air gunners and air gunners, returned to the UK for advanced and operational training before joining squadrons. The emergence of the four-engined bombers in 1941, in line with the rapid development of Bomber Command, for example, demanded a great influx of aircrew for the huge offensives of 1943/4, as did the creation of Tactical Air Forces for the invasion of Europe. Fifty per cent of U-boats sunk in the Second World War were destroyed by aircraft, and Coastal Command, who had suffered shortages earlier, had to be supplied with more aircrews to man its more advanced long-range aircraft.

Thus the Empire Air Training Plan became a dominant factor in achieving victory in the air, and control of the air became the prime requirement for any invasion force. This narrative focuses the spotlight on the evolution of the great Scheme which enabled Stanford and his associates to play their role.

* * * * * *

THE TIMES

Letters to the Editor, December 1990

From Mr M. R. Hardwick QC

Sir, in the crisis of 1940, Britain did not stand completely alone because in September 1939 the old Dominions entered the war at once, voluntarily.

Dominion support included participation in the Empire Air Training Scheme. Commencing just over fifty years ago, from populations of about 19 million people of European race, the old Dominions provided 41 per cent of the total output of qualified aircrew. Altogether over 34,000 Dominion aircrew were killed, mostly in the air war against Germany and Italy. They have been described as 'amongst the finest and most highly-trained material in the British Empire'.

But it is impossible not to regret the apparent disinclination of British authorities to pay more regard to that enormous Dominion contribution and sacrifice by providing sufficient funds to widen displays at appropriate museums and at St Clement Danes (RAF) Church. Unlike those who served from Allied countries, the Books of Remembrance in that church do not identify the Dominions of origin of the airmen who fell.

There appears now to be an oblivion in Britain characterised by a lack of interest, will and money adequate to acknowledge such a debt of gratitude.

Yours sincerely,

MALCOLM HARDWICK,
Wentworth Chambers,
180 Phillip Street,
Sydney, Australia

Mr Hardwick's letter to *The Times* coincided with the 50th anniversary of the Empire Air Training Scheme. His points are well made: the fact that the Dominions provided nearly half the total output of qualified aircrew from a combined population of only 19 million, that over 34,000 Dominion aircrew were killed, and that Dominion aircrew were described as 'amongst the finest and most highly-trained material in the British Empire.' He points out that, regrettably, we in Britain have not even identified the Dominions of origin of the airmen who fell. It is hoped that this book will reawaken interest in the Scheme, and make people aware of the enormous contribution and sacrifice made by the Dominions.

Ironically, the Scheme is very much alive today amongst the surviving aircrew who participated. Their journey across the globe in their youth was undoubtedly an experience of a lifetime—so much so that, some 50 years later, reunions are still taking place throughout the Empire and Commonwealth. The Fifth Commonwealth Wartime Aircrew Reunion in Winnipeg, Canada, in September 1988, for example, attracted over 5,000 aircrew and their ladies from all parts of the Commonwealth and the Western world. In October 1991, on the other side of the globe, the third reunion was held in Cape Town, South Africa.

Over the past few years, aircrew associations have blossomed. There are currently over 90 branches and 12,000 members of the Aircrew Association, sponsoring the lively and well-produced quarterly magazine *Intercom*. This Association is international in character, with branches throughout the Empire and Commonwealth, America, France, Spain and Cyprus. Those who trained in America under the various schemes formed independent associations which are extremely active today. The Arnold Scheme Register, for example, was formed in 1986 as a society to extend wartime experience, and to register all who entered or related to the Scheme. Such associations and others like them cross-fertilize with their conterparts all over the world, maintaining a dialogue and arranging reciprocal visits.

Those who took part in the Empire Scheme are now in the evening of their lives. Their recollections and varied experiences in those faraway places inject life and reality into this book. The collation of these images also reflects the reception, hospitality and style of each country concerned during those war years, when air cadets continued to arrive from all parts of the globe and make their impact on the local community. Thus, apart from examining the statistics, aircrew training, aircraft types, and political and financial implications during the evolution of the Scheme, its theme becomes an ongoing human story.

While the prime function of the Plan was to train aircrews and technicians for offensive operations, instructors played a key role in the exercise. The valuable and sometimes dangerous service given by flying instructors and ground crews has to date received little distinction or credit. Their skills, views and attitudes when training men to go to war highlight the challenge faced by Flying Training Command.

This project was a gigantic and highly complex operation, with major political and economic overtones. At its peak it employed over 100,000 men and women in Canada alone, including some 12,800 civilians, operating 105 flying training schools and 184 support units. The Royal Air Force and the British Government were naturally prime movers in the exercise, and the Scheme reflected Flying Training Command's UK operation, format and style, except in the Towers and Arnold Schemes in the USA, which were strictly US Navy and US Army Air Force flying training operations.

This book tells the story. The evolution of the Scheme, against a background of doubt and uncertainty, unveils a fascinating glimpse of 'horse-trading' on a global scale. International currencies, lend-lease agreements, manufacturing opportunities, commercial gain, politics both local and national, Service rivalry, bureaucracy, and wheeler-dealing are all ingredients of the package which made up the Scheme. Sir Maurice Dean politely called it 'one of the most brilliant pieces of imaginative organization ever conceived'.

However, blood ties linking the 'Mother Country' to her Dominions and Commonwealth were strengthened by the advent of war. Only 21 years had elapsed since the end of the First World War, and tradition dies hard. When danger confronted Britain, this family association provided an impetus which overcame financial considerations. But the autocratic British attitude adopted by Lord Riverdale very nearly caused the Scheme to founder.

The end-product of the enterprise was the mass output of trained aircrew, and flying was the powerful magnet which attracted youth from all over the world. Flying provided the 'icing on the cake' during months of intensive training, and the ultimate challenge for all those involved. Personal experiences of what life was like while training thousands of miles from home are an integral part of the story.

1. A seed is sown: the background to the scheme

IN MID-1916 FIELD Marshal Haig asked for more Royal Flying Corps squadrons. He needed to increase his force to 56 squadrons by the spring of 1917, in preparation for the great Somme offensive. Flying training was rather primitive in those days. To qualify, a pilot had to have flown at least 15 hours solo, carried out a cross-country flight of 60 miles incorporating two landings, climbed to 6,000 ft, made a successful precautionary landing without engine, and made two night landings. Later, these qualifications were drastically reduced!

Skilled workmen were in short supply, not only for manufacturing the R.E.8s, Pups, Camels and other types of new aircraft, but also for servicing and maintaining aircraft needed for the expansion. Hilary St George Saunders, in his book *Per Ardua*, wrote that: 'Unskilled men were given special training, the Dominions were combed for suitable recruits, so were the ranks of the Army and the factories; *a number of squadrons, forerunners of the Empire Air Training Scheme of a generation later, were raised and maintained in Canada*' (italics mine).

So a small seed was planted in the New World in the middle of the First World War in aid of the Royal Flying Corps. Those concerned can have had no idea that they had pioneered a Plan which would yield a vast harvest during the Second World War some 24 years later!

By the mid-thirties events in Germany had proved so disturbing that aircrew training began to occupy the minds of senior officers. The expansion of the Royal Air Force began to gain a little momentum in 1934, the year that the Austrian Chancellor Dollfuss was murdered and Hitler became Dictator of Germany. In that year Air Commodore Arthur Tedder became Director of Air Training. He was deeply concerned when he found that only 300 pilots were scheduled for training over the next 12 months, and he said, 'The expansion of Service Squadrons must be based on a reasoned training expansion programme. If we attempt, as we did in the last War, to make our training programmes fit a hypothetical squadron expansion, we shall again fall between two stools, and secure neither the squadrons we want nor the training which is requisite.'

Trenchard had described training as 'that on which the whole future of the Royal Air Force depends', and Tedder thought likewise. However, Tedder's clear, analytical mind and his dogged perseverance failed to overcome opposition from Treasury officials. They weren't interested in the length of flying training, the extension of operational training by qualified instructors, or night flying (no night flying had been taught, even to those destined for bomber squadrons). They regarded the expansion of the RAF as a short-term consideration, not as a means towards creating a permanent, larger, highly efficient force. In consequence, all planning appeared to be on a contingency basis, and there was continual bickering and disagreement.

This pinch-penny and myopic attitude on the part of the Treasury, and Mr W. L. Scott in particular, continued until 1936 when war clouds began to gather. Germany repudiated the Locarno Treaty, then came the occupation and remilitarization of the Rhineland, while Italian troops occupied Addis Ababa. The likelihood of war breaking out brought with it a sense of urgency which hitherto had been lacking, even amongst Service chiefs. To ratify and implement any new proposals regarding training programmes during this period was a lengthy affair. The training process remained under five different Commands and two Departments of the Air Ministry until the summer of 1940, when it was at last co-ordinated into one Command and for the first time was directly represented on the Air Council!

As it became obvious that war was almost inevitable, intense expansion began to take place. Arrangements were made for civilian flying schools to provide three months *ab initio* training, while training at Service Flying Schools was cut to six months. The civilian scheme proved to be a great success, indirectly bringing back into service many experienced instructors who had previously served with the Royal Air Force.

On 30 July 1936 the Royal Air Force Volunteer Reserve was instituted as part of the RAF. Reservists were to train as weekend flyers with civil flying clubs at airfields near larger towns. The Treasury agreed that they should be paid a retaining fee, and ten shillings per day flying pay, providing they were subject to discipline and Service contract. The equation had to be balanced, as far as the Treasury was concerned. This was a real step forward, because it was agreed in principle that 800 reserve pilots should be trained each year for the next three years. Thirteen centres were set up in various parts of the country using existing airfields, and a further ten were under immediate consideration.

The Air Ministry was well aware that bad weather, cramped conditions and enemy action could seriously affect flying training in Britain. One incident proved the Air Ministry to be absolutely right about the vulnerability of airfields. It happened on 16 August 1940. Two Junkers 88s made a daring attack on the training airfield at Brize Norton in Oxfordshire. They approached with wheels down as if entering the circuit, and their bombs hit hangars crammed with fuelled-up aircraft: 46 were destroyed and seven damaged. Eleven Hurricanes at a maintenance unit on the airfield were also destroyed.

The British climate was another major factor which influenced flying training and caused the Air Ministry to consider overseas schemes. The majority of training aerodromes in Britain were grass, runways being comparatively new ideas in airfield construction, necessitated as they were by the arrival of heavy bombers with their greatly increased bomb loads. In consequence, any prolonged period of rain was likely to make aerodromes unserviceable. There were RAF flying training schools in Egypt (including the oldest Service flying school at Abu Sueir) which had more considerate climates; but the Air Ministry decided that, if war became inevitable, it would have to call in the New World to facilitate flying and technical personnel training on a vast scale.

In this context, and alongside the reserve schemes in progress, the Air Ministry had been investigating the possibility of flying training in Canada; Australia and New Zealand were considered too far away. The RAF had traditional ties with the Royal Canadian Air Force, as with other Empire Air Forces, which helped in lobbying the Canadian Government.

Several approaches were made to Canada in the mid-1930s. No part of the British Empire could match the inducements which Canada could offer: good flying conditions, especially during the long days; aircraft production facilities of her own, being in close proximity to the mighty industrial resources of the USA; and a strategic position within the Empire.

These probes, however, were vigorously opposed by the Canadian Government on the grounds that their sovereignty might be affected, and that their freedom to remain neutral in the event of war could be inhibited by the presence of a 'foreign' military force on Canadian soil.

This blunt rejection was understandable at that particular time. The Prime Minister, Mackenzie King, who had lost his office in 1930, had just been re-elected in 1935, when Canada was emerging from the depression of the early thirties. Although a modified scheme had been suggested, it would still have involved heavy capital expenditure, and Mackenzie King was facing both political and economic problems at home.

Despite these reservations, the Canadian Government agreed in 1936 to two schemes. The first was to send to the United Kingdom each year 15 officer cadets, who had already been trained in Canada for one year, and who would serve for five years with RAF squadrons. Secondly, the Canadian Government agreed to select and medically board 25 officers each year for complete training in the United Kingdom, followed by four years with an RAF squadron.

Both Australia and New Zealand sent a limited number of trained cadets for service with the RAF. Shortly before war was declared, New Zealand offered substantially to increase its number of cadets, and offered facilities for RAF training. Southern Rhodesia had coincidentally formulated an air unit to work with the RAF, and also offered facilities for training. The only flying school within the Commonwealth had been instituted by Kenya.

It is difficult to speculate on what might have happened if Canada had agreed to participate in the modified plan in 1936/7. Certainly its operation would have enabled the RAF and the Dominions to extend flying training courses, and build up a reservoir of highly trained aircrew and flying instructors. But this needed careful planning to avoid having large numbers of trained aircrew available without the aircraft and the back-up to keep them occupied! The Plan would have assured a supply of technical personnel, and revitalized the aircraft manufacturing industry. It might even have persuaded Hitler to have second thoughts. But pushing the button too early and setting the machinery in motion might well have had serious consequences.

With hindsight, the early discussions were in reality a 'sounding out' operation to find out how Canada would react to the RAF's idea of decentralizing flying training in her Dominion. Nobody had any clear idea as to its scope and requirement. But a proposal was put forward and rejected.

Stanley Baldwin had regained the British premiership in 1935, the same year as Mackenzie King. His record was one of appeasement, being a dove rather than a hawk, and he was opposed to spending money on military expansion. The climate in the mid-1930s reflected this attitude, and if the Scheme had got off the ground, public reaction and political bias could have stifled it. One has to remember that, a little later on, Winston Churchill was 'crying in the wilderness' when he exposed weaknesses in the RAF; he was labelled a warmonger.

The Scheme was shelved, and the governments concerned adopted a 'wait and see' attitude. They regarded Britain as the 'Mother Country', but there was no emergency. War might be brewing up, but it was not yet a reality. Their countries were thousands of miles away from the European theatre, and not vulnerable to air attack. Distances between cities and towns in Canada and Australia are vast, and communities far more isolated than in Britain. The land area of Canada, for example, is 41 times greater than the UK, that of Australia 32 times, and New Zealand 1.1. Canada's population of 10,500,000 was less than one-third of Britain's, Australia's 7,000,000 was less than that of Greater London, and New Zealand had only 1,500,000.

Communications were primitive by modern standards. The world was no oyster for the masses, unlike today when jet transport has enabled most of us to travel the globe. Ironically, in 1936 Frank Whittle formed his Power Jets Company, and began to build his first jet engine. Britain might well have had jet fighters in 1940 if the Establishment had given him backing in 1930! In those days people crossed the oceans in steamships, on journeys taking weeks. There was no television to influence and persuade the public at large, and any government would have had problems in substantiating a co-operative flying training scheme.

While the proposed Empire Scheme remained in limbo, RAF expansion continued, although the Service was totally ill-equipped to meet the rapidly growing strength of the Luftwaffe. In February 1937 the

Treasury more than doubled the Air Estimates from 50.1 million to
137.6 million, providing a basis for further expansion and development,
particularly in aircraft production.

As far as training was concerned, the RAFVR 'weekend' flying
scheme was underway and four new flying schools had been added to
the existing five, but they had only 247 pilots on strength. A further eight
schools had been planned for 1938, but there weren't sufficient experienced pilots to staff them! These would have had to be taken from
squadrons, which was considered to be too great a risk. Consequently,
the burden of advanced and operational training was thrust upon the
squadrons. By early 1939 there was a deficiency of well over 1,000 pilots
targeted for training. From 1935 to 1939 the RAF accepted under 7,000
air and ground crew for initial training. (By comparison, in 1942 alone
Canada trained 30,177 aircrew, of which 14,135 were pilots!)

Incredible though it might seem today, the Air Ministry at that time
regarded only pilots as full-time operators. Air observers combined the
function of gunners, and personified the amateur status of aircrew. They
were mainly volunteer ground crews; their flying was regarded as a
spare-time occupation, and they were paid accordingly. In late 1937, Air
Chief Marshal Sir Edgar Ludlow-Hewitt, Commander in Chief of
Bomber Command, wrote:

> . . . we have been ready to go to great expense in providing highly skilled
> maintenance personnel, the best possible aircraft and equipment, and all the
> very costly overheads required to maintain an efficient air force, yet when it
> comes to the climax of the whole operation, namely the crew of the aircraft,
> we have considered economy before efficiency. Consequently, our crews fall far
> short of practical war requirements, and are not well devised to carry out the
> very duties for which alone the force as a whole exists.

Modernizing and rationalizing the aircrew structure required finance
which was not available. Neville Chamberlain had taken over from
Baldwin in 1937, and the following year he appeased Hitler with the
shameful Munich agreement. Spending money on military investment
was anathema to him; his prime concerns were economic stability, and
the avoidance of war at any cost. The aircrew problem only began to
sort itself out in line with technical development: for example, the
introduction of the power-operated turret divorced the observer from
the air gunner. But it was not until January 1939 that the Air Ministry
began to tackle the status question of aircrew other than pilots. In
December 1939 air gunners were at last made full-time, and given the
rank of at least sergeant, together with their famous 'AG' half-wing. It
took Ludlow-Hewitt over 12 months to get the Ministry to agree to a
ten-week navigation course for observers. This was long overdue,
because even in late 1939 more than 40 percent of his bombers could
not pinpoint a target in a British city in broad daylight!

RAF training for pilots was of a high standard, and this was generally
recognized throughout the world. Cranwell was the university of the air.

The accent was on quality, in that cadets were well educated (public school, preferably), came from higher social backgrounds, and were good at sport. Their counterparts in Auxiliary squadrons comprised an élite, moneyed society in which a club atmosphere prevailed. University air squadrons spoke for themselves. There was also a scheme in which skilled tradesmen were taught to fly, becoming sergeant pilots when they qualified. After qualifying, they could return to their trade with the rank of sergeant, provided they passed their necessary trade examinations.

The emergence of the RAFVR in 1936 altered the social structure of entrants, in that it took men from a wider, middle-class stratum of society. The VR scheme was a milestone in RAF training history. It was the forerunner of a vast expansion to come, and it proved invaluable in that it provided a reserve of pilots when they were desperately needed. Over 40 percent of the pilots who fought the Battle of Britain, for example, were sergeants, most of whom had joined the RAFVR in 1937/8 as weekend flyers.

It was against this background that the Royal Air Force entered the war in September 1939. Flying training still did not have its own Command, nor representation on the Air Council, yet was coming under increasing pressure to produce urgently needed pilots required by front-line squadrons. By comparison, the Luftwaffe had reached a peak of efficiency, and presented an awesome challenge.

2. The enemy

A PRIME CONSIDERATION for transferring flying training overseas was the growing strength and power of the enemy. Since the First World War ended, the Germans had been planning to rebuild their air force, and from the mid-thirties onwards its development had been greatly accelerated by political motivation. Aircrew training together with aircraft production between the wars had been vital factors in making the Luftwaffe a dominant force.

The outbreak of the Second World War in September 1939 greatly assisted the birth of the Empire Flying Training Scheme. The significance of this bold undertaking, however, can only be really appreciated by reviewing the progress of the Luftwaffe pre-war—'Know thine enemy' is an old maxim!

Generalleutnant Adolf Galland, looking back over pilot training in Germany during the Second World War, made the following comments:

17 January 1991

Pilot training was performed in Germany in the AB training without instrument flying in about 40 hours. Then these pilots were sent to the fighter pilot training schools where they got 20 to 30 hours on fighter aircraft. After that, these pilots were sent to the Fighter Operational Training Units (OTUs) of which each fighter wing had its own squadron.

Pilot training was never sufficient. We had not enough aircraft, not enough time, and finally not enough fuel.

I have been twice to Winnipeg for the Commonwealth Wartime Aircrew Reunions. I have admired your training organisation which was owned by a rich Air Force.

Generalleutnant Adolf Galland, Knight's Cross of the Iron Cross with Diamonds, Oak Leaves and Swords, Cross of Honour.

Generalleutnant Galland was one of three fighter pilots in his family and he became one of Germany's most famous airmen in the Second World War. A general at the age of 29, he became Commander-in-Chief of the German Fighter Force and was intimately connected with tactics and planning. His comments regarding the basic training of Luftwaffe aircrew are of particular interest, as are his remarks concerning our global aircrew training operation. German aircrew training had reached a high degree of quality and intensity by 1939. However, from 1942, in spite of its territorial expansion throughout Europe, the German training organization began to break down.

While the differences in style between RAF and Luftwaffe training merit consideration, the prime factors in achieving command of the air were the supply of aircrew in line with the changing pattern of the war, and the availability of aircraft types. Hence the German aircrew training operation both pre-war and during the war is the criterion upon which we can judge the success of our own operation, the 'numbers game' being vital as the war progressed.

In September 1939 the Luftwaffe was in many respects the most powerful and efficient air force in the world, possessing some 4,300 aircraft manned by highly trained crews with battle experience (in Spain) and high morale. After three years' invaluable operational experience during the Spanish Civil War, Goering boasted that his Luftwaffe had achieved ultimate supremacy over other leading air forces, which he considered would be maintained for years to come. However illegal, this was no mean achievement, as the Air Clauses of the 1919 Treaty of Versailles had stipulated that Germany was no longer to maintain or develop military or naval forces. In the event she circumvented these legal requirements by subterfuge and careful military planning over 15 years, 'cocking a snook' at world opinion and criticism.

During the pre-Hitler period, in 1926, the German civil airlines, which survived the Treaty of Versailles, were incorporated within a new and brilliantly efficient company called Deutsche Lufthansa. This company, enjoying a complete monopoly in German commercial aviation, established a network of airlines which gave Germany the clear lead in civil aviation in Europe. From 1929 onwards the nucleus of the Luftwaffe was created under the guise of civil aviation activities.

Lufthansa pilots were trained in special schools known as D.V.S.—German commercial air schools—and many of them received 'under cover' military training at Lipetzk experimental centre and other auxiliary airfields in the Caucasus (by arrangement with the Soviet Union). In July 1933 the first intake of German pilots—posing as South Tyrolean soldiers—secretly crossed the border into Italy to train with the Regia Aeronautica. Many had been flying for Lufthansa. They were issued with Italian Air Force uniforms and accepted as students on an operational training course.

The Regia Aeronautica at that time was one of the most efficient and modern air forces in Europe, and the German pilots were able to engage in every aspect of aerial warfare. During the warm summer months of 1933, in collaboration with the Italian army, the Germans created and developed the blitzkrieg technique for air support for an invasion force.

Subsequently, graduates of the Italian course were placed on the Air Force active list and became commissioned officers of the Luftwaffe.

Under the civil umbrella of the Lufthansa airline, German aircrew gained additional invaluable experience for military flying via aircraft factories, experimental establishments, wireless and meteorological stations, and long-distance flights. At the end of 1935, after a decade of so-called commercial and sporting flying, the newly formed Luftwaffe was able to muster 1,800 front-line military aircraft and 20,000 officers and men in spite of legal restrictions.

Thus, in the mid-1930s, Goering had a nucleus of enthusiastic and experienced pilots to help train and develop his air force. One of his first priorities was to overhaul the existing system of flying training provided by the commercial and sporting flying organizations. In 1936 these were put on a war footing, and a special training inspectorate at the Air Ministry was created to centralize control and to ensure the highest possible standards in all flying training schools.

Before hostilities began in 1939 the Luftwaffe had about 50 basic training schools across Saxony, the Rhineland, Bavaria, Silesia, East Prussia and Pomerania. As the war progressed, basic training schools were established in Poland and Czechoslovakia, and advanced flying schools in France, Belgium, Greece, Norway, Denmark and Italy, making a total of 75 to 100 schools. At the outbreak of war the Luftwaffe training scheme was turning out between 10,000 and 15,000 pilots a year. Thus, Germany had a surplus of pilots in 1940, and created operational and reserve training units to re-absorb them. At this juncture the Empire Flying Training Scheme was emerging from its embryo and becoming a reality. During 1940, 1,101 aircrew of all types (including 728 pilots) were trained under the scheme.)

This territorial expansion of Luftwaffe flying training compares favourably with the extent of the RAF global scheme, so the Luftwaffe was not lacking in training establishments. But training establishments need a continuous intake of pupils, and recruitment, as in the RAF, was a key factor. Goering and company formed the National Socialist Flying Corps in 1937 for pre-training Hitler embryo pilots. The idea was to 'catch them young', preferably at the age of about eight years, indoctrinate them and send them to regular Luftwaffe Flying Training Schools for gliding experience. There they gained theoretical knowledge of aircraft, air experience, and—more particularly—political prestige. Thus, from the outset, many German cadets were politically motivated, as was the Luftwaffe itself. The RAF later drew recruits from the Air Training Corps, and this was similar in some respects, but it had not the slightest political pressure.

Initial Luftwaffe training—corresponding broadly speaking to the RAF ITW stage—was quite different from our own. German recruits, including officer candidates, spent from six to twelve months primarily on an infantry regimental course. Here they had a strong dose of Prussian discipline, learning to goose-step, fire small arms and be toughened up on the parade ground. This was somewhat akin to the

American system for training officers (break them down first and then build 'em up as you want them), which RAF cadets in the United States found frustrating!

On passing out from the Recruit Depot they spent two months at a pool known as the *Fluganwaerterkompanie*, learning general aviation subjects before being posted for *ab initio* training. Luftwaffe pupils arriving for this training were therefore highly disciplined in true Teutonic tradition, and politically motivated. The RAF system, by contrast, allowed more freedom for the individual, and in many ways was more sophisticated as far as basic flying training was concerned. There is little doubt that by the time a German pupil had graduated, the effects of political motivation had worn progressively thinner!

A Luftwaffe pilot was given his wings after he had completed 100–150 hours' flying; then he would be selected for specialist training as a bomber, fighter or reconnaissance pilot. The first 'A' course (our EFTS) consisted of some 30 hours of dual and solo flying. Aircraft he might fly included the Focke-Wulf Fw 44, Heinkel He 72, Gotha Go 145, Arado Ar 66 or possibly a Bücker Bü 131. These aircraft had a top speed of between 110 and 130 mph and a landing speed of between 45 and 55 mph.

The course was considerably shorter than our EFTS, and so was the 'B' course (corresponding to the RAF SFTS), during which the German pupil would do about 70 hours' flying before he qualified. An RAF cadet would log between 200 and 300 hours, depending where he trained, before he got his wings.

One Englishman managed to arrange some flying hours at a large German flying school in March 1938. He wrote about his experience in *Flight* magazine under the pseudonym 'Kismet' in January 1940. He didn't reveal its location, or how he was able to arrange the deal as a civilian visitor.

The writer had been flying for some time, so he received rather more advanced instruction than an absolute beginner. Naturally he was interested in comparing the methods employed by the Luftwaffe for basic flying training with our own. He said that German manufacturers often ran their own flying schools, under the control of the German Air Ministry—in England there were only two such instances he could recall. The advantages were obvious: ease of maintenance by the factory itself, spare parts on the shelf, and opportunities for technical experts to see daily how their machines performed. In addition, pupils could visit the factory to see how their aircraft were constructed, and the design features which determined flying characteristics.

The writer was taken up in a Bücker Bü 131 Jungmann primary training biplane. This was probably at Berlin Rangsdorf, because at the end of 1935, a new and enlarged works and main offices had been established there. His first big surprise was to find that there was no telephonic communication between instructor and pupil; instead, the instructor used hand signals or sharply pulled the controls to take command.

The German onlookers had laughed at *der Engländer*'s helmet, with its novel ear fittings, and even more so when 'Kismet' did a smart ground loop when taxiing out—the Jungmann was fitted with a tailwheel rather than the accustomed skid! However, after that slight setback, he wrote:

> *I headed into wind and took off as carefully as possible, it being the first time that I had flown an aircraft with duplicate ailerons. In spite of my care, the take-off was bad, and the controls were pulled sharply out of my hands.*
>
> *After a few seconds the instructor waved both his hands above his head in token of having quit the controls, and I again took over. Climbing with plenty of speed in hand failed to please him, and a series of violent upward jerks with his extended right arm made me steepen the angle until the Earth had disappeared altogether, and I was convinced that we were going to stall; but we did not.*
>
> *A downward stroke of the right arm, and I eased the stick forward for straight and level flying. The left arm extended with fingers pointing left; I turned left, but not steeply enough, as extra pressure is put on the stick and we are turning vertically, or rather the machine is turning itself vertically, as there are the instructor's hands above his head again, and mine are gripping the seat!*

'Kismet' soon got the feel of the machine and, after carrying out a few landings, which he admitted he did after a fashion, he passed on to the next stage of his tuition. He was told to take the machine up himself to 1,500 metres over the nearest lake, do a right-hand turn and then a left-hand spin. 'You must take off, and land, on the left-hand half of the aerodrome, whatever the wind direction happens to be,' his instructor said 'the right-hand half is always reserved for military flying. Also, you will never perform aerobatics, except over water. That is a compulsory order to all pupils, at all flying schools.'

All use of controls, their functions and objectives were explained on the ground first and then performed in the air by the instructor. This was understandable because his instructor told him that he had never seen a pair of headphones until that day! Having performed satisfactorily in the Jungman, 'Kismet' was allowed to fly the Bü 133 Jungmeister—a more powerful single-seat biplane trainer which all fighter pilots learned to handle. Aerobatic training consisted of loops, half-loop followed by a roll, looping while gliding, inverted flying, slow roll right and left, continuous roll in right- or left-hand rotation, spinning, inverted spin, knife flight and vertical slip-over wing, in that order. All these aerobatics were first performed dual in the Jungmann.

Twelve to fifteen hours of dual instruction was a fair average before a pilot was sent solo. Both Bücker trainers had a deservedly good reputation for their pleasant handling qualities. Other aircraft used for Service training included the Gotha 145, the Arado 66 or the Focke-Wulf 56, the Arado and Gotha being biplanes and the Focke-Wulf a parasol monoplane.

During the 'B' course, as the flying tempo increased, pupils were watched carefully and selected for the various commands. Then they were sent to specialist schools—fighter, dive-bomber, bomber, observer, etc. The creation of operational and reserve training units in 1940 was partly to reabsorb some of the surplus aircrew from specialist schools. 'Kismet's' experience, however, provides an interesting insight into German pre-war basic training. In retrospect it seems incredible that the Germans had to use hand signals which made the instructor seem like an automaton. Verbal contact in the air was an essential ingredient of flying training for most of us. However, hand signals were used when instructing on the American Stearman primary trainer, and there are other similarities between the German and American systems for pilot training. The West Point disciplinary code was enforced to train officers as a prime function, flying being part of the process and the American flag symbolic. The Germans applied Prussian discipline in its regimental form, coupled with political persuasion. Without being too dogmatic, this regimental approach by the Germans and the Americans alike was reflected in their methods of flying instruction, which employed a copying or follow-through technique, as described above.

On the eve of the outbreak of war the German training organization was turning out more pilots than the Luftwaffe could readily absorb. The RAF had only just sorted out the aircrew status problem and the newly formed RAF Training Command was hampered by its own very high standards. While the incredible optimism of Goering and company prevailed in Luftwaffe High Command, the RAF was busy laying the foundations for mass-produced aircrew on a global basis. At this juncture the Luftwaffe was geared up for lightning strikes producing quick results, with the expectation of light casualities. It achieved these results during its advance across Europe, although both sides lost about 1,000 aircraft each during the Battle for France.

During the summer of 1940 in the Battle of Britain, the Luftwaffe suffered its first—and very unexpected—defeat, losing some 3,000 aircrew. Although able to absorb such losses, it proved a salutary lesson to the powerful and arrogant Luftwaffe. Apart from staving off an invasion, this victory enhanced the RAF image, and acted as a great stimulus for encouraging young men to volunteer for aircrew both at home and throughout the free world.

The losses sustained by the Luftwaffe during the battles of France and Britain were substantially increased when Germany invaded the Soviet Union in June 1941 (in that year, ironically, the RAF had a surplus of aircrew, due to shortage of aircraft). By 1942, in spite of the territorial expansion of the Luftwaffe training organization throughout Europe, it began to fragment. The major training schemes of 1940, 1941 and 1942 were being clipped or cancelled. Courses had to be shortened in order to replace combat losses, and there was a shortage of flying instructors and of twin-engined training aircraft. The Luftwaffe training organization was short not only of pupils but also of ground staff, who were being diverted to infantry regiments to fight, mainly on the Russian Front.

By 1942 the Luftwaffe was fighting on three fronts: the Soviet Union, the Mediterranean and the Atlantic. The manpower difficulty and shortened courses had to affect the quality of aircrews. In contrast, courtesy of the global training scheme and accelerating aircraft production the RAF was undergoing the biggest expansion in its history. During this period the United States had entered the war, and the US Army Air Force was using the UK virtually as an unsinkable aircraft carrier. Thus, the numbers game in men and machines began to make its impact on the air war.

The emergence of the four-engined bomber, and the growing European bombing offensive, began to suck in aircrews like a vacuum cleaner. The planning and timing of the overseas training programme was perfect because it began to peak at that particular time. In 1942 the Commonwealth Scheme alone (The Empire Air Training Scheme was re-established as the Commonwealth Air Training Plan in June 1942), produced 44,338 trained aircrew, and in 1943 this increased to 58,601. In addition, during 1940–45 over 88,000 RAF aircrew were trained in the UK, and over 14,000 in the USA.

Germany, by comparison, was totally unable to compete with this vast training organization which, at its peak, had three times the number of German training establishments serving the Empire Air Forces. Germany's production of aircrews depended upon its national availability of manpower. Healthy, educated youths born in the years 1922–4 provided the basic reservoir for potential Luftwaffe recruits. With a population of some 88 million, Germany had about double the number of likely UK pupils. But the global scheme was able to draw upon members of these age groups throught the Commonwealth, and the USA, with a population of 188 million, tipped the scales heavily in Allied favour, via the US Army and Navy.

Generalleutnant Adolf Galland's concise comments reflect the Luftwaffe's situation from 1942 onwards: 'Pilot training has never been sufficient. We had not enough training schools, not enough instructors, not enough aircraft, not enough time, and finally not enough fuel.'

The unfolding events of the Second World War in relation to the rising number of aircrew trained overseas illustrate, without a shadow of doubt, the enormous contribution the Scheme made to ultimate command of the air. The Scheme throughout was an extension of the format and style of RAF training and it provided the basis for the development of Commonwealth and Dominion air forces. In so doing it provided the impetus for the regeneration and development of the aviation industries of the countries concerned.

3. Southern Rhodesia— the opening bat!

It is quite remarkable that No. 25 EFTS Belvedere, near Salisbury, commenced training on 24 May 1940—some weeks before the first of the schools in Canada became operational.

Sqn/Ldr Francis Butcher, 'Vital Command'

AT THE OUTBREAK of war, Southern Rhodesia, now Zimbabwe, was part of the British Empire, and there was no thought of Unilateral Declaration of Independence or indeed of independence at all. Such matters were unthinkable, and Rhodesia's loyalty to the Mother Country was deeply held and utterly unshakeable.

Air Training at that time was negligible, although a scheme had begun in 1937 under Major D. Cloete MC AFC as part of the country's territorial forces. This involved the Rhodesia Regiment only, training Southern Rhodesians by seconded Royal Air Force instructors on aircraft supplied by Britain. Aircraft from this small scheme consisted of four Hawker Audax and six Hawker Hart trainers, together with ten other assorted machines, including those needed for *ab initio* instruction. Two RAF officers and 12 other ranks made up the personnel.

This training plan, such as it was, was tied to an Agreement with the United Kingdom committing Southern Rhodesia, in the event of war, to send a unit to Kenya for service with the Royal Air Force. In consequence, during August 1939 a major part of the contingent left for Kenya to operate in the North Frontier District, forming up, in due course, with 237 (Rhodesia) Squadron RAF. This move, honouring as it did the original Agreement, virtually decimated flying training at home. With few aircraft and spares, and limited instructors, matters quickly approached a crisis level.

Major Cloete had retired and gone to live in South Africa. He was replaced by Lt.-Col. Charles Meredith, who arrived from the UK as Rhodesian Staff Officer and Director of Civil Aviation. His first task was the depressing one of dispatching the unit to Kenya.

It was clear that a great deal had to be done if Rhodesia was to play any significant part in the war while at the same time retaining her identity, and Meredith set about this task with great drive and enthu-

siasm. Colonel J. S. Morris was at that time commanding Southern
Rhodesia Forces, and on his own admission knew very little about flying
matters. He depended almost entirely on Meredith, who made out a case
for the supply of Rhodesian aircrew to man three RAF squadrons, and
the setting up of Training Stations to be known as the Rhodesian Air
Training Group.

Meredith was authorized to discuss matters with Sir Godfrey
Huggins, then Prime Minister, and convinced him that his plans were,
without doubt, feasible and viable, provided that the right assistance
was forthcoming from the UK. There was no delay. Huggins cabled
London with the proposals, and offered to send Meredith on a one-
man mission. In retrospect, it is quite remarkable that so much was
achieved by one man with a brief containing nothing but the bare
outline of a scheme, and absolutely nothing regarding its very large
financial implications.

Nevertheless, Meredith arrived in London in October 1939 and
started discussions with Air Ministry officials, setting out his modest
proposals. He immediately generated a great deal of interest, and it soon
became apparent that the UK's thinking embraced a much larger scale
of operations than Southern Rhodesia had contemplated.

In fact, Meredith had made his approach at the right moment. The
Air Ministry and the British Government had become exasperated by
Lord Riverdale's delay in coming to an agreement on the Empire Air
Training Scheme with Canada, Australia and New Zealand. The sands
of time were fast running out, and there was a paramount need to
disperse flying training away from England. It was in the interest of
the Air Ministry to 'hedge its bets', and Southern Rhodesia's offer of
mutual collaboration had to be exploited. Thus, Meredith suddenly
found himself enmeshed in a much bigger deal than he had imagined,
and for which he had not been prepared. Fortunately he was a man
of considerable resource and administrative talent, which enabled him
to take these developments in his stride.

It was initially agreed that the scheme should embrace three EFTS
supplying three Service Schools, and one Initial Training Wing for
ground training and selection. This involved establishing six aerodromes
and handling a large influx of trainees. Originally the project was to
train Rhodesians only, but its enlargement called for an influx of recruits
from other countries, with all the attendant problems.

Meredith had been authorized only to negotiate flying training in
Southern Rhodesia, and had no authority to enter into financial
agreements. It was obvious, however, that he had to make some
tentative and no doubt rather nervous enquiries as to how the bill
was to be met. The Air Ministry, desperately worried about the
apparent failure of the Canadian negotiations, had no hesitation in
putting Meredith over a barrel. At this particular time the Canadians
wanted to use apple exports to offset some of their share of the costs,
to the British Treasury's dismay! The British adopted a somewhat
cavalier attitude towards Meredith, telling him, to quote his own

words, to 'buzz off and get Air Training going in Rhodesia before the Canadian scheme is bogged down in apples'.

Meredith was told to obtain whatever finance was needed from the Southern Rhodesian Government, and that the United Kingdom Treasury would settle up later. So Meredith returned home with an agreement, and apparently unlimited resources. He had obtained much more than he had anticipated, and had vastly increased his country's participation in the war. The desperate co-operation of the Air Ministry, and a UK Treasury promise to pay later, had made it possible—a blank cheque which Southern Rhodesia, to her great credit, honoured immediately. (Incidentally, the country's white population at that time was about 45,000, less than one-thousandth that of Britain!)

There was much work to be done in very little time, and Meredith wasted none of it. On arrival in Salisbury he set to work implementing the proposals without much concern as to who should meet the bill. An early decision by the Government was to separate the Air from Defence and inaugurate a Department of Air, introducing Air Force uniforms and ranks. Meredith, who became a Group Captain and soon an Air Commodore, commanded the Rhodesian Air Training Group, and combined with it the post of Secretary for Air.

A detailed plan was quickly formulated embracing the design of airfields, erection of hangars, repair shops, messes, accommodation and a multitude of other details concerning the building of Service aerodromes and Training Wings. There was pressure from the Air Ministry in London as the shipping of personnel, aircraft and equipment had already been scheduled. Moreover, training had been based on periods of six weeks at each phase, and it was essential that pupils should pass from each phase to the next without the progress being impeded. The excellent Rhodesian climate was a great asset, but in the initial stages it was essential that all training stations were ready for their first intake when needed.

The fact that on 24 May 1940—the day on which the German Army occupied Boulogne—No. 25 EFTS, at Belvedere, near Salisbury, commenced training before the Canadian scheme became operational was a truly remarkable achievement. This was followed by the RATG Air Station at Guinea Fowl, near Gwelo, which was completed in 12 weeks. Carved out of the bare veldt, it consisted of an aerodrome, all ancillary buildings, water supplies, sewerage, and its own railway siding. On the day it became ready for use a train conveying 500 cadets arrived, and they sat down to a breakfast of bacon and eggs!

As the war progressed, the Rhodesian contribution flowered. The original programme of six schools was increased to eight, plus a Bombing, Navigation and Gunnery school. Six relief landing grounds were added, together with two Air Firing and Bombing Ranges. Later, a School for the instruction of flying instructors was established, bringing the total of RATG Air Stations to ten.

Meredith was the prime co-ordinator of this great contribution to the war effort, and he was able to concentrate on the operational aspect without worrying about the financial implications. These were conducted by the Secretary to the Treasury, C.E.M. (later Sir Cornelius) Greenfield, who negotiated with the British Treasury. The 'blank cheque' given to Meredith in London resulted in the following agreement:

Southern Rhodesia accepted responsibility for:

(1) The capital expenditure on land and buildings and ancillary works for the whole of the RATG, including quarters and housing.

(2) The cost of all barrack equipment at Air Stations.

(3) The cost of Headquarters.

(4) All pay and allowances for Rhodesian personnel serving in Southern Rhodesia.

(5) Make-up pay and family allowances for Rhodesians serving abroad—that is, the difference between RAF and Rhodesian rates.

(6) A cash contribution of Canadian $800,000 pa towards the operating costs of the Air Training Scheme.

The provision of aircraft, equipment, petrol, oil, transport, and the pay and allowances of RAF personnel were met by the British Air Ministry.

The total cost to the Southern Rhodesian Government was £11 million, which was no mean sum in those days for a comparatively poor country. Pupils were trained from Australia, South Africa, Greece and the UK, in addition to the considerable number of Rhodesian volunteers. In all, some 10,000 aircrew were produced by the Air Training Group, of which 7,600 were pilots (one of them was Ian Smith, who was later to become Prime Minister). This was a superb effort by so young a country in coming to the aid of the Motherland. Its trust and loyalty is perhaps hard to understand today! Furthermore, the sacrifice of so many Rhodesians, not only in the Air Force, was the ultimate one which younger generations should remember with pride and gratitude.

After the war, Southern Rhodesia was able to recover some of the heavy expenses incurred during the scheme. Many of the buildings were converted for civilian use as houses or apartments. Three stations were taken over by schools, and one became a Bata shoe factory. Meredith, now Sir Charles Meredith, in his Memoranda on the Rhodesian Air Training Group, from which this chapter largely emanates, quotes from *Huggins of Rhodesia* by Gann and Gelford:

The air training scheme in fact formed Southern Rhodesia's greatest individual contribution to the war, and in an unexpected way also provided a major economic boom. Farmers and industrial firms suddenly found an almost insatiable market, and Guest calculated that Imperial expenditure on the scheme alone almost equalled the indirect benefit which the country derived from its entire gold-mining industry.

* * * * * *

Flying over 'bush' country in Southern Rhodesia could be a bit hairy
if one was unlucky enough to have to force-land. The same applied to
the alligator swamps, known as the Everglades, in Florida. Snakes and
alligators have nasty habits. All a pilot had to do after a forced-landing
or bailing-out in Florida was to spread his parachute in a circle—first,
to make the search easier, and secondly—providing he stood or sat in
its centre—to give him maximum warning of the approach of the
'crawlies'. The Everglades aircraft would then locate him and drop a
bunch of goodies plus a revolver and ammo. All he then had to do was
to await the arrival of the 'swamp buggy', which was radio-controlled
and directed from the aircraft above—an efficient and typically American solution to a local problem! In Southern Rhodesia, however,
the unfortunate chap who descended into jungle territory could find
the local native tribe crawling through the long grass towards him!
Ian Black, who was posted to Rhodesia as a flying instructor in
March 1944, recalls two instances when this happened. He was operating from Guinea Fowl, an EFTS station half-way between Gwelo and
Selukwe.

His first story concerned a pilot who had force-landed and been taken
in by the natives, who fed him and gave him a bed in their kraal. Ian
said that 'during the night they murdered him, because the food on
which he had dined was giraffe meat, and giraffe was royal game. They
were afraid he would report them for this, and so committed this crime.
Unfortunately, one of these natives, before they disposed of the pilot's
body, took his wrist-watch, and that was how they were eventually
caught by the British South Africa Police'.

The second episode was not quite so grisly! 'One pupil was doing his
solo cross-country flight from Guinea Fowl to Induna, and got lost.
The next day, ten aircraft from our station', Ian said, 'took off flying
half-a-mile apart in line-abreast to search for him. We did a search that
must have covered some 200 square miles, to no avail. Some three days
later the pupil turned up at a District Commissioner's home well out
in the bush. We discovered that he had been uncertain of his position
and had turned to find the railway line and "Bradshaw" his way to
Bulawayo.

'Unfortunately, in turning to find the railway line he had not realized
that he had already crossed it, with the result that the more he carried
on looking for it, the further off course he got. He eventually put down
in a field. He got out of his aircraft, and after a short time a number
of natives appeared and looked at him through the long grass but went
away again. He was somewhat afraid to contact them because he had
heard about the murder of the pilot given giraffe meat.

'The young trainee pilot was not disturbed by the natives and spent
the day emptying one tank (using the cover of the upper identification
light) into the other. He spent the night with his aircraft, taking off the
next morning. After flying around for some time, and realizing that he

had no idea as to his whereabouts and was running short of fuel, he landed again in a field, damaging the aircraft.

'On this occasion he had no alternative other than to approach the natives who came to see him. He used drawings which showed himself being led by a native to habitation of white man's house, railway lines and trains. He agreed to pay the natives one pound then and a further pound at the white man's house. They set off just as dusk was approaching, at a trot, and ran through the night. The pupil was terrified, as he could hear all sorts of strange noises in the bush, and he was also not as fit as the natives. In fact, he was stopping to rest for ten minutes after every mile or so of trotting. They eventually arrived at the District Commissioner's office, who radioed RAFHQ to report his safety.'

The chap had obviously experienced a nerve-wracking ordeal, but showed a cool head and great enterprise in his liaison with the natives. His Tiger Moth, however, had to be cannibalized, as it was too damaged to repair on site.

As in South Africa, Elementary and Service schools were grouped together, in the north around Salisbury, in the Midlands around Gwelo, and in the west around Bulawayo. During the period 1941–4 the RATG fed trained aircrew into the UK and Middle East theatres, and had to be flexible to meet the changing pattern of the war.

Southern Rhodesia was primarily concerned with training pilots, although a number of navigators and wireless operator/air gunners were also trained. In mid-1942 the system required some 300 instructors per year to service the schools, and naturally had to feed itself. The CFS flight at Belvedere couldn't possibly cope, and so a new CFS school was established at Norton, west of Salisbury, and was renamed No. 33 Flying Instructor School. At that time an instructor's tour was 12 months, but by early 1943 this was increased to 18 months.

Flying training courses likewise were shortened or lengthened according to operational requirements. In June 1942, for example, pilots' courses were lengthened to 12 weeks for EFTSs and 24 weeks for SFTSs, involving 225 hours' flying before graduation. This additional flying time was used for night and bad-weather flying, a sensible arrangement because there was a severe shortage of operational training units in the Middle East theatre and such additional training was a considerable asset.

Southern Rhodesia's contribution to the overseas training of aircrew was amazing, especially when one recalls that the Rhodesians, via Lt.-Col. Charles Meredith, were the first to activate the Empire Air Training Scheme. Such an example must have helped to motivate the Union of South Africa sitting on the doorstep. The fact that a large percentage of the aircrews trained in Southern Rhodesia were sent to the Middle East theatre was significant, bearing in mind that this territory was a prime operating area for the South African Air Force.

Instructing at Gwelo, Southern Rhodesia, October 1941–October 1943

'The remarkable feature of that experience', said Flt. Lt. T. S. Kilpatrick, 'was that during the whole of those two years, a full flying training programme was carried out on every day except one. That day was lost, not because of anything the weather was doing up aloft, but because torrential rain had so soaked the grass field that it was wisely decided not to spoil its surface by allowing any traffic on it for 24 hours.' Substitute Gwelo for Brize Norton in England, and the mind boggles as to how many days one would have been able to carry out a full flying training programme during a like period! Kilpatrick's experience, however, illustrates beyond any shadow of doubt the invaluable climatic advantage gained by training overseas. He goes on to say:

'Southern Rhodesian weather was utterly predictable. The dry or "winter" season lasted from March until October, to be followed by a similar six-month period of the wet or "summer" season. Consistently throughout the dry months, the sky was a clear, bright, blue dome. No drop of rain, no hint of cloud, relieved what for many became the sheer monotony of perfect weather, and, indeed, October was known as the suicide month as, for some, the monotony actually became unbearable. The "wet" season followed, with humidity to contrast with the crisp preceding months, and with rain showers which, however frequent, were usually of comparatively short duration.

'Towering and quite beautiful cumulus clouds would build up, clouds in which there was little turbulence to worry anyone; and the rain storms would approach, quite visible and quite defined, lasting for perhaps 20 minutes or less, so that they could be avoided and flown around with no effective interference to the flying training schedules. In the under two years of actual operations, the writer logged 1,100 hours of instructing, and that was fairly typical.'

Such conditions enabled pupils to concentrate on their flying without having to worry about sudden changes of weather conditions. This was also conducive to a more relaxed attitude but, like many ideal situations, it had its drawbacks, as Kilpatrick pointed out:

'One problem about flying in these conditions was that there was little chance to gain experience of anything other than almost ideal flying weather. A pilot could bash through the highest cumulus with impunity. Visibility, when there were no defined rainstorms around to interfere with it, was for practical navigation purposes almost unlimited. The one hazard to beware of was a bank of thin, low cloud locally called *guti*, which occasionally drifted along from the east in the evening, and which could interrupt the night-flying programme.

'Flying began at 0600 hours each day, stopped at about 1300 hours, to be followed by night flying on a gooseneck flarepath starting at dusk (between 1800 and 1900 hours according to the season) and finishing at midnight. Flying programmes and schedules were completed on time, what with perfect weather and the excellent serviceability of the Harvards.

'All this meant that every succeeding course of pupils was put through the training programme bang on time, and qualified pilots were churned out as if by a sausage machine. It also meant that instructors' leave periods were both scheduled and regular—six weeks' instructing, one week of leave.

'There was a somewhat sketchy social life around Gwelo, whose white population of 1,300 was literally swamped by the 3,000 or so Service personnel stationed at Thornhill SFTS, Guinea Fowl EFTS and Moffat Navigation School. Other stations in the Rhodesian Air Training Group were clustered around the larger cities of Bulawayo and the capital, Salisbury. Gwelo, with its one hotel and one bioscope (cinema), had to cater for its own invasion, so regular leave was a godsend.

'A favourite leave venue became the Victoria Falls to the north-west, and Durban, some 840 miles south on the coast of Natal, was another. The drill was that, as our Harvards were shipped from the USA crated and in pieces, they were assembled and test flown at Durban, and were then available for instructors to fly them up to Rhodesia at the end of a week's leave on the coast.

'This meant that the journey to Durban by train was paid for by the RAF; and a splendid hotel in Durban itself, the Mayfair, became a popular base at the cost of a mere 11 shillings a day, which provided a jolly good room and private bath plus four marvellous meals daily. Even a Flying Officer's pay of 18s 2d a day contrived to cater for that!' During his Rhodesian posting, the writer made that trip no less than 19 times, usually bringing back a full locker of wines and brandy from South Africa for the Mess; the average price of a bottle of good South African wine was 1s 3d (8p in today's money).

'If weather at the coast delayed the return flight, then living expenses became a charge on the RAF; and if a late start in the day meant an overnight stay after an immediate landing at Swartkop, between Johannesburg and Pretoria, then the Officer's Club in Brea Street, Johannesburg, offered a room for 2s 6d.

'Surely no other country in the world could have beaten the Rhodesian record for producing pilots regularly and to schedule. The weather remains the overriding memory of those flying years—the weather, the horizon a hundred miles in front, the slow rolls at night over Gwelo with the Harvard's twin landing lights on, revolving around each other, the take-offs in the early dawn before the Sun had risen, to see the Sun rise after getting airborne and set again on descending; then, from ground level, to see it rise for the second time—these are but a few of the memories which in total could fill volumes.

'In the middle of 1943 the Station Commander, Group Captain Clare-Hunt, announced at the end of a church service one Sunday morning that there would be a week of celebrations to commemorate the founding of No. 22 SFTS two years earlier. He said there would be a formation fly-past over Gwelo on the Monday, a sports day for local children on Tuesday, a dance in the Sergeants' Mess on Wednesday, etc, etc, culminating in a cocktail party and dance in the Officers' Mess on the Saturday evening.

'The pause that followed was broken by a voice, loud, clear and anonymous, from the middle of the 800 or so airmen who had listened in silence. The tin walls and roof of the Bellman hanger echoed the voice with efficiency: 'Wot about the * * * * War?'

Kilpatrick's story makes Southern Rhodesia sound like a flyer's paradise. He ended up saying:

'Well, it is true that 22 SFTS was a long way from the battlefields of both Europe and the Far East. But the contribution it made should not be forgotten, and there must have been, and still will be, very many who have reason to be grateful to the blue skies and lovely clouds which, in one or other of the seasons, made their flying here so beautiful and, for the RAF, so rewarding.'

Kilpatrick's words ensured that the spirit of No. 22 SFTS, Thornhill, Gwelo, Southern Rhodesia, was not forgotten. They were published in the Souvenir Programme of the Fifth Commonwealth Wartime Aircrew Reunion held in 1988 in Winnipeg, Manitoba, Canada, which attracted over 5,000 aircrew and their ladies from all parts of the Commonwealth and Western world.

After serving as a flying instructor in Southern Rhodesia, Kilpatrick returned to the UK to Bomber Command and was shot down on his 23rd trip over Germany in March 1945, some four hours after being promoted to Squadron Leader as OC 'B' Flight of 77 Squadron based at Full Sutton. He claims to be the shortest-serving Squadron Leader of the war years!

Passport to the Middle East

Many aircrew who graduated in Southern Rhodesia and South Africa were posted to the Middle East. Derek Wilkins, who became a pilot, was one of them. He sailed from Liverpool on 14 December 1943 on the SS *Orbita*, an old converted troopship, on a long and uncomfortable journey of six weeks, ending up somewhat hungry! Nobody had any idea of their route or destination, and the RAF contingent was housed in 200-man troop decks, several decks down near the engine rooms. They ate at long tables, sleeping over them in closely packed hammocks at night. The food was inadequate, and sometimes bad, as the boat had had no time to revictual adequately.

The convoy sailed south-west close to Brazil, then across the South Atlantic towards West Africa and up to the dangerous waters of the Straits of Gibraltar. Christmas 1943 was celebrated by a special ration for the troops consisting of a small bottle of beer or a packet of sweets! There was danger from German aircraft near to Crete prior to entering the Suez Canal at Port Said, Egypt. The voyage then continued southwards through the Red Sea to the north of Aden and then round the Horn of Africa to Mombasa, Kenya, where the ship docked to disembark and embark civilians and military.

At about this time the ship had virtually run out of food; the troops were starving, and many were forced to eat their emergency-ration tin of rough chocolate. The ship finally docked at Durban, South Africa, on 23 January 1944. Everyone was greeted by 'The Lady in White' singing her welcome from the dockside as she did for each ship. The RAF contingent disembarked, and was taken to Clairwood Racecourse to be installed in concrete 'pigstyes', well pleased to leave that awful ship!

After four years of air raids, black-out and food rationing in England, South Africa was a paradise. Derek particularly remembers lights, unlimited bread and huge tins of Koo melon and lemon jam! The effect of even moderate amounts of food on shrunken stomachs was devastating, and it took days to settle down. The party was then allowed a few days' leave to sightsee before embarking on a troop train for Southern Rhodesia.

The route to Bulawayo, in Matabeleland, the western part of Southern Rhodesia, was north through the Union, into the Bechuanaland Protectorate (now Botswana) and then into Rhodesia. The contingent was inducted at the RATG's ITW at Hillside, Bulawayo. From there cadets were sent to the various EFTS airfields for flying training. A priority was to visit an Indian tailor to modify the ridiculous baggy tunics and long shorts which had been issued at Heaton Park, Manchester, and which were the object of derision by those who had already 'got their knees brown'. The huge topees were rarely worn.

Wilkins was sent to No. 27 EFTS at N'Thabusinduna, a grass airfield near a prominent kopje (hill) to the east of Bulawayo, the ex-HQ kraal of Lobengula, the famous Matabele king. The aircraft at Induna were Tiger Moths, and later American Fairchild Cornells. Wilkins soloed at 8 hr 45 min, and completed about 117 hours' flying between 13 April 1944 and 28 July 1944. He and Derek Dempster were on the same course and indulged in strictly forbidden dogfighting in their Tigers! Night flying, including night cross-countries, featured towards the end of EFTS, using gooseneck flares on the grass.

Southern Rhodesia in the 1940s was wild frontier country. In the west, around Bulawayo, it was mainly arid flat savannah, 5,000 ft above sea level. This part borders on the Kalahari desert, and was alive with hordes of elephant, buffalo and other wildlife. Landmarks were minimal and so accurate dead-reckoning navigation was essential—not easy in a bucking Tiger Moth, with only a compass and an airspeed indicator. Survival training, 'bundu bashing', was included in the course. Flying weather was generally favourable, but in the summer there was extensive cumulo-nimbus and then a season of occasional *guti* of low cloud.

Wilkins moved on to 21 SFTS at Kumalo, Bulawayo, on Course 38B from 28 July 1944 to 6 February 1945. Bulawayo, founded by Cecil Rhodes, was laid out by him in a grid pattern; it was mainly a railhead, and in some parts was fairly primitive. Kumalo had been its civil airport and had a runway, with a sewage farm at one end and a cemetery at the other. The aircraft were mainly twin-engined Airspeed Oxfords, but North American Harvards and Avro Ansons were also flown. During the course there were several flying fatalities, but the cadets were only dimly aware of them as a veil of secrecy was drawn over them by the staff—presumably so as not to affect morale. The story of the lost aircraft, the giraffe hunters and the murdered pilot was generally known.

Social life was to hand in the limited spare time available. The Rhodesians were most hospitable, and entertained cadets in their homes. The prettiest girls attended the Baptist Church. For those with coarser tastes, the Bodega Bar provided the support of South African brandy with guaranteed desperate hangovers. Cigarettes were very cheap, genuine gaspers, the main brands being 'Springbok' in a white packet and 'C to C' (Cape to Cairo) in a yellow-and-brown packet. Wilkins tried some, and is a non-smoker to this day!

SFTS Kumalo had satellite airstrips, the main one being Woollandale, on which was held a course under canvas, simulating 'off base' operational conditions for air and ground crews. Bombing practice formed an important feature of advanced training, both at low level and from 5,000 and 10,000 ft, by day and by night, and on the ground using a camera obscura. During the early days of RATG a joker had christened two bombing ranges used by Kumalo as Miasi and Mielbo, which sounded obviously authentic African names! The names were solemnly printed on all maps and charts used by the RATG, and may still be used.

At the end of the course a landing competition was held at Woollandale. The instructors had heavy bets on their favourites. Also, a mass formation of about 12–15 Oxfords, led by an instructor, flew over Bulawayo to celebrate the occasion and to thank the very hospitable Rhodesians for putting up with the lads. Wilkins logged about 234 hours at Kumalo—a total since beginning flying of 349 hours of day, night and instrument flying. Although courses were shortened or lengthened to meet aircrew requirements at any particular time, this was considerably more than most pilots logged—200 to 250 hours was about average, and this in its turn was far more than a German or Russian pupil would manage.

Wilkins graduated at a Wings Parade at Kumalo on 2 February 1945, and was granted an Emergency Commission. He was rated an 'outstanding cadet' and offered the opportunity to remain in Southern Rhodesia as an instructor. He declined, in favour of joining a squadron after OTU.

He was then posted to 61 Air School, South African Air Force, at George, Cape Province, to do a Maritime Reconnaissance Course. This was a specialist navigation course in preparation for Coastal Command duties. It included astro-navigation, aerial photography and ship recognition, including those of the German and Japanese navies.

The course lasted from 12 February 1945 to 13 April 1945. Wilkins logged another 43 hours day and night flying in Ansons on southerly exercises far out to sea between Port Elizabeth and Cape Town. One had to be careful not to put red on blue—the next landfall was the Antarctic! Pigeons and Mae Wests were carried: care was required in ejecting the pigeon, as a severe loss of feathers ensued if he or she was pushed out into the slipstream backwards. All shipping was identified, photographed and logged, and a sharp eye was kept open for enemy submarines moving round the Cape to the Indian Ocean.

Wilkins' next posting was to the Middle East. The group flew from IFTC Durban in a Short 'C' Class flying boat, the *Coorong*. Prior to embarking, the RAF were issued with temporary passports and civilian clothes so that Mozambiquan (Portuguese) neutrality would not be impaired, as they had to transit Lourenço Marques. The flight to Cairo took four days, landing each evening on sea, lake or river via Dar es Salaam (Tanganyika), Entebbe (Uganda), Khartoum (Sudan) and Wadi Halfa (Egypt), and finally on the Nile at Cairo.

Wilkins, having done a Flying Control Course in Palestine, was posted to 216 Group HQ, Middle East Flying Control, at Heliopolis as a duty officer at Aircraft Safety Centre. He was engaged in controlling the flow of service aircraft through the Middle East and Eastern Mediterranean until he returned to the UK. By this time the war in Europe and the Far East was well over. Lend-Lease had long since run out, and the RATG was closing down.

Wilkins' story is particularly interesting because, after some 46 years, he remembers so much in detail about his flying training in Southern Rhodesia and in South Africa. Like most others, his progress throughout his career in the RAF was dictated by the date of his birth, and the time he entered the Service. Born in early 1925, he was bound to find himself graduating during the final phase of the European war.

The Rhodesian Air Training Wing post-war

Bill Gunston, ex-Technical Editor of *Flight* magazine and author of more than 300 books, was born in 1927 and was a DOPE cadet (in for the Duration Of the Present Emergency). In late 1946/47 the bullshit had reappeared in force, and there was no war on the horizon. A Labour Government had been returned, and the RAF was in a state of flux, having little idea as to its future strength and commitment. Furthermore, Sir Frank Whittle had given Britain an invaluable lead in jet technology and the aviation industry was being revolutionized. Overseas flying training schemes had been closed down in 1946, and Cranwell, which had been shut down late in the war, had reopened but was not yet working to its full capacity. Trained aircrews were being demobbed in large numbers, and others, partly trained, were having to remuster. In this climate of confusion and uncertainty it is extraordinary that arrangements were made for reopening flying schools and resuming aircrew training in Southern Rhodesia.

This was the 'icing on the cake' for Southern Rhodesia, which had given such tremendous backing to the Mother Country at a crucial stage in late 1939 and early 1940. She held a special place in RAF esteem and, no doubt, deserved special consideration. But there were other factors. The peacetime RAF was looking for cadets with a higher standard of education and background for regular commissions, more appropriate to post-war requirements. The vast majority of Bill Gunston's associates had been educated at well-known public schools, and they had been selected from several hundred candidates for intakes either at Cranwell or in Rhodesia. Cranwell could only absorb a few cadets at that time, which made Rhodesia an attractive proposition. Ground crews were diverted from the Middle East, and reopening the stations was not difficult.

Bill Gunston's experience of training in Rhodesia is interesting because, unlike previous intakes, there was no war at the end of it. Cadets, of course, were keen to fly, and maintained discipline for fear of being eliminated from the course. But the atmosphere and style differed, because these young men were more of the upper-crust student fraternity, and their background affected their attitude to flying training and to life in general.

Bill Gunston himself had been one of 22 cadets who had spent 12 months in 1945–6 at University College, Durham, and had flown Tiger Moths from RAF Ouston. In the following narrative Bill captures the atmosphere of his Rhodesian adventure, and the style of life in surroundings which had not changed since the wartime intakes graduated.

'I remember the thrill I felt when I read in *Flight* just after VJ-day that future aircrew training would be carried out in Southern Rhodesia. The dream came true. I became part of No. 1 Course, and we sailed from Tilbury aboard the troopship *Chitral* on 29 November 1946. We docked at Durban on Christmas Day, to find ourselves surrounded by things totally unfamiliar: hot sunshine, giant fruit sundaes, cigarettes in boxes of 50 (price 1s 3d), flashy American cars, electric shavers, colour film and modern 35 mm cameras, fresh or canned fruit, chocolate, and more liquor than we could take. Austere post-war Britain was 8,012 miles away, and it seemed like it.

'After two days in trains we unloaded at Bulawayo, spent a day or two at RAF Station Kumalo and then a week or two at 4 FTS, Heany. During the war the Rhodesian Air Training Group had grown to include 15 airfields, using de Havilland Tiger Moth IIs and Fairchild Cornells for elementary pilot training, and Avro Ansons and Airspeed Oxfords for twin-engined qualification and, especially, for training navigators. The RATG and SRAF headquarters was at Cranborne, outside Salisbury.

'Along with the rest of what had become the British Commonwealth Air Training Plan, the RATG was shut down after VE-day, the stations being put on a Care & Maintenance basis. But the incoming post-war government decided to reopen three stations as the RATW. I would not presume to know the reasons, though obviously the weather was far better than in the UK, and probably overall costs would be lower. The three stations were: Kumalo, HQ and wing admin; Heany, No. 4 FTS; and Thornhill, 5 FTS.

'After the short spell at Heany about half No. 1 Course, myself included, got back on a train and arrived at Gwelo. This pleasant town was the capital of the Midlands, with Matabeleland on one side and Mashonaland on the other. Today it is called Gweru, and is quite a big city, but 45 years ago Gwelo was a small chessboard of straight streets with one or two substantial buildings and a much larger collection of single-storey shops and dwellings mostly of corrugated iron. It had the air of a Western frontier town, but we loved it. The amazing width of the main streets was explained to us: before the age of the car the streets had to be wide enough to turn a wagon with a long team of oxen.

'A mile or two outside the town was RAF Thornhill. Its layout followed a familiar pattern. The straight road ran past the guardroom at the main gate. Entering the station, you soon came to a roundabout, with SHQ facing you on the far side and the flagmast in the centre of the grass circle. From this point the station's built-up area was arranged in concentric semi-circles. Around the outside edge were the four pairs of giant hangars. The latter were of T2 type, but with a row of windows on each side. They were of silver corrugated steel, and so was virtually every other building on the station; I can't recall a single thing made of brick or wood. Everyone knows the old saying, "If it moves, salute it; if it doesn't move, paint it white". This applied to the RATW 100 per cent. Post-war bullshit ruled the day, and the entire station was lined with many hundreds of white-painted rocks. But no problem; this was nothing compared with No. 1 Aircrew Officers' School at Hereford, which many of us had survived.

'The AOC of the RATW was Air Commodore G. G. Banting. He was a Grade A1 flying instructor, and he certainly impressed me. We would have seen little of him, but one day another cadet and I happened to meet him in Salisbury. We were in civvies, but he knew who we were instantly, grilled us at great length and put right most of our many beefs almost overnight. Station Commander was Grp Captain F. W. Stannard, a no-nonsense cigar-smoker who looked and acted the part, though I suspect the Adj, Flt/Lt Hagger, did the routine work. CFI was Wg Cdr Dennis Weston-Birt, who probably wished he was back busting Panzers in the Western Desert as CO of 6 Squadron. SAdO was Wg Cdr E. L. A. Walter, the most hirsute man I ever met; hair bushed out from his cuffs. He was a fitness fanatic, and was heartily disgusted to find hardly anyone on the station who was eager to spend his spare time boxing.

'The instructors, whom it was my privilege later to join, were naturally ex-operational types who in some cases regarded the job as a chore to be suffered for a short time until their number for release came up. The erks, a splendid lot, were almost all ex-Palestine or Egypt. We soon learned that the truck taking those off duty into Gwelo each evening was actually "a gharry". And, incidentally, I never found one who didn't wish he was back in the Middle East.

'Like most of Southern Africa, Southern Rhodesia is on a high plateau. Though more than 1,000 ft lower than Jo'burg, Thornhill was still 4,680 ft up, so a Tiger was getting on for half-way to its ceiling before we took off. We began on Tigers, and because most of us had already done lots of "gash" flying we soloed pretty quickly. Ian Stebbings made it in 3 hours, and I took 4 hr 50 min. I am sure we had no "washouts". It was a difficult period for the Air Force but we were lucky in getting plenty of flying in mainly glorious weather with no prospect of being shot at. The very fact that the war was over removed from most of us our reason for being in uniform. Many cadets, especially the navigators, were mature chaps—real oldies, over 25—who had been through the war in ground trades, remustered as aircrew and, from 1944 onwards, had spent their time mowing lawns and cleaning out latrines, in between fierce kit inspections and staying up half the night varnishing the coal in the mirror-like scuttles and polishing the soles of their boots. As for the instructors, most were simply counting the days.

'Half the time, classroom lessons were made up on the spot. F/O Johnson, a nav instructor, thought one day he'd teach us about map grid references. Then he called a cadet out to demonstrate. "Bish" Pope strode up to the blackboard and quickly drew a map and a grid, with the letters QO, RO, SO, TO, etc, and TA, TB, TC, etc. Marking a point, he said, "This is grid reference ROTB 1947." The whole class was convulsed, because this was a belligerent chant heard day and night, ROTB standing for "Roll on the boat" (to take chaps back to Blighty).

'Somewhere in between we did a lot of things. When we arrived, our khaki drill shorts reached to our knees, but having seen the vast expanse of bronzed thigh and leg exposed by the local white Rhodesians, we soon cut 10 in off. We got on well with half the locals, though I recall we had an official complaint from the Gwelo Rugby Club who couldn't take the RAF team's brandy-soaked breath (this on Sunday mornings, mark you). The other half, of Afrikaner origin, had lain low during the war, but now they came out looking for trouble, and the young ones—locally called Yarpis—caused fights in the town almost every night. Down the road was a town reputed to be 100 per cent Boer—Enkeldoorn—and we were told if we went there we would be unlikely to come back. We didn't test the belief. On the other hand the congregation of St Cuthbert's, Gwelo, included several hospitable Afrikaner families who found the aggro embarrassing.

'We also rehabilitated the station itself, and in our spare time uncrated 115 Cornells, took out the map cases with beautifully hinged lids, which could serve many purposes, and then sledgehammered them into pieces small enough to be loaded into trucks. The Lend-Lease Act precluded their post-war use, and the USA didn't want them back. We also played a lot of water polo, built a theatre in a hangar, and built dozens of giant flying models powered by Ohlsson petrol engines bought from a shop of the Das Brothers (we'd never seen such things before). In odd moments we learned to fly Harvards. One day two Spitfire IXs arrived with officers of the SAAF who promised us what sounded like an air marshal's pay, but I don't think they got many takers. Several of us, myself included, though totally unqualified as instructors, stayed on to help teach No. 3 course. I can only remember one prang in two years. S/L Hyland-Smith, a brilliant aerobatic pilot, got caught in a whirling dust devil as he practised his routine in a Tiger for a forthcoming air show. He lay encased in plaster in Gwelo hospital, where the nurses spent much of their time rolling him over to see what we had written on him.

'Southern Rhodesia obviously has many happy memories for me. The RATW was finally closed in March 1954. Subsequently, Thornhill was to go through dark days in which white Zimbabwe AF officers were tortured during investigations into sabotage of Hawk jet trainers. I hope that by now they have got their act together.'

4. Canada—the big deal

I am convinced that the idea that we shall be able to fight the next war with mass-produced pilots and crews, as we did the last war, is fallacious.
Air Chief-Marshal Sir Edgar Ludlow-Hewitt

THE ADVENT OF war is a great motivator, because national survival is in the balance. Preconceived ideas, plans and programmes are subjected to the winds of change and the test of battle. Ludlow-Hewitt, whose prime argument had been that all war planning was hypothetical without operational efficiency, was wrong about mass-produced aircrews, but right when he stated categorically that aircrew training was more important than any other factor.

At 11 am on 3 September 1939 Great Britain declared war on Germany as from 5 pm on that day. Much to our everlasting gratitude, the Dominions immediately placed themselves alongside the Mother Country. Exactly 23 days later Prime Minister Chamberlain lit a fuse under the proposed Empire Air Training Scheme in a direct approach to the Canadian Prime Minister, Mackenzie King. This outlined in broad terms the vital importance of training and stressed the overstrained and limited facilities available in the United Kingdom:

CYPHER TELEGRAPH

To the Goverments of Canada, the Commonwealth of Australia and New Zealand. (Sent 3.30 am 26 September 1939)
Unnumbered.
MOST SECRET AND PERSONAL.
Following for Prime Minister from Prime Minister, begins.
To Canada only.
I am sure you will agree that the scheme outlined in the following message is of the first importance. For this reason, and because it invites the co-operation of Canada to a very special degree, I want to make a special personal appeal to you about it. I feel that so far-reaching a project will strike your imagination, particularly as it concerns an all-important field of war activity

in which Canada has already made so striking and gallant an individual contribution.

May I therefore ask that the matter should receive very urgent attention? To all

1. During the last few days War Cabinet have been considering whole problem of future requirements in air strength and nature of effort likely to be required. Conclusion reached is that problem is one of vital importance, especially in light of success obtained by German air force in helping to achieve rapid subjugation of Poland. It is now abundantly clear that an overwhelming air force will be needed in order to counter German air strength and, in combination with other military measures and economic pressure, to bring ultimate victory.

2. With this in view War Cabinet have sanctioned immediate instructions to direct further expansion of aircraft production and training. Objective is to build up gradually and maintain in continuous operation a greatly enlarged air force. In view of unfortunate fact that wastage rate of air force when engaged in continuous and heavy operations is exceedingly high, it is expected that there would be required not less than 20,000 pilots and 30,000 personnel of aircrews annually for the maintenance of this large force. To provide these, it is estimated that about 90 elementary and advanced flying training schools, with some subsidiary aircrew and ground schools, would be necessary.

3. In this respect we find ourselves under a grave disability in that the training organization now required is more than twice the entire training capacity available in the United Kingdom, having regard to limited space, opertional restrictions and vulnerability to air attack.

4. It seems to us that there is a problem in the solution of which the overseas parts of the Empire may well be able to play a decisive part. If about one-half of this vast training organization—say 50 flying training schools (of which 25 would be for advanced training) with some subsidiary schools—could be built up elsewhere than in the United Kingdom it would be in our judgement of inestimable value to the common cause. We have therefore been thinking over the lines on which such an effort might be realized, and venture to put forward for the consideration of your government a scheme of which the following is an outline.

5. Schools for elementary training would be established in each Dominion according to its capacity. Whilst all Dominions enjoy equal immunity from risk of enemy interference, Canada has the special advantages of nearness to United Kingdom, greater potential for manufacture of service type of aircraft and proximity to vast resources of United States of America. For this reason the conception of the scheme involves general agreement on the part of all Governments concerned that advanced training for trainees from the elementary school should be centred in Canada. There would be a continuous flow of trained personnel from the elementary training schools through the advanced training schools in Canada to the theatres of operations. It would also be our intention that a number of those who have completed elementary training in the United Kingdom should receive their advanced training in Canada.

6. We appreciate that any such scheme of rationalized training must depend on adequate provision of training types and advanced Service types of aircraft. It is our hope that existing resources of the Dominions for the production of trainers and their engines will be fully utilized and expanded to meet the requirements of elementary schools, as determined by the extent to which each Dominion may decide to participate in the general scheme of training. It would not be the intention to retard or interfere in any way with projects already embarked on for Dominion production of Service types. We are working out the numbers and types of aircraft, both training and advanced, that we think would be required and we should be in a position to let you have particulars at an early date.

7. We would wish to do everything in our power, as for example by the loan of personnel, to help in building up the organization outlined above.

8. It is of course contemplated that the first call on Dominion personnel who had received their training in the schools under the scheme would be for such air force units of the Dominions as the several Dominion Governments might be prepared to provide and maintain.

9. If a scheme on above lines is acceptable in principle to your Government we suggest, as a first step, joint discussions between experts. We think that these discussions might most conveniently take place in Canada. We ourselves are ready at very short notice to send to Canada a mission of high standing specially qualified for this particular purpose, and we hope that it might be possible for it to discuss questions arising with similar missions from other Governments concerned.

10. We hope that you will agree to the immense influence which the development and realization of such a great project as that outlined in this telegram may have upon the whole course of the war; it might even prove decisive. We trust therefore that this cooperative method of approach to the problem will appeal to your Government. The knowledge that a vast air potential was being built up in the Dominions, where no German activity could interfere with its expansion, might well have a psychological effect on the Germans equal to that produced by the intervention of the United States in the last war with the cumulative strength of its vast resources.

11. It would be most helpful if you could let us know at the earliest possible moment whether your Government approved the suggested scheme in principle and whether they are agreeable to join discussions in Canada in order that immediate arrangements can be made to that end.

12. I have conveyed the substance of the above scheme to the Prime Ministers of Australia and New Zealand also. Ends.
Australia and New Zealand
Canada and New Zealand
Canada and Australia also. Ends.

Chamberlain must have wondered at that time what sort of reply he would get from Mackenzie King. Response to previous negotiations through the British High Commission had been remarkably intransigent, due largely no doubt to the Canadian Premier's anxiety over a pending election, and the effect that any full-scale assistance to Britain might have on the French Canadian vote in the Quebec Province. Chamberlain received the following reply on the eve of Russia's attack on Finland.

CYPHER TELEGRAPH

CANADA

From the Government of Canada.
Dated 28 September 1939. Received 9.07 am, 29 September.
Unnumbered message, 26 September. Most Secret.
Following from Prime Minister for your Prime Minister, begins.

1. I have received and discussed with my colleagues the situation outlined in your telegram under reference.

2. We have noted the conclusion of the War Cabinet that a greatly enlarged air force, in combination with other military measures and economic pressure, has become of vital importance. We have therefore given immediate consideration to the Secretary of State for War's scheme outlined in your telegram, and in particular to the part Canada could play in recruiting and training pilots and other personnel on co-operative plan proposed.

3. I can say at once that our Government fully agrees that Canadian co-operation in this field would be particularly appropriate and probably the most effective in the military sphere which Canada could furnish. We would therefore be prepared to accept the scheme in principle.

4. There are necessarily certain important points which would have to be considered in determining what on our part may be possible.

5. The first requirement to ensure maximum effectiveness is the provision of sufficient planes to permit of training the large numbers contemplated. Canadian aircraft production is only just beginning to expand, and cannot hope to provide the aircraft necessary for home defence and the initial supply of intermediate and advanced training aircraft in time for the scheme to develop quickly, therefore these initial aircraft for this scheme must come from Britain or the United States. Canadian production could probably look after subsequent replacement. Canada can provide a surplus of elementary trainers which would be available for other Dominions. Engines are not available in Canada at present and must be supplied from Britain or the United States. Canadian manufacture of engines, if started now, could hardly produce useful results in less than 18 or 20 months. It would be desirable to consider whether it would be possible to expand the Canadian production by the transfer of some of the United Kingdom plant to Canada.

As regards the United States, it is unlikely to provide either air frames or engines in large quantities for quick delivery, except by the diversion to Canada of aircraft now ordered by Britain. In event of the repeal of the arms embargo, United States plant will still be engaged far ahead with domestic and other orders including orders from neutral countries. Some recent quotations indicate 18 months as minimum time for delivery of new orders, though we believe that this could be speeded up.

The views of the United Kingdom Government on all of the above points would be very helpful.

6. As to instructors available here, full details will be sent very shortly. It is however plain that the number at present available is far below what would be necessary for rapid and effective co-opeation, and that the loan of personnel from the United Kingdom at the outset would be essential in ensuring the training of the maximum numbers in the minimum time. Particulars on this point would therefore be of great assistance. The facts as to existing and potential aerodromes and training stations are being collected and will be furnished shortly.

7. A third point of importance is the financial aspect. In order to decide the best possible extent of participation in the proposed air training plan, and in the light thereof to review the plans already made for military and economic co-operation, it will be necessary to be informed in general terms what your Government has in mind as to the distribution of costs of air training amongst the several co-operating Governments. I should perhaps mention that the question of financing British purchases in this market, to which reference was made in our telegram No. 82 of 21st September, is still unsettled, though we hope that the Treasury representatives will be able to discuss it with us in the course of the next few days.

8. We are entirely in agreement as to the desirability of joint discussions in Canada between experts at the earliest possible date and would be pleased to receive the missions from the United Kingdom suggested in your telegram, and also similar missions from other parts of the Commonwealth.

As a result of these exchanges the Canadian Government agreed to receive the mission proposed under the leadership of Lord Riverdale KBE. Its initial purpose was to discuss in detail, and if possible reach agreement on, proposals which had been put forward by Captain Balfour, Under-Secretary of State for Air. These concerned the Dominion Air Training Scheme in which Canada, Australia and New Zealand would be involved. Canada was expected to be the prime mover and to undertake the lion's share.

On 10 October 1939, Air Minister Sir Kingsley Wood informed the House of Commons that the Dominions concerned had signified their agreement in principle to an overseas air training scheme, and that a mission would shortly be going to Canada. Regarding South Africa, he said: 'For various reasons the Government of the Union of South Africa does not consider this scheme of air training applicable to the circumstances of the Union, and they consider that their Air Force personnel should receive their full training at home. I am, however, authorized to say that the Union authorities intend to make their training as complete as possible, and to expand their Air Force to the fullest extent of their resources . . . '

The mission arrived in Canada on 14 October 1939—the day that the battleship *Royal Oak* was sunk in Scapa Flow with the loss of 810 lives. In addition to Lord Riverdale, it consisted of Air Marshal Christopher Courtney and Mr F. T. Hearle, managing director of the de Havilland Aircraft Company. Unfortunately, Hearle was taken ill on arrival, and returned to England after attending only one meeting. Courtney had replaced Air Marshal Sir Robert Brooke-Popham, who was not immediately available. Australia and New Zealand were represented separately, as the plan proposed to include the training of aircrew in Canada from both of those Dominions.

The preliminary meeting with Canadian Ministers closely concerned achieved the object of convincing them of the need for a training scheme of such magnitude; but it became clear that they were alarmed at the size of the proposal, and at its probable cost. They insisted that they should not be regarded as committed to the scheme until the question had been fully investigated.

On the assumption that the scheme would be working at full capacity by July 1942, the Royal Canadian Air Force authorities, together with British experts, set to work preparing estimates. (A total of 30,177 aircrew were actually trained in Canada during 1942, consisting of 14,135 pilots, 7,404 navigators, 1,742 air bombers and 6,896 WOP/AGs and AGs. During 1943 this figure was exceeded by 9,001, which made 1943 the peak year for those trained in Canada.)

When the true costs started to emerge, the Canadian authorities began to have grave doubts about the whole scheme, and these doubts were shared by the Australian and New Zealand missions. At this stage RCAF estimates for the scheme were showing a probable expenditure of $900 million over three-and-a-half years, to be offset by the United Kingdom's offer of $140 million in kind. Matters came to a head when Prime Minister Mackenzie King opened the proceedings of a meeting to consider estimates on 31 October 1939.

He started by reading Chamberlain's telegram of 26 September outlining the proposed scheme, and added that his reason for doing so was to emphasize that the proposals were those put forward by the British Government. They had not been suggested by his Government, which had no primary responsibility for them. It was a scheme devised in Great Britain for training pilots and aircrews in Canada, and Canada had done no more than express her willingness to co-operate in such a scheme. She had not agreed to accept responsibility for it.

These were harsh words on Mackenzie King's part, contradicting the earlier impression given by his telegram to Chamberlain. His blunt statement was a serious setback for the mission. But clearly his main concern was the balance of financial contribution, and this formed the basis of future talks.

Riverdale and his colleagues urgently needed a settlement. Riverdale himself pointed out in vain the enormous sums that the UK had expended on defence since the rise of Hitler, and he emphasized that Britain's current defence budget would exceed £1,300 million. But Mackenzie King and his Ministers were lukewarm, and recalcitrant in their attitude to Riverdale's approach.

Personality clashes can change the course of history, and there is little doubt that Mackenzie King and Lord Riverdale disliked one another. The bluff, hearty, yet domineering manner of Riverdale did nothing to ease the distrust which had been aroused, and his somewhat airy assumptions, particularly relating to cost, which he seemed to regard as irrelevant, almost led the mission to founder from the start. Although

Riverdale was an astute Northern businessman with a great deal of experience in public affairs, he personified all the characteristics of an Englishman so resented by King.

To be fair to Canada, particularly with regard to the attitude she adopted at this early stage, one has to understand her priorities. She already had a heavy commitment to the Royal Canadian Navy and the Canadian Expeditionary Force which could not be abandoned. The Prime Minister had earlier outlined her defence policy in precise detail. He explained that it was imperative for her to place in the forefront the defence of her coastline, the protection of internal security, and the stability of her economic and financial position.

Co-operation with the United Kingdom, he said, would have as its primary objective the safety of the main trade routes, especially those emanating from the St Lawrence, which would include the security of Newfoundland and Labrador. Further measures would include economic co-operation, the control and security of essential commodities, and the prevention of trade with the enemy.

Apart from the problems highlighted by Mackenzie King and his Ministers, both Australia and New Zealand voiced pungent criticisms of their own. It seemed that the plan originally put forward by Balfour, admirable in its far-reaching concept, had presumed far too much, and that too little preliminary consultation had taken place with the countries concerned. Both Australia and New Zealand expressed the view that the majority of training of their own men should take place in their respective Dominions, pointing out the difficulties of obtaining Canadian dollars for training in Canada. They felt it would be far better for them to spend their money on training in their own countries, which, furthermore, would be simpler and less costly. By this means training could be accelerated, and pupils would be happier being trained at home.

Additional doubts were also raised by Australia regarding their ability to find the number of pupils envisaged in the original scheme, but they undertook to try. New Zealand, however, were adamant that their quota should be reduced considerably, to 3,350 pupils of all categories of aircrew per year. As a result, fresh estimates had to be prepared.

The mission was impressed by these views because they argued in favour of a reduction in costs to Canada. Both Australia and New Zealand insisted that the share assigned to them was larger than justified by their small populations and resources.

With hindsight, it seems that Balfour and his Treasury advisors had acted in a heavy-handed manner when drawing up the scheme. They should have given far more consideration to the interests of their Dominion partners. New Zealand, for example, was already committed to heavy capital expenditure on additional training facilities at the express request of the British Air Ministry! Consequently, the UK ran the grave risk of torpedoing a great idea before it was afloat. In the event, Britain was forced to accept more of the financial burden during the following days of horse-trading, which failed to reflect in any way the vital urgency of the situation. Naturally, Mackenzie King wanted to do the sort of deal that he could sell to his electorate. He knew that he had been asked to accept the major share, but was reluctant to admit that he was indisputably in a far better position to do so.

As Britain was forced to agree her contributions, so Canadian Ministers reopened the question of the form these contributions should take. They made the point that such contributions were fixed in quantity, but not in value. They insisted that, should the total cost of the scheme exceed the estimated cost, the UK should make a supplementary payment in kind or cash to cover it. This resulted in Australia and New Zealand re-examining their own positions, and temporarily withdrawing their original agreements. Hence, there were drastic rearrangements of flying schools in Australia, and those to be provided by Australia in Canada.

At last, on 17 December 1939, almost two-and-a-half months after the mission had arrived in Canada, the formal Memorandum of Agreement was signed by Prime Minister Mackenzie King on behalf of the Canadian Government, and by the other delegates on behalf of their Governments. This was not before the Canadian Government had insisted on five points, namely:

1. Confirmation by the Government of the United Kingdom of the agreement which had been provisionally reached between Captain Balfour and the Minister of National Defence in regard to the higher organization and control of the training scheme in Canada.

2. That the Government of the United Kingdom would be prepared to help the Government of Australia and New Zealand to raise the Canadian dollars which they would require in order to pay for their shares of the cost of the training in Canada.

3. That the United Kingdom Government regarded participation in the air training scheme as more effective assistance than any other form of co-operation which Canada could give; and they wished to be at liberty to give publicity to the assurance of the Government of the United Kingdom on the latter point.

4. That the financial discussions taking place in London between their representatives and the representatives of the United Kingdom Government led to a mutually and reasonably satisfying agreement on the general financial questions outstanding between the two Governments.

5. That arrangements satisfactory to them would be made for identifying Canadian pupils with Canada to the maximum extent possible after the completion of their training.

To her credit, Canada had driven a hard bargain, but it was significant that her Ministers had not wished it to be felt that the training scheme should take the place of or overshadow the commitment of her forces in the field. Neither should Canadian airmen, wherever trained, be absorbed into Royal Air Force squadrons without being easily identified.

Such fears proved to be unjustified. Canadian squadrons were to be found in almost every Command, and each officer and airman was clearly identified by shoulder flashes. They had a great and glorious record in all theatres of the war.

The agreement was signed on the day that the pocket battleship *Graf Spee* scuttled herself in the entrance to Montevideo harbour. Some time after the event, the crews of HMS *Exeter*, *Ajax* and *Achilles* marched through the City of London to martial music and a hero's welcome. The three little cruisers, like ferrets, had cornered the far more powerful German battleship, and in so doing had aroused public admiration throughout the free world.

This incident could not have come at a better time.

Had it not been scuttled, the *Graf Spee* could have done untold damage let loose in the Atlantic. As it was, a few months later British aircrew cadets were crossing the Atlantic to dock in Halifax at the beginning of their journey across Canada for training!

Turbulence and triumph

The Scheme was introduced to the Canadian Parliament in Ottawa on 19 December 1939 by Mackenzie King, and Mr F. Jones, Defence Minister representing New Zealand. Coinciding with Canada's call to arms, it was enthusiastically received. Apart from Canada's dominant role in this momentous undertaking, which appealed to national pride, there was an intense interest in flying throughout the Dominion. Trans-Canada Airlines, for example, carried more air freight than their counterparts in the USA, and there was intense rivalry between the two. Air transport had opened up isolated areas in the North, carrying machinery and supplies. There were a great many bush pilots, many of them operating floatplanes using the myriad of lakes and rivers. These were pioneering days for air travel across this vast continent which naturally stimulated interest in aviation, especially amongst the youth. Canada had, in fact, more pilots in proportion to her population than any other country.

As far as the Royal Canadian Air Force was concerned, the Empire Scheme provided the biggest challenge and opportunity for growth in its short history. Initially, one of the prime objects of the Scheme was to train Canadian volunteers, with about 20 per cent of the total number coming from overseas to do advanced training. It was envisaged that some 1,400 cadets would be turned out as trained aircrew each month when the Scheme was running at full throttle in 1942; thus the RCAF, which had only 11 regular squadrons and 12 part-time squadrons, had 'the ball at its feet'. Naturally it played this ball with the utmost vigour in helping to make Canada a monumental training ground for the Empire, and in so doing to establish itself as a major air striking force.

Its tradition dated back to the first Canadian Air Force Wing, which

was formed in August 1918 as part of the Royal Air Force. Famous air
aces who joined the wing included Lt.-Col. 'Billy' Bishop VC, Lt.-Col.
W. H. Barker, Majors Earle Godfrey, McKeaber and Don McLaren,
and Captain C. E. McEwen. These flyers had made their reputations
with the Royal Flying Corps (predecessor of the RAF). The newly
formed Canadian Wing never saw action, being financially disbanded
when the Canadian Expeditionary Force returned home.

In 1926 the part-time Canadian Air Force was formed, with material
supplied by the RAF. Four years later, in 1930, it was granted the prefix
'Royal', when it had a complement of 61 officers and 262 men. Its
uniforms and general style were modelled on the RAF, except for
buttons and wings embodying the letters RCAF, and the RAF provided
the equipment.

This tiny force was hardly capable of guarding Canada's vast
coastline. Run by the Department of National Defence under the
control of the militia, its duties were mainly of a semi-civil nature, such
as aerial surveys, forest-fire detection, anti-smuggling patrols, crop
dusting and the exploration of far north territories. During the
depression of 1932–3 its budget was reduced to such an extent that
its few personnel had to be cut by half. However, by the end of
1936 the force had grown to 253 officers and 1,829 men on a
regular basis, and 87 officers with 820 airmen on a volunteer, part-time
basis.

At this time it was withdrawn from the General Staff and placed
under its own Air Council, with a Chief of Staff in Ottawa. Provincial
governments and commercial operators had taken over the semi-civil
work, and the RCAF began to develop along Service lines. The force
was divided into three Commands. Western Air Command, with its HQ
in Vancouver, had bases in British Columbia, Alberta, Saskatchewan
and Manitoba to protect the Pacific coast; Eastern Air Command had
its HQ at Halifax and units in New Brunswick and Nova Scotia; and
the third Command was Training Command, with HQ at Toronto.

It was shortly after these developments had taken place that officials from the British High Commission and the RAF began to sound
out the possibilities of joint co-operation as a means for the RAF to
decentralize flying training. RCAF Training Command became the
nucleus around which the Empire Scheme was formulated and programmed. Organized on a functional and not an administrative basis
and, unlike the RAF, having a one-Command structure, it became the
vital piece in the jigsaw. Close liaison and mutual links between the
two Services had enabled Lord Riverdale and his associates to lobby
Parliament and public figures which, at times, had caused some friction
with Canadian Ministers.

Some details of the deal must have been leaked to the public before
the official announcement was made, and even then estimates and
programmes were later modified. It was understood that Canada's
contribution to the Scheme would start with setting up 67 training
schools, the construction of 60 new aerodromes, and the enlargement

of 20 existing ones. Concerning the schools, there were to be three large schools for initial training, 16 Service flying schools, ten observer schools, ten for bombing and gunnery, two for navigation and four radio schools. Staffing was estimated at 40,000 men, of whom 2,700 would be commissioned officers, 6,000 civilians, and 30,000 NCOs and airmen engaged on servicing and other work.

The initial reaction from the public at large to this grandiose project was enthusiastic. People began pressing for details of the new airfields which would be necessary. The Toronto *Financial Post* reported that '. . . thousands of communities across Canada have been prodding their local members to 'get one for us'. Over 7,000 euphoric young men volunteered for aircrew training, and it looked as if the Scheme was off to a splendid start.

However, in early 1940 Canadian public opinion became intensely critical of the way its Government was implementing the Scheme, and demanded prompt action. The *Financial Post* reported that:

> *Scaled down from the gigantic enterprise mooted for months, the so-called Empire Air Training Scheme emerges as very largely Canadian. Though of less magnitude than long indicated at Ottawa, the air training plans involve a vast building and construction programme, which will affect many communities, and many lines of business. Apart from providing an undisclosed number of advanced training machines, and perhaps sending a few recruits here for advanced training and to serve as instructors, Britain has hardly more than a nominal connection with the Scheme. Australia and New Zealand are only to send a few of their men to Canada, and only for advanced training.*

Modifying the Scheme in order to launch it was undoubtedly a necessity for 'getting it off the ground', but it disappointed some Canadian financiers because in its revised form it did not offer so much profit as originally envisaged—but then, a few profiteers exist in every country! This criticism, however, put the pressure back on Britain to do more, and was another reminder that the Scheme had not been thoroughly thought out and researched beforehand.

There were also some notable people at home in Britain who had their doubts about the plan. The provocative C. G. Grey, Editor of *The Aeroplane*, commented on 16 February 1940 in his article entitled 'The Canadian Training Scheme' that:

> . . . *The scheme for the sending of British pupils to Canada never looked very sensible to me. There seemed no reason why a pupil should cross the sub-infested Atlantic twice so that he might ultimately fly over Germany or Russia. And the idea that recruits should take ship to Canada, learn to fly there, and then fly back to England as the crews of Canadian-built big bombers of 'Flying Fortress' enormity suggested a long period of training. Such things take much building.*

Writing about other areas that he considered suitable for aircrew training, he said, '. . . But there are vast areas available in France, which, although they might be expensive to hire, would certainly cost less than shipping people across the Atlantic. The Royal Naval Air Service had a gigantic training establishment in Central France at Vendôme, from about 1915 to the end of the war.' Grey must have known that work had already started on five airfields in the Loire area, but fortunately this was overtaken by events. It is a horrifying thought how many valuable aircraft, instructors and pupils, together with equipment and men, might have been lost during the collapse of France had the scheme come to fruition! Similar proposals in Kenya were discontinued as being impractical after Italy's entry into the war.

However, to be fair to the incomparable C. G. Grey, he concluded his article by saying that, taking the Empire Scheme all round, it seemed quite sound to him, although he thought that Australia should be able to train her own pilots past advanced training stage.

Fortunately for the Free World, the Empire Scheme did not founder on the rocks of financial viability and self-interest. Hard-pressed by Canada and the other Dominions, Britain was forced to increase her commitment. She proposed the transfer of entire flying schools, but Canada went further and insisted on the supply of aircraft as a condition of acceptance. The United Kingdom reluctantly agreed, and the programme went ahead as planned. By April 1940 the first training school at Toronto had opened, and the first batch of British cadets had safely crossed the Atlantic.

A matter of some urgency

The Empire Scheme slowly gathered momentum against the backcloth of Hitler's blitzkrieg machine powering its way across the Low Countries and France during May and early June 1940. The Panzers were unstoppable, and the battle to save France soon became a lost cause. The Germans occupied Paris, and newsreels soon showed Hitler standing triumphant at the Arc de Triomphe, looking down the Champs Elysées, while his Luftwaffe regrouped for the Battle of Britain.

The enemy had reached a pinnacle of success in becoming the masters of Western Europe. To Britain's astonishment, the Luftwaffe had acquired a vast network of airfields stretching from Norway across to the tip of Brittany, providing operational, transport, supply and training bases. The Germans began making plans to establish basic training schools in Poland and Czechoslovakia, and advanced schools in France, Belgium, Greece, Norway, Denmark and Italy, making an eventual total of some 75–100 schools.

Such was the strategic background in Europe when the first few training schools in Canada began operating. During 1940 the foundations upon which the Empire Scheme was built were laid across the vast expanses of Canada (geographically bigger than Western Europe). It was a matter of some urgency, because the RAF was poised to undergo the biggest expansion in its history, and likewise the Royal Canadian Air Force.

Over the skies of Southern England the Battle of Britain, one of the most decisive battles of all time, had been fought and won and an immediate invasion of the United Kingdom averted. Such an invasion would have had a paralysing effect on overseas training and Britain's ability to survive! The successful conclusion of this battle, however, ensured the survival of the Western democracies, and bought time for rearmament and training. Plans were being aired in the corridors of power at the Air Ministry and Whitehall which demanded a force of some 4,000 heavy bombers to make Bomber Command a major offensive strike force. The inauguration of such a plan, which took place in mid-1941, required a continuous and substantial intake of trained aircrews. This plan, known as 'Target Force E', had been designed to expand Bomber Command to 250 squadrons, and four-engined bombers were already in service. Canada was destined to provide the lion's share of all overseas-trained aircrew, and there was little time to lose!

The advent of war stimulates action, and unfetters the restraints of a peace-time economy. Following the signing of the Empire Air Training Agreement in December 1939, Canada was faced with the monumental and complex problem of implementing the Scheme. The enormity of the project, even by today's standards, is difficult to grasp. For example, to locate and construct over 80 airfields across 3,000 miles, and then to build and furnish 67 training centres to house the various training schools, was a massive undertaking.

The airfields project got off to a good start, because of the airport expansion programme instituted in 1936. New airports had been constructed along the Trans-Canada Airlines route across Canada, and over 20 of these were allocated to the flying training programme. Further construction work was required to meet the requirements of flying schools, and satellite airfields had to be provided to avoid congestion at main bases. However, 60 or more airfields had to be located before the Scheme could be fully operational in April 1942, two years after the first school opened.

Most of the administrative, design, contract and construction planning was done in Ottawa. Those involved included the Canadian Department of Transport, RCAF, RAF specialists, and representatives from Australia and New Zealand. In the early summer of 1940, during the first phase of the operation, the Canadians got to hear about the negotiations taking place between Britain and the USA regarding flying training in the States, and this created political turmoil.

Public opinion in Canada at this juncture had become discontented at the apparent lack of progress. People had expected to see work put in motion at the drop of a hat, and couldn't appreciate that tens of thousands of blue-prints had first to be prepared and construction programmed, although hundreds of contracts had been sent out. Their

frustration boiled over when word got around that the USA was to
become involved, which was a natural reaction because there was great
rivalry between the two countries.

All this led to a serious situation, and the Canadian Minister for Air
threatened to resign. Ironically, this political upset helped the Scheme
along. The RAF agreed to provide more aircraft quickly, ensuring
that an additional three SFTSs would be in operation before the end
of 1940.

The supply of aircraft for the deal was primarily the concern of the
RAF. Some 3,500 training aircraft were required to launch the project in Canada, and the UK Government agreed to provide the lion's
share at a cost of about $185 million, or about one-third of the total
cost of the scheme. However, there was a problem with the type of
aircraft. The vast projected expansion of Bomber Command swung
the balance heavily in favour of multi-engined pilots (about five or
six being needed to each single-engined pilot) and sufficient Oxfords
and Ansons could not be provided. Consequently, potential bomber
pilots had to be trained on single-engined Harvards.

Breakaway

When the Empire Air Training Scheme was being formulated, in
1939, proposals had been put forward to transfer some RAF SFTSs
to Canada. No final decision was reached at that stage, because it
was thought that too much valuable training time would be lost
during the process of transfer and re-establishment. This matter was
brought to a head some months later when the Luftwaffe began to
focus attacks on RAF Training Command airfields. Even then, in
August 1940, there was strong opposition from Lord Beaverbrook,
who held the newly created post of Minister for Aircraft Production
and felt that degutting such reserves would remove a second line of
defence. His attitude was supported by the Prime Minister, by now
Winston Churchill. Furthermore, it was considered to be politically
imprudent from a public morale point of view to transfer instructors
and aircraft when the Battle of Britain was raging overhead. However, this postponement was short-lived because of the following
considerations.

During the summer and autumn of 1940, enemy air attacks on
aerodromes had made life very difficult for Training Command in the
UK, especially for night flying. Flarepaths for night training were a
natural target, as were the unarmed and unprotected aircraft flying
predictably round the circuit. Night flying was therefore carried out at
satellite airfields some distance away from the main base, and these had
only the minimum of equipment.

Dispersing, however, did not solve the problem, as the flarepath,
consisting of gooseneck paraffin flares, had to be relaid if the wind
changed sufficiently to make landings too difficult. In the event of a
raid, these flares could not be extinguished with any speed, and they

could be seen by enemy aircraft from a considerable height.

Some relief was obtained by hooding the flares, thus making them invisible from above 3,000 ft, but this greatly increased the difficulties of instructing comparatively inexperienced pupils. The introduction of a primitive glide path indicator and, later, the Chance light—which, generator-operated, provided a floodbeam only at the moment of landing and was then switched off—gave some further relief, but night instructing continued to be a very dangerous business. Under black-out conditions on the darkest of nights, often accompanied by low cloud down to 1,000 ft and with no discernible horizon, circuits were completed by using instruments alone. By October 1940 things had reached the stage where Flying Training Command was ordered to continue flying irrespective of any form of enemy attack.

A typical example of the hazards of night flying training during this period happened at RAF Kidlington, near Oxford. Although it was August, the night was dark and the horizon barely visible, but night flying continued despite an Air Raid warning Red. Suddenly a stick of light bombs straddled the flarepath, causing surface damage, but subsequent air-to-ground fire severely damaged seven Oxford aircraft. During this time two Oxfords were airborne, one piloted by Flt. Sgt. Olsen and the other by LAC Blair, another pupil flying solo for the first time. After the ground attack, the Ju 88 picked up the trail of the Oxfords and shot them both down.

Night intruders, both at high and low level, lightning daylight raids on airfields, bad weather conditions, congested airspace and black-out all slowed down the tempo of flying training in the UK. Because of disruption by weather, every hour available had to be utilized, and dawn-to-dusk flying was a matter of routine, followed by night flying. Instructors were expected to fly seven days a week, until the accident rate rose to such an extent that it was decreed that they took one day off in seven. Such was the situation in the UK when it was finally decided to transfer some complete schools to Canada and South Africa.

The first four schools to be transferred to Canada were No. 7 SFTS Peterborough, which became No. 31 SFTS Kingston, Ontario; No. 10 SFTS Ternhill became No. 32 SFTS Moose Jaw, Saskatchewan; the third SFTS was a new school from Wilmslow, Manchester, which became No. 33 SFTS Carberry, Manitoba; and the fourth, a school of navigation at St Athan near Cardiff, became No. 31 ANS in Canada. As time progressed, a further ten RAF schools were transferred to Canada, and five other types of RAF school were operating, which gave the RAF a considerable presence in the Dominion!

Although these schools came under RCAF administrative control (covered by the Visiting Forces Acts of Canada and the UK 1933), they were operated by RAF personnel. They had simply been uprooted from the UK and transplanted some 4,000 or 5,000 miles distant in Canada, to continue operating as before. They were a by-product of the Empire Air Training Scheme, but not part of it. EATS schools were operated by the RCAF, and it had been agreed that ten per cent of all places allocated for pupil pilot training in these schools could be filled by pupils supplied by the UK. Thus, it might be said that the RAF had the best of both worlds, in that it ran its own schools and was also plugged into the EATS programme!

However, there was another factor of concern to everybody. By mid-June 1940 the 'Wolf-Packs' of U-boats were out in increasing numbers, as the first phase of the Battle of the Atlantic began to inflict heavy shipping losses. There was also a chance of bumping into a lone surface raider, which happened to 32 SFTS personnel on their journey across. They became spectators of a naval battle between the German heavy cruiser *Admiral Scheer* and convoy HX84.

Being crowded together below decks in cramped quarters and a hothouse atmosphere was an eerie experience for most cadets. They became acutely aware of a change in the throbbing of the powerhouse, the piercing shriek of ships' sirens, or a change of course. Eyes were usually fixed subconsciously on the friendly escort destroyer weaving alongside, giving everybody a touch of Nelsonian naval confidence. She immediately became a focal point of conjecture and debate if she suddenly vanished, leaving everybody 'on the hop'.

Dennis Hickin, an instructor, was on the first outbound convoy carrying No. 7 SFTS from Peterborough: 'We were attacked by the *Scharnhorst* and defended by the armed merchant cruiser *Jervis Bay*, which was sunk. Our boat, the *Duchess of Richmond*, travelling between Liverpool and Montreal, broke ranks and proceeded solo, with every rivet vibrating for 48 hours.'

Britain needed all the help she could get in the Atlantic, and a few months later President Roosevelt authorized Defense Plan No. 5, whereby the US Navy undertook to escort the Empire Air Training Scheme convoys. This released British naval forces in mid-Atlantic, instead of them having to make the passage the whole way across.

A vast amount of work was carried out by all concerned to get the Empire Air Training Scheme under way during 1940. By the end of the year the four SFTSs transferred from the UK were in operation, as were 36 Empire Schools; 520 aircrew were trained, of which 240 were pilots. These foundations provided a basis for rapid development during the following year, when the output rose to 16,653 aircrew, including 9,637 pilots.

There were naturally many teething problems with an undertaking of such magnitude. For example, some British cadets arrived at their RAF school to find that the construction work was still in progress. Expecting to get down to groundwork and lovely flying, they were organized into labouring gangs to help finish the job. Also, there was nothing more frustrating than to arrive at an airfield in the middle of nowhere to find that the aeroplanes hadn't turned up!

In early 1941, all RAF pupils going to Canada had completed EFTS training beforehand. As the elimination factor was high during primary training, this ensured that cadets making the long journey to Canada had already shown aptitude in the air. It was also considered to be more cost-effective, transport being an expensive factor! However, the value of synchronized or 'all-through' training at adjacent airfields far outweighed the disadvantages. The continuity of 'all-through' training in a stable background was much better for pupils working very hard for long hours both at EFTS and SFTS. Grading schools were established in the UK to deal with the aptitude problem, and in the summer of 1941 (with the agreement of both parties) the RAF began opening EFTSs in Canada.

The RCAF had used a number of civilian flying clubs before the war to carry out primary training on its behalf, and this practice continued throughout. John Johns, an RAF cadet who trained at Canadian schools, said that at 5 EFTS, RCAF High River, Alberta, 'the dining room had small tables, complete with white tablecloths, waitresses and menus, together with properly laid out crockery and cutlery. No washing up of one's own "eating irons"—luxury indeed! There were comfortable chairs in the crew rooms, a good library and cinema, and essential shops on the base'.

Johns, like the vast majority of cadets, found the local population to be very hospitable. 'The first weekend they organized a trip to Banff in the Rockies, which included sightseeing and meals. Thereafter, invitations were constantly being received to spend a weekend on a ranch or a shooting lodge. We were plied with meals and hospitality generally. All we had to do was to talk about the UK.'

1941—a year of destiny

While the Empire Air Training Scheme was taking root across the globe, Operation *Sealion*—the code-name for the German invasion of England—had been shelved in mid-September 1940, when the Germans began dismantling their assault transport facilities round the Channel coast. Thereafter, the German High Command had focused its attention on planning the invasion of the Soviet Union, code-name Operation *Barbarossa*, which erupted along a front of some 1,500 miles at 11 o'clock on the Saturday morning of 22 June 1941.

The Luftwaffe had sustained substantial losses during the fall of France and the Battle of Britain, probably in the region of 2,500 aircraft. Goering's air force had suffered its first defeat, and had taken a psychological caning in the process—Goering had boasted at the commencement of *Adlertag* that his Luftwaffe would neutralize the RAF within a few days, and gave his orders accordingly. Just as the romance of the successful battle in the skies over southern England had induced young men throughout the civilized world to fly in combat, so in reverse, the shining image of the Luftwaffe began to tarnish in the eyes of German youth.

But Hitler had few problems. By mid-1941 his forces were reporting victories in Yugoslavia, Greece and North Africa. In his Directive No. 21, dated 18 December 1940, Hitler said that the German Wehrmacht must be prepared, even before the conclusion of the war against Britain, to overthrow the Soviet Union by a rapid campaign.

Goering was one of the few men who wanted Hitler to defer his attack in the East until the Luftwaffe had had the chance to recuperate and rebuild its strength. Combat losses had had to be replaced, which entailed shortening flying-training courses and depleting reserves. Notwithstanding, the Luftwaffe was able to amass more than 2,000 aircraft for the opening phase of the huge assault. In the event, Germany had embarked on a course which not only restored a European ally to Britain, but proved fatal to the Nazi regime. The sheer size of the Russian campaign became the first turning point of the Second World War.

The second turning point came on 7 December 1941, when the Japanese attacked Pearl Harbor, sucking the USA into the war. The world's greatest powerhouse officially entered the war arena, having previously developed collaboration with the UK to a remarkable degree. The war suddenly ignited across the globe, with two colossal Allies on the military chessboard whose military strength was to outweigh by far the capacity of the British Empire. In the short term, Britain could hold her own as a major influence strategically, but her status as a great power was to be reduced in the long term.

The invasion of the Soviet Union and the Japanese attack on Pearl Harbor had an immediate effect on the RAF. The Russians were soon in deep trouble, and demanded a Second Front in Europe to alleviate the terrible pressure on them—by the end of 1941 they admitted casualties of over four million! It was impossible for the British even to contemplate an assault on Europe. Apart from agreeing to send much-needed supplies to Murmansk and Archangel, it was left to the RAF to provide a military response.

On 9 July 1941 Bomber Command received new instructions: to direct the main effort of its bomber force towards dislocating the German transport system, and of destroying the morale of the civil population as a whole, and of the industrial workers in particular. Fighter Command was to make offensive sweeps over Northern Europe, to force the Luftwaffe to increase its presence along that front, and to escort bombers on daylight raids. Hence the situation in the East quickened the pace of Bomber Command's projected expansion. It had become the RAF's only means of delivering the required military clout across Europe, and the plan code-named Target Force E (a strike-force comprising 4,000 bombers) was on the road to reality. Significantly, the Lancaster made its maiden flight on 31 October 1941—the first of over 7,000 such machines manufactured during the Second World War. The other four-engined 'heavies', the Stirling and the Halifax, had entered service in the winter of 1940–41.

The value of the supporting role of the overseas flying training schemes was becoming increasingly self-evident. Although, ironically, there was a surplus of aircrew in the UK in 1941, due to shortage of aircraft and accident rates during operational training, all Allied air forces were to undergo the greatest expansion in their short histories.

The Japanese attack on Pearl Harbor had widened the theatres of war considerably, and stretched them across the globe. Countries operating overseas training schemes were strategically placed to feed these areas—for example, Southern Rhodesia and South Africa supplied the Middle East, and graduates from Australia, New Zealand, the USA and Canada were posted to the Far East.

The Riverdale agreement which had got the Empire Air Training Scheme off the ground was due to expire at the end of March 1943, and the scheme needed to be extended. The war was obviously going to be a prolonged affair, and although the Scheme had been remarkably productive throughout the Dominions and Commonwealth in 1941 (23,676 aircrew graduated), the moment was ripe in view of urgent requirements to review its operation and efficiency.

Convened by the Canadians, the conference which had met to deal with this became a major international affair, during which all systems of aircrew training were re-evaluated in an attempt to standardize and co-ordinate them throughout the North American continent. In addition, the economics and efficiency of the project were carefully studied. This resulted in the signing of the Ottawa Agreement on 6 June 1942 (an appropriate date, in view of the Normandy landings two years later!) which took effect from 1 July 1942 until 31 March 1945.

This agreement embodied major changes, not least a change of name—from the Empire Air Training Scheme to the British Commonwealth Air Training Plan. Under the control of the Royal Canadian Air Force, all schools and supplementary units, together with resources, were administered from one power-base in Ottawa. All SFTSs were to be expanded, and RAF EFTSs brought under civilian operation. Basically, the Ottawa Agreement made for greater efficiency, laid the foundations for greater expansion, and clarified legal points. It also provided an invaluable forum for representatives from host countries who were providing overseas training at a crucial time during the expansion of their own air forces.

The year of 1942 was like the 'curate's egg' for the Allies—good and bad in parts, but mostly bad! The German/Japanese/Italian Axis was in the ascendancy, and the Allies, generally speaking, were bottoming out. Some of the following major events of the year reflect the situation: the Japanese conquered about one-quarter of the globe, U-boats carried on slaughtering shipping, the retreat and advance in the Middle East ended with the El Alamein offensive, the first 1,000-bomber raid hit Cologne, the battle for Stalingrad began, the ill-fated raid was made on Dieppe, the Allies invaded North Africa (against the wishes of the French), and the French scuttled their fleet at Toulon. Hitler occupied the southern half of France.

Command of the air played a key role in defeating Rommel's army in the desert, and many lessons were learned in tactical air support. The role of the fighter-bomber and strategic bombing by day and night are two examples. Many graduates who trained on Harvards found themselves flying Spitfires, Typhoons and Tempests in this respect. But the RAF discovered in North Africa that covering an advancing army was not simply a question of providing air cover in a supporting role, but a total commitment in ensuring air supremacy throughout the region.

Operation Millenium, the 1,000-bomber raid on Cologne on 30 May 1942, was followed by another saturation raid on Essen the following night. Such tactics were indicative of things to come, but not with any frequency at this juncture, because throughout 1942 there was an acute shortage of aircraft everywhere. The Cologne raid, however, proved to be an interesting and fruitful public relations exercise in more ways than one. It uplifted the British public in general, and especially those who had been ravaged by the Luftwaffe; equally, it demonstrated to Allied High Commands what Air Marshal Harris, chief of Bomber Command, had in mind for the future.

One of the most interesting facets of Operation Millenium from the point of view of this book was Training Command's involvement. This was not the first time that Training Command had taken part in operational exercises, but bombing Cologne was a big deal, and many were itching to have a go. The following story highlights the difficulties in using Training aircraft to fill the gap!

In early 1942 Harris had indicated to Portal, Chief of the Air Staff, his intention of amassing 1,000 aircraft in one raid over a single German target, and outlined his reasons. Portal agreed enthusiastically, but asked Harris not to proceed without first informing him of the date and proposed target, in order that he could liaise with Churchill. Harris then proceeded to muster his forces, but the magic figure of 1,000 could not be obtained without help from other Commands. The response from these sources was not as great as he had hoped, except from the Army Co-operation Command, who offered Blenheims, which were hardly suitable for so long a distance, and from Flying Training Command. Air Marshal Sir William Welsh, Later C-in-C, FTC, replied as follows:

My Dear Bert,

I received your DO 42 of 20 May this morning. I will certainly let you have everything I have got which is of any use to you, but I am afraid it is not a big contribution.

At first glance it looks as though I can give you about 8 Wellingtons IA and IC, 9 Whitley I and III and 13 Hampdens. In addition to this, there are about 80 Blenheims, but I doubt these will make the distance. I am having these figures checked as discreetly as possible.

These aircraft are, or should be, in every way fit for operations, but as they have not been used for these purposes for some time they should be checked over by the operational Group. I would suggest as time is short that those you want to take should be sent, complete with their crews and a member of maintenance personnel, to whatever station you detail. They would then come under your Station Commander for final equipping and checking. I would make the attachment under the guise of giving the crews experience of an operational station, and would not stir up too much excitement and guessing by exercising Plan Banquet-Training [Plan Banquet was the code-name for Operation 1,000.] While I hope to increase the number of aircraft mentioned above, if this is not possible I could, if you are short, lend you some trained navigators from my instruction staff.

Will you let me know if you want any of this type of aircraft, and where I should send them? I will assume if I can find more I should send these too.

I will let you know the result of my further check, and, as I said above, I will let you have everything I can scrape together.

Yours ever,

It was agreed that training aircraft so deployed should report as an attachment to a Bomber Command station to prepare for the operation, and for them to be checked as to their suitability for such an enterprise. Seven Hampdens together with supporting staff left Jurby on the Isle of Man for Syerston in Nottinghamshire, but the manner of their arrival was not encouraging. Group Captain Gus Walker, commanding Syerston, later reported that on 25 May three Ansons, two Blenheims and three Hampdens left Jurby for Syerston. Of those, one Anson arrived before dark, and two Blenheims, one Hampden and one Anson arrived after dark. One Anson landed at Lichfield, one Hampden at Newton, and another crashed near Doncaster. On the following day, 26 May, the Anson and Hampden which had strayed off course arrived, together with two more Hampdens direct from Jurby.

Walker went on to say that a casual inspection showed that the Hampdens were in no way fit for operations, and all the resources of his Station had to be put at the disposal of the detachment. The radio equipment, which could be so vital, required 24 hours' work to bring it up to the minimum standard required.

An oil consumption test on a night cross-country exercise showed that the Hampdens produced figures far outside those permissible for the Pegasus engines, and it was decided that these aircraft were totally non-operational. Despite the intense disappointment of the aircrew, the decision had to stand, but some were included as members of the Hampden or Manchester crews of No. 61 Squadron which raided Cologne on the night of 30/31 May. They included Flt. Lt. Gray DFM, Flt. Lt. Sheering and FO Dewer.

As noted above, Harris decided on one more saturation raid the following night before a stand-down on Operation Millenium, and this time the target was Essen. Wg/Cdr. MacDonald and Flt. Lt. Sheering again acted as crew members of 61 Squadron, while Wg/Cdr. Edwards, whose previous operational experience had been two sorties in Coastal Command, flew a Hampden. His crew consisted of Flt. Sgt. Smith (observer), Sgt. Hamilton (WOP) and Flt. Sgt. Brown (air gunner), all from Flying Training Command at Jurby.

Gus Walker drily remarked that Edwards had an eventful trip. While over Essen, one of his two engines failed at 11,000 ft, shortly after releasing his bombs in the target area. Edwards set course for base and, although the engine came to life for a short period, it failed completely after ten minutes.

Edwards was engulfed in searchlights and consequent flak forced him to take evasive action, forcing him down to 1,000 ft as they crossed the Dutch coast. Everything possible was jettisoned, and somehow they gained height to 2,000 ft. Single-engine flying in a Hampden required great skill under any circumstances, but Edwards was an exceptional pilot and he was soon to need those talents! As he arrived over Norfolk his remaining engine flickered and died, but he managed to belly-land his machine on an aerodrome under construction, without injury to himself or his crew. Later he was awarded the DFC.

Summing up the whole question of using training aircraft for such an operation, the AOC Flying Training Command wrote: ' "Hack" aircraft can never be maintained at full operational efficiency, partly because they do not carry all the essential equipment, partly because schools are not issued with the appropriate equipment, partly because what we have is mostly obsolescent, and partly because our ground equipment is not up to that of an operational unit.' By scraping the bottom of the barrel Harris was able to deliver his message to the German people via 1,076 bombers—about a quarter of the total projected strength of Bomber Command UK!

1942 was a year during which accelerated aircraft production, coupled with the expansion of aircrew training, had become prime objectives. At the end of the year the output of pilots and other aircrew trained in the Dominions had reached a total of 44,338. Canada's contribution had reached the staggering total of 30,177. A further substantial number of cadets had also graduated in the UK and USA.

The output from Dominion sources had, in fact, doubled during the previous 12 months. In Canada, the SFTSs had been expanded to take more pupils, and more schools were opened. When the Ottawa conference was taking place there were 68 EAT schools and 27 RAF transferred schools. By the end of the year these had increased to 92 BCATP schools supported by 62 ancillary units.

More flying instructors were needed to service this rapid expansion, and three new flying instructor schools had been established in August. Thus, the British Commonwealth Air Training Plan was geared up to reach a pinnacle of performance in the coming year.

Saskatchewan, 1942

Bob Stanford was one of 14,135 pilots who graduated in Canada during 1942. He had gone solo in a Magister from 15 EFTS Carlisle, embarking on HMS *Batory*, bound for Halifax, Nova Scotia, on 16 May. Aged 18, he had never been abroad before, and he found the cramped conditions somewhat uncomfortable crossing the

Atlantic. The Polish ship was infested with rodents, and had wooden bunks from floor to ceiling, with minimum headroom.

The ship lost convoy in mid-Atlantic because of engine trouble, and life became a staccato pattern of sirens and lifeboat drill. The motherly destroyer, which had appeared out of nowhere from time to time, had vanished, leaving them to fend for themselves. Most cadets were optimistic and cheerful, except those who were troubled by the eternal pitching and tossing of the boat. The crossing took ten days, and everybody was glad to disembark at Halifax and get a first glimpse of the New World.

Stanford was posted to 34 EFTS at Assiniboia, about half-way across the continent, a CPR journey of over 1,500 miles, taking in Montreal, Toronto, Winnipeg and Regina. Fleeting impressions after leaving war-torn, blacked-out Britain remained in his memory: lights, and advertising signs blazing at night—platforms crowded with women carrying trays of coffee, sweets and little Union Jacks—relaxed, warm, friendly greetings—casuals, tartans and Canadian brogue—coloured attendants trundling down the train corridor with trays of goodies—the steam whistle 'whoo whoo' from the engine—a never-ending scenario of lakes and forests—then into the vast golden cornfields of prairie landscape.

The journey took three days and, after changing trains at Moose Jaw to cover the last 65 miles, No. 51 Course finally arrived at Assiniboia. Stanford couldn't believe his eyes when he got off the train. The vista could have come straight out of the old movie in his local cinema on Saturday mornings. There were duckboards on either side of a rough main street, a station hotel, two or three shops, a few wooden shacks, the odd horse and cart, and a few battered old farmers' trucks. The sun outside was strong and high, and a light wind raised the dust, as the cadets were formed up and transported to No. 34 EFTS a mile or so outside the town.

The EFTS occupied a grass airfield, with newly constructed hut accommodation. The aircraft type was the DH 82C—a standard Tiger Moth equipped with a sliding Perspex canopy. The station was, in fact, a standard RAF EFTS plonked down in the middle of the Canadian prairies, with RAF flying instructors and Service back-up. Flying conditions were ideal, and cadets were able to have four or five lessons in a full day's flying.

Stanford recalled that everybody was razor-keen, instructors were like gods, and most pupils had great affection for the man who first sent them solo! He had had a problem initially, in that he found it difficult to relax in the air. It had taken him longer than average to go solo in England, and his greatest fear when he arrived at Assiniboia was that he would fluff it. Again, he had the same tensed-up feeling, and it was only the patience and skill of his instructor that enabled him to overcome this psychological problem.

Learning to fly becomes a series of airborne experiences, like those endured by a fledgling who has flapped his wings and left the nest. The fledgling gathers the tricks of the trade by emulating the parents, as does the pupil pilot with his instructor. But, unlike England, in Canada the process was far easier. Navigation was simple because roads and rail lines ran directly east and west, south and north, in symmetrical fashion. The grain elevators, standing up like giants in the prairie corn, displayed the name of their location. The air was clear, with visibility of 50 miles or more, and there was little turbulence. A pupil pilot could gain confidence without having to cope with the changing pattern of English weather, or the complexities of its congested landscape—or the Luftwaffe! Thus, Stanford and his colleagues had ideal conditions for flying training, and no distractions to keep their minds off ground school studies.

The town offered little in the way of entertainment, as one would expect from a small and isolated farming community. Stanford remembered taking an evening walk once through a fire lane which bored a track through the acres of standing corn. The sun was hot, and all was still except for the rustling of the gophers in the wheat. His mind was preoccupied with the day's flying, and he felt pleased with himself. His instructor, Mansfield, had congratulated him on his recovery from spins. Spinning, he thought, was the most violent condition of flight and he had mastered it without doubts or fears.

Suddenly he came upon a track leading off to a wooden shack, and wondered what the hell it was doing there right out in the wilds. An attractive girl came out and waved to him. He discovered later that she was the schoolmistress, whose flock rode to school on horseback. On the way back to the airfield he met a fellow cadet. They both stopped and stared at one another, realizing that they had been in the same form at school in Bath. He learned that eight out of their class of 24 had volunteered for pilot/navigator training, which, he considered, was probably 'par for course', because their maths master Jock Brody had been an RFC pilot!

The wags in flippant mood had said that the hierarchy put bromide in the tea to curb their sexual desires. But there weren't many opportunities for exuberant youth in that part of the world, except for the Saturday night barn dance—a real hill-billy affair for all age groups. Assiniboia was a close community, whose womenfolk gathered news and gossip by listening to each other's telephone calls. They could tell the recipient by the number of rings, and often joined in the conversation, so there were no secrets. Good behaviour by the cadets in town was therefore essential, but it was generally observed, for fear of getting slung off the course. Another directive related to Indians, although few ever appeared. It was a very serious offence to give hooch (alcohol) to a member of this fraternity.

One Saturday evening at the barn dance, Stanford met 'Wee Darkie Wood', who farmed 75 square miles of wheat. Woodie was a fascinating character, who years ago had ridden shotgun on the stage coach to Moose Jaw. But Woodie had another, more appealing, attribute as far as Stanford was concerned—he had five good-looking daughters. He invited Stanford, who had a 48-hour pass, back to the farm for the weekend, promising to return him to camp for Monday.

Stanford and the girls climbed aboard the wagon, and Darkie drove the horse to a large, rambling wooden farmhouse. Stanford, always an optimist, was keyed up, thinking he was on to a good thing, but Woodie had the last laugh. No sooner had they drunk a hot punch, during which Stanford was doing well with number two daughter, when Woodie handed him working gear. 'Bob,' he said, 'Get these on and come do a bit of "stooking". See howya make out on this little old farm of ours.' The men had arrived with the combine harvester, and under floodlight Stanford found himself 'stooking' the sheaves. He soon discovered that throwing sheaves of corn onto a slow-moving truck behind the combine was painfully hard work.

He will never forget staggering in for breakfast. A vast old wooden table was groaning under a great weight of food, including fried eggs, steaks, doughnuts, sausages, ham, bacon, butter and sweetcorn. On Monday he found it hard work to climb into the cockpit of the Tiger Moth, and he never did make it with any of the daughters!

A few weeks later he was recording details of a flight in his RCAF Pilot's Flying Log Book—everybody had been issued with them—when cloud floated across the sun, and gusts of wind slammed the door of the flight hut. Outside, the eastern horizon was dark, and ground crews were feverishly tieing down the aircraft. The acting CFI, Fl. Lt. Macbeath, was issuing orders, emergency recall black balls were being hoisted, and Tiger Moths were fluttering like butterflies, struggling to get down against the wind.

The prairie storm lasted for about 20 minutes, with driving rain leaving the airfield waterlogged. Stanford remembered seeing chaps pulling down Tigers trying to land—some flying backwards—and others being picked off the ground like handkerchieves, and blown upside-down into the distance. The whole place was in a shambles, but the episode was a lesson to everybody about the vulnerability of light aircraft in high winds.

Stanford's last flight at 34 EFTS was a cross-country from Assiniboia to Caron and return, on 14 August 1942. Caron was about 50 miles due north of base, and west of Moose Jaw, where Stanford was to do his SFTS course. Navigation was relatively simple in those parts, and he hit the button by flying directly over the centre of Old Wives Lake; the rest was easy. WO Mansfield, his instructor, certified his landing at Caron as good, and 1322882 LAC Cadet Stanford had completed his primary flying training course with an 'average' assessment as a u/t pilot. His total flying time was 78 hr and 50 min, of which 38 hr 50 min was solo.

Passing the EFTS course was a personal achievement for any cadet, and boosted his confidence. Stanford had been fortunate in that his instructor, a Warrant Officer, had a great deal of experience, and was a patient and understanding character. He knew within himself that it was Mansfield who had got him through, and he was genuinely sorry to leave him. Also to leave the little Canadian Tiger Moth with its sliding canopy. These had been fitted to cope with the Canadian climate, but the weather during his three months at Assiniboia had been fine, except for the prairie storm!

His instructor at No. 32 SFTS Moose Jaw was Sgt. Randell, a small, wiry, round-faced chap of cheerful disposition and infectious grin. Randell had a dry sense of humour, and was quick to note the reaction of his pupils, especially when they first sat in the front cockpit of the Harvard IIA. Being confronted with a mass of instruments and controls, including undercarriage lever, propeller pitch control, inertia starter, flap controls, etc, and staring up through the windscreen only to gaze at the rounded top of the big radial Pratt & Whitney engine, was a sobering experience for most cadets.

Stanford was no exception, and his first thought was not to touch anything in case the machine fired into life or collapsed on its belly. His eye caught the boost gauge calibrated in inches of mercury which meant nothing to him, and it was a pensive and subdued young man who clambered out to face his instructor. 'Bit different from a Tiger Moth, eh, Stanford?' he said. 'But you'll soon get the hang of it with me behind you. You'll see.'

After 8 hr 20 min dual in the Harvard, Stanford went solo, feeling very pleased with himself, especially as Flt. Lt. Draper DFC had checked him out. Having the air ace sitting behind him had made him rather nervous at first, but the training he had had from Randell enabled him to overcome his anxiety. He did four trips that day and felt very tired but happy at the end. After his check with Draper he felt confident that he would complete the course and get his wings. That feeling of true confidence (not over-confidence) is of enormous importance.

After Assiniboia, everything at Moose Jaw was on a grand scale. No. 32 SFTS was a large RAF station, complete with hangars (to protect aircraft from the extreme Canadian climate in winter) and runways. But Moose Jaw was only one of five RAF SFTSs in the Province of Saskatchewan—No. 32 at Moose Jaw, No. 34 at Medicine Hat, another at Swift Current, and two new ones, No. 41 at Weyburn and No. 39 at Estevan. Thus, three were ensconced in Indian territory, while the other two were isolated in the dust bowls of the far south.

Cadets and staff at 32 SFTS were fortunate in having a large town on their doorstep. There were many training establishments across Canada sited out in the middle of nowhere. Moose Jaw boasted a main street with shops, including a large barber's establishment with a plate-glass, full-length front window, a Chinese restaurant, and a pleasant park. The timber houses were double-skinned and arranged in open fashion. The barber's shop always seemed to be the centre of activity, with people on both sides of the window gesticulating and shouting to one another!

Although cadets frequented the town, there were no problems that

Stanford could recall, not even on Saturday nights in the Chinese restaurant. The discipline was in-built because graduating was all that mattered. Unlike the American system, the RAF allowed the individual his freedom as long as he didn't break the rules. Very few were tempted to cross that Rubicon for fear of being put back a course, or remustered as other aircrew.

Life revolved around flying, and the Harvard IIA, similar to the US AT-6C, was a fine machine for training young potential fighter pilots. Stanford's instructor, Sgt. Randell, for all his humour and easy manner, was a stickler for the finer points of flying, and very firm. He never lost his composure even when Stanford lost height in steep turns, but would tell him how much height he had gained or lost, and make him do the exercise again and again until he got it exactly right. Similarly with cross-wind landings: the Harvard started to swing, and Stanford over-corrected. Instantly, Randell took over, to avoid a ground loop which could have damaged the aircraft. Then he made Stanford do more landings until he was able to control the Harvard before the swing gathered momentum.

One afternoon Stanford had made four turns of a spin from 10,000 ft. He corrected the spin and was pulling out when he felt a tap on his shoulder. Looking behind, he could see Randell grinning and waving his control column as a gesture of confidence.

In mid-October they started night flying. Light KDs had been discarded for heavier blues, gloves and overcoats for the coming of winter. Trees were in full 'fall' colour, and the air at night was crisp and cold. Going round and round the circuit in moonlight, watching the flarepath and the lights of Moose Jaw, presented few problems. There was little turbulence, and lowering cloud would herald a cancellation. By day, formation and instrument flying were added to the exercises as the landscape became covered in a white blanket of snow.

With temperatures of 60° or more below zero, Balaclava headgear became essential. Double-skinned Canadian timber homes were hot and stuffy inside, while out on the street one had to be careful of frostbite. On 18 December 1942 Stanford received his wings in a vast heated hangar, and became a sergeant pilot. He had 203 hr 5 min flying in his log book, and his SFTS course had lasted for just three-and-a-half months.

Then followed an unforgettable week in New York. He got the idea when the CPR train stopped in Montreal. Spending Christmas in New York was a dazzling thought, so he caught the 10-hour special, bound for Grand Central. On the train he was approached by Raymond Massey, the actor, who treated him to lunch, and told him about free board at the Forces Hotel, and where to go in New York. The next few days were memorable: meeting Claudette Colbert in the Stage Door Canteen, driving through New York on the back of a fire-engine with the Mayor, Fiorello La Guardia, parties in Greenwich Village, Dempsey's Bar, Christmas lunch in White Plains, the première of

Random Harvest in Radio City, round-the-clock hospitality, and doing all those things he had never dreamed of.

A fast run home in the vast *Queen Elizabeth*, in company with thousands of American troops, ended his Canadian adventure. It had been a journey of some 10,000 miles, and seven months of intensive flying training.

Advance and retard

The year 1943 was the peak for Canadian output of aircrew, during which 39,178 graduated. The Plan had been running at full throttle, with further substantial increases from other countries (excluding the USA) bringing the total to 58,601. The supply of trained aircrew had been increasingly dramatically, and the significance of this build-up can only be appreciated in the context of the demand situation dictated by the pattern of events.

During early 1943, Bomber Command had played a major role in the anti-U-boat battle, before concentrating its growing resources and awesome power upon the total destruction of the German military and economic system. Harris had also been determined to undermine the morale of the civilian population, to weaken its resolve. Apart from attacking specific strategic targets, Bomber Command, from mid-1943, concentrated on three major areas, namely the Ruhr, Hamburg and Berlin, with continuing and increasing ferocity. Strategic air power, in the hands of the RAF by night and the US 8th Air Force by day, was reaching its peak during this year.

Much has been written about the heroic deeds and almost unbelievable dedication of the crews of Bomber Command during the Second World War. The fact that over 55,000 RAF bomber aircrew were killed reflects the grim and dangerous job performed by the Command. This figure alone represents roughly one-third of the total number of aircrew who graduated under the overseas training schemes! Operational flying is a dangerous business, and taking into account casualties sustained by other Commands in the various theatres of war, the continued expansion of the British Commonwealth Air Training Plan was vital—in 1943 there was no end in sight, either for the war in Europe or in the Far East!

The performance of our aircrews as the war in the air intensified, particularly over Europe, reflected their selection and training. The quality of training was becoming increasingly important as more advanced aircraft and technical aids emerged. The Mosquito, Mustang, Typhoon and Tempest are examples of new machines, while bombers were being equipped with aids such as Oboe and H_2S radar.

Higher degrees of skill were being required from a growing supply of aircrew which had been rapidly got together, trained and then committed to combat. High Command was naturally concerned about the quality of aircrew in these circumstances. The formation of the Pathfinder Force in 1943 was an example of having to provide a 'hand-picked' group to make operations more efficient—an admission, perhaps, that quality had not been maintained throughout.

However, training is no substitute for combat experience, and members of 'élite' forces had been case-hardened to a high degree in battle! Training engendered professionalism, while strong moral fibre had to be a key ingredient in the make-up of all aircrew at war. The RAF system of training aircrew, employed throughout the overseas schemes, made life very competitive for the individual. The fear of being eliminated or 'washed out' motivated every cadet. Hard work over long hours kept their noses to the grindstone. The atmosphere in which they lived fostered a competitive spirit—a natural characteristic of youth! All these factors, coupled with a determination to join the airborne fraternity and wear the brevet, bred confidence within.

Fear was perhaps the operative word. One chap who was washed out in 1940 wrote: 'This has given me the opportunity, perhaps once and for all, to exorcise the most crushing disappointment of my life. So what follows may not be quite what you require for your book. I am sorry if you are bored reading all this, but I needed to get it out of my system.'

Thus, the training experience had a profound impact upon the individual. Apart from teaching him his job, it toughened his character and imbued him with the RAF spirit and attitude. Uniform quality of training was almost impossible to achieve: courses were shortened or lengthened from time to time, there were shortages of specific aircraft and updated equipment, instructors varied in style and standard, and so did the cadets themselves.

The vast majority of ex-aircrew, when looking back over their basic training, described it as very good indeed. And so it was. Their varying flying experiences during the course of their RAF training confirmed it. Generally speaking, they looked back on their overseas training as a journey of a lifetime, which remains a vivid memory nearly 50 years later. There is no doubt that this experience, away from war-torn Britain, set them up both mentally and physically.

Mental and physical toughness was essential, because continuous operational flying made enormous demands on the moral fibre of all aircrew, whether they admitted it or not. 'Lacking in moral fibre—LMF—was a label attached to those unfortunates who couldn't face up to operations, and to those who were unable to take further punishment. Anybody showing signs of LMF was carefully watched. The RAF regarded this malaise as a form of cancer, which could spread rapidly if not removed.

If a chap was suddenly posted off his squadron as 'LMF', few people discussed the issue. Most felt sorry for a chap who had genuinely suffered from operational fatigue, and sorrier if he happened to be an NCO, because many felt that NCOs were more unfairly treated than officers in this respect—they were stripped of their rank and flying brevets, and made to do menial tasks.

The historian John Tremaine discussed the subject of moral fibre at length in his classic book, *The Right of the Line*. He said:

It is of interest to note that during the twelve months July 1943 to June 1944, the statisticians obtained the total percentage of aircrew with LMF submitted from the whole of Bomber Command including OTUs. This was less than 0.4 per cent. It will be realised that, by nature of the operations and intensive flying carried out by Bomber Command during that period, they submitted most of the cases under the Memorandum. Therefore, the total percentage submitted from the whole of the Royal Air Force would be less than 0.4 per cent. It is, however, clear that less than 0.3 per cent of the total aircrew have been classified under the Memorandum. This is indeed a grand record.

It is also a fine tribute to the British Commonwealth Air Training Plan, whose performance had peaked in 1943 when the war in Europe was about to reach a climax. Denis Miller-Williams was one of 15,894 pilots who trained in Canada that year, and describes his experience:

'I was lucky in that I moved from one course to the next without a hiccup. In retrospect, I am amazed at the high level of activity that was maintained throughout the course, not only in the air but on the ground. Every minute of the day seemed to be filled. Fond and not-so-fond memories of the NCOs that ruled our early days? I remember our first "fatal" and the shock that hit us all... The witness of a public humiliation of a sergeant pilot who was stripped at a station parade for low flying... The anti-climax of the "wings" parade because of the realization at that time that flying was a serious matter... The severity of the Canadian winter in North Saskatchewan, when temperatures sank to levels which stopped flying, and the summer which produced sudden high winds... The blanket haze produced by forest fires, the smell of burning from stubble even at great heights... And, of course, the fascination of the diverse characters of one's colleagues.

'As always, the quality and personality of the instructor was the most important factor. He could literally make or break you, though the system had adequate checks and opportunity for changes built in. I had one instructor who hated aerobatics, so I never achieved a perfect slow roll, but I could make a near-faultless GCA landing.

'Although I rebelled against being made an instructor, I was thankful for the experience, and had approximately 1,400 hours in the log book by the time I became a Transport Command Captain in the immediate post-war period in the South-East Asia area.

'I am always filled with admiration for those who flew four-engined bombers with full loads at night with little more than 250 hours' experience. That, for me, is the real tribute to the excellence of the training we received in the British Commonwealth Air Training Plan.'

As far as the quality of training was concerned, Miller-Williams remarked:

'I believe the training course for pilots, worked out by the CFS, trained them to the highest level in the minimum number of flying hours. Some of my pupils went out to OTUs and took to Mosquitoes with not too many hours. The structure of the course was designed to allow the pupil to build up confidence in line with his experience. As training progressed the tasks grew more difficult, as other activities such as bombing and formation flying were introduced.'

Miller-Williams sums it up neatly, as one would expect from a legal man who was later Called to the Bar by the Inner Temple! He certainly appeared to have had a smoother passage than some of his contemporaries throughout his flying career in the RAF. He admitted rebelling against being sent to FIS to become an instructor, but there was nothing that he could have done about it. By a like token, an associate who might have set his heart set on becoming an instructor could have found himself flying Lancasters with a mere 250 hours in his log book!

Deceleration

In late 1943 and early 1944 there were 98 training schools and 184 supporting units in Canada. The system began to overheat, resulting in a substantial surplus of trainees in Canada, and trained pilots back in the UK. The brakes had to be applied, resulting in lengthening courses, raising the elimination rates, and closing schools. The journey to graduation for many cadets became a lengthy and often frustrating process. Having graduated, there were also considerable delays waiting for postings.

The winds of change which swept through the British Commonwealth Training HQ in Ottawa were generated by something even larger than the Plan itself. It became known as Operation Overlord—the code-name for the invasion of Europe. The Canadian Army was going to need all the manpower it could get, and its urgent need for increased manpower was given priority. This change of policy automatically affected the RCAF, because no air force can be an independent arm of the Services' structure. Its production of aircrews and aircraft is relative to the overall war situation concerning the nation. Its deployment is in the hands of the high command.

Undoubtedly there was some hard argument in the corridors of power in Ottawa at the time, particularly as fierce battles by day and night were raging in the skies over Germany, as the RAF and the US 8th Air Force were in the process of destroying German aircraft production. Over past months the Luftwaffe had inflicted heavy casualties on Allied bomber forces, and there was no sign of any capitulation in that respect.

In retrospect, the decision to run down the Commonwealth Plan could have been taken earlier, especially as this had to be a gradual process. There were thousands of cadets in the pipeline at various stages of training. Cycles needed to be completed in line with closures. The immediate effect of the revised manpower policy was to divert recruitment into army channels, which in itself reduced intake. A new agreement was signed on 16 February 1944 designed to reduce the number of schools by about half, from 98 to 47, within a 12-month period.

Within a few weeks 13 schools were closed, and the winding-down process had begun. Yet, despite the continuing reduction of schools, over 30,000 aircrew graduated during 1944—a drop of about 30 per cent on the previous year. Although the British Commonwealth Air Training Plan officially ended on 31 March 1945, the RCAF carried on providing limited training facilities for pilots and navigators for a further year.

Thus ended a scheme which played a major role in achieving victory in the air during the Second World War. Official figures reveal that 137,910 aircrew were trained during its operation. Statistics, however, do not bring to life this vast enterprise, which Prime Minister Mackenzie King described as 'an undertaking of great magnitude'. It is left to Commonwealth Wartime Aircrew Reunions in Winnipeg, Manitoba, to recreate the atmosphere and style of those days. These reunions have attracted thousands of ex-cadets from all over the world.

5. Arrival back home

WHEN OVERSEAS FLYING training schemes got under way, it soon became evident that, well-trained as they might have been in overseas schools, pilots and navigators were totally without experience of British weather conditions, the black-out, and map-reading over a crowded landscape. In December 1941 it was proposed to establish Advanced Flying Units not merely to provide a means of keeping pilots in flying practice, but as a definite stage in their training policy.

RAF Flying Training Command had faced a traumatic and challenging period during the first two years of conflict, having to intensify flying training in the UK in difficult and often dangerous conditions. At that time there were 13 Service Flying Training Schools in the UK and one at Abu Sueir, Egypt. These establishments were fed by the civil schools already in operation, but the total output was still very small when measured against squadron needs. However, by May 1940 5,300 pilots were being trained annually, against an average of 300 in the mid-1930s. (Yet 12 months later, Canada alone was training nearly 10,000 pilots—almost twice the number graduating in the UK!)

Initially, the expansion of training both of aircrew and ground staff became a vicious circle, because, as the need increased, training requirements were indirectly absorbing their own output. In consequence, the pressure on staff resulted in high accident rates, with a subsequent loss of aircrew, aircraft and equipment. Relief would have been afforded by schools in France and even in Kenya, but, as noted earlier, events proved otherwise.

At this stage most Training Schools were operating with aircraft long obsolete. Hawker Harts, Hinds and Audaxes, together with other Hart variants, were standard. All were biplanes with open cockpits and equipped with very limited navigational instruments. Radio was not normally fitted on such aircraft, and the consequent lack of communication was a severe handicap.

Gradually the Miles Master and the American Harvard trainer became available, whilst the old work-horse, the Anson, together with the Airspeed Oxford, proved invaluable for the production of twin- and multi-engined aircrew.

Such was the shortage of pilots during the Battle of Britain that an extremely risky, and in the event unprofitable, experiment took place. Pupils were taken from Elementary Flying Schools and placed in Operational Training Units on what were called 'X' courses. At this stage they had done barely 50 hours' flying, of which only a little less than half had been solo, and all on elementary trainers. Some were sent to RAF Abingdon to fly huge twin-engined Whitleys, and others to RAF Bicester for conversion to Blenheims. The course lasted 12 weeks and involved 120 hours' flying, about one-third of which was at night. Pupils were specially selected for this accelerated treatment and they were exceptionally keen, but the loss rate, both during training and subsequently at squadrons, made it inevitable that there was no advantage in such a method.

Simultaneously, the Empire Air Training Scheme commenced, which was to have such a profound impact on Flying Training Command's operation in the UK. In mid-1941, a number of SFTSs began to be moved *in toto* to Canada and South Africa. One can readily appreciate that this systematic degutting of the Command posed innumerable problems, both in its operation and composition. Furthermore, the restructuring of the Command to meet the requirements of trained aircrew arriving from overseas required urgent action.

Fortunately, remnants of one or two SFTS establishments remained, and it was upon this structure that it was proposed to build the AFUs. In the first place, single courses were introduced into selected SFTSs; later, the SFTSs were converted into AFUs. The first single course was commenced at No. 2 SFTS Brize Norton, and by the end of January 1942 six other SFTSs were taking part. In the same month new AFUs were starting to form, and in February the total conversion of SFTSs into AFUs began. By the end of 1942, eight SFTSs had been converted and five new AFUs formed, bringing the total to 13.

In the initial stages there was no set course, units simply confining themselves to correcting any particular faults and providing refresher flying. However, it quickly became apparent that a regular syllabus was essential, with a different approach for single-engine pilots and twin-engined pilots.

Aircrew returning from overseas started with one week in the pre-flying section, where kitting-up and flying control instruction was carried out. This initial week was followed by a standard syllabus lasting eight weeks for twin pilots and four weeks for single pilots.

Twin-engine pilots completed some 80 hours' flying on Oxfords, including 20 hours' night flying, 10 hours on beam approach training, and 20 hours on advanced day flying, during which simulated night flying was carried out. Single-engine pilots completed 40 hours on Miles Masters, during which 20 hours were spent on day flying, 10 hours on night flying and 10 hours on advanced day flying. The nature of the English winter demanded flexibility, and courses were extended to 12 weeks and six weeks respectively if necessary.

Advanced Flying Units continued to operate until the end of the war in Europe, and were then gradually phased out in 1946. They had surpassed by far their original purpose of providing flying practice and acclimatization and had become an integral part of the flying training process.

6. American involvement

IN MAY 1940, with the need for aircrew becoming ever more urgent, the British Government held tentative talks with the US Government regarding pilot training in the USA. They were told, however, that all military flying schools there were fully occupied with their own needs.

It was then suggested that primary training could take place in American civil schools, but the authorities in Washington expressed the view that pupils would be better trained in Canada, using American aircraft and instructors. Understandably, the US Government did not wish to compromise its neutrality, and although the Canadian offer was accepted, only very few United States aircraft and instructors were provided.

In August 1940, when the Battle of Britain was entering its crucial phase, the project was reopened. The British Government was desperately anxious to explore any possibility of additional training, and this time it was proposed to set up civil schools in the US to train British pilots under direct, paid contract. The problem of neutrality was again a stumbling block, but was circumnavigated by proposing to sell non-military training on a commercial basis. This solution did not, however, dispel all the difficulties, the main two being the enormous dollar cost to the UK, and the lack of suitable training aircraft in the USA for civil school use.

Nevertheless, the scheme was put into operation, but due to the shortage of aircraft it was delayed until July 1941, shortly after Germany had invaded the Soviet Union. The aircraft shortage was greatly alleviated by the introduction of the Lease-Lend Act earlier in the year, enabling the US not only to provide the aircraft so urgently needed, but also to build six British Flying Training Schools (BFTSs), bearing a large proportion of the costs themselves.

It is quite remarkable that the United States should have made such a considerable contribution to RAF aircrew training *before* the Japanese attack on Pearl Harbor on 7 December 1941 brought her into the war. It is also typical of US efficiency and drive that the six BFTSs were operative within a matter of a few weeks.

Side-by-side with this fine American effort, their civil schools were training their own citizens who had volunteered for the Eagle Squadrons, and who were to prove such a great support to the Royal Air Force both physically and morally. In addition, navigators from Britain were being trained under a contract with Pan American Airways at their school in Miami.

When in March 1941 additional Service schools were badly needed, the British Government agreed a further scheme with the United States. This was entered into despite a great eagerness on the part of the Canadian Government to increase its already heavy commitment and its wholehearted involvement in the war. It could well be that the financial aid available under the Lend-Lease legislation (signed by President Roosevelt on 11 March) influenced the issue, against Canada's earlier reluctance to accept the heavy monetary responsibilities involved. But whatever the reasons were (and they have not been revealed), the United States agreed to train RAF pupils in Army schools. Over 14,000 RAF aircrew were trained in America altogether, which in itself was an invaluable contribution. Such involvement also enabled the air forces concerned to understand mutual problems, and to share techniques covering a wide field of operations.

Apart from the BFTS operation, which was under RAF control, there were two other schemes: the Towers Scheme, named after Admiral Towers, US Navy, and operated within the US Navy organization; and the Arnold Scheme, operated within the South-east Army Air Corps Training Center, with HQ at Maxwell Field, Montgomery, Alabama. This was named after General Henry 'Hap' Arnold, Chief of Staff of the US Army Air Corps (as it was in 1941).

It was General 'Hap' Arnold who, on a fact-finding mission to Britain in March 1941, was astonished when, by chance, he came across the Whittle project. Convinced that this British jet invention could become the springboard of America's entry into the jet age, he rapidly made arrangements for Whittle's X.1X engine to be shipped to the USA, and picked General Electric to build it under licence. This was an important event, because it established beyond doubt that even though Whittle had had to wait seven years to get any support, Britain was in the forefront of aviation technology. This must have had a bearing on deals between the two countries at that particular time.

As a result of these schemes being set up in the USA, British pilots under training were faced with a variety of methods. Some went at first to the civil schools, which worked to RAF requirements. Later they found themselves under American Army discipline at the Arnold Service schools, or under Naval discipline on the Towers courses, which produced either flying-boat pilots or those destined for Fleet Air Arm service.

As with the civil schools, the rate of introduction of both the Arnold and Towers schemes was prodigious. Both were agreed in April 1941, and both were fully operational in June, little more than two months later! Even more exceptional was the immediate output of 500 pilots in the first year. As the war progressed, so the supply of aircrew began to fulfil the requirements of squadrons, but standards were still an important factor, not only for the fighting units but for the survival of the aircrew themselves.

The British Flying Training School scheme in the USA

They were called BFTSs, and there were six of them. Nearly 7,000 RAF pilots and over 400 USAAF pilots graduated under this scheme, which was the most productive of all the Anglo-American ventures. The brainchild of General 'Hap' Arnold, in collaboration with Air Commodore Pirie, the Air Attaché and a prominent member of the British Purchasing Commission in Washington, the scheme was finalised in March 1941.

It formed part of an American package deal which included both the Towers and the Arnold schemes. After the Lend-Lease Bill had been cleared by Congress, on 23 April 1941 President Roosevelt formally authorized the setting up of six schools for the training of British pilots. A sum of $21,337,165.62 (an enormous amount of money in those days!) was appropriated to cover the cost until 1943 under the heading of 'Defense Aid'.

This was a massive deal, comprising the setting up of the following schools: No. 1 Terrel, Texas; No. 2 Lancaster, California; No. 3 Miami, Oklahoma; No. 4 Mesa, Arizona; No. 5 Clewiston, Florida; and No. 6 Ponca City, Oklahoma. The cost of aircraft, operating costs, etc, was covered under Lend-Lease terms. The establishment and operating costs were complex, as illustrated by Falcon Field, at Mesa, Arizona.

The 720 acres of Falcon, and the 640 acres of its auxiliary field, were acquired at a nominal cost, but the construction costs ultimately amounted to $352,330.80. It was initially agreed that the Southwest Airways Company would be paid the following rates: primary trainers, $21.60 per hour; basic/advanced trainers, $32.00 per hour; and Link trainers, $5.00 per hour. In addition, board and lodging was costed at $25.00 per person per month (good value), and haircuts at 50 c. per fortnight (very expensive!). The airfield and buildings were constructed in 12 weeks, while Courses Nos 1 and 2 commenced at Thunderbird Field. The main contractors, C. T. & W. P. Stover of Claremont, worked on a cost-plus-fixed-fee contract.

A novel feature of the BFTS scheme was that it provided a complete training course from primary to graduation at the same station—a continuous production-line process! To remain at the same station throughout his training was a bonus for any cadet, and the fact that the RAF had taken a firm hand to ensure that the syllabus covered all aspects of EFTS and SFTS training was also an advantage. Furthermore, the RAF supplied a Chief Flying Instructor, a Chief Ground Instructor, an Adjutant and a disciplinary NCO for each pair of schools.

Naturally there were teething troubles in getting the scheme 'off the deck', and the time factor was vital for the RAF. One can imagine how long it would take for a British town council to select, approve the plans for a site, and start building! Their American counterparts regarded the project as a challenge, and set about it with typical enthusiasm and efficiency. No. 1 School at Terrel, a small town about 30 miles east of Dallas, Texas, for example, was ready within eight weeks of the selection of the site. In a like spirit, General 'Hap' Arnold had agreed to give 260 primary and 285 basic trainers to make the scheme operational.

The schools took 200 cadets for a 20-week course, flying Stearman PT-17s or Fairchild PT-19s at primary, and North American AT-6 Texans (Harvards) or Vultee BT-13A Valiants at basic and advanced. Thus the BFTSs could only provide graduates who had been trained on single-engined aircraft, a disadvantage for RAF Bomber Command! The instructors were all civilians, most of whom had had a great deal of flying and instructing experience. Phillip Murton (later Sqn/Ldr), who trained at No. 6 School at Ponca City, Oklahoma, comments that:

'The quality of instruction is a difficult one to assess. Generally the flying instruction was good, in that the instructors sure could fly. But they were, for the most part, unable to explain in the air or on the ground why an aircraft did certain things, or what one had to do in order to fly correctly. From the student's point of view it was largely a question of copying.' This was described by Bill Williams, who also trained at Ponca, as a 'sitting by Nellie' technique!

Others have made similar observations, particularly those who were later trained at an RAF FIS and became flying instructors. The fact that the American system of instructing differed from ours didn't necessarily make it a bad system. Murton admitted that he must have been a pretty good 'copier', because he went on to fly Hurricanes, Spitfires, Typhoons and Meteors without any dual! Perhaps their civilian instructors had the last laugh, because Murton said: 'One of the things that amused us was that our flying instructors were paid for their flying to the nearest minute, so that, when I got my wings, I had 200 hours and 4 minutes!'

About 20 per cent of each course was taken up by American cadets who trained alongside their British equivalents at BFTSs. Americans are always sensitive to competition, and did everything possible to ensure that their chaps put up a good show by comparison. Their cadets were carefully selected, and any with anti-British feelings weeded out. Also, they had previous flying experience and had shown aptitude in the air.

Any cadet who had the good fortune to be trained at a BFTS was a lucky chap. He wasn't confronted by the harsh discipline in the West Point tradition at the Army and Navy schools—there was no 'honours system', no 'square meals' or 'hazing'. The flying was less rigid. His quarters were new, roomy and airy, and the food excellent. A swimming pool and cafeteria on site were 'par for course'.

Apart from the constant scream of 'needle, ball and goddam airspeed' engraven on his memory to this day, Phillip Murton's memories of Primary at Ponca City included the coloured lady who, every morning after breakfast, when they were all using the lavatories, used to come in and cry, 'Lift up your legs, boys'—and they'd all lift their legs off the floor so that she could mop along the complete line. The instructor who occasionally turned the petrol off was noted, and word passed round. On a solo cross-country they all had to do one day, six of them formed up some way away from the field and, led by a chap who was good at navigation, they all got down on the deck and flew low all the way round the triangular course. The instructors turned a blind eye to it!

The superb weather, which was virtually guaranteed, enabled courses to proceed day and night with only an occasional storm or Sirocco wind spiral. With extraordinarily good visibility, and roads and railway lines running north and south, east and west, navigation and dealing with weather conditions was relatively simple in that part of the States. Recommencing flying in the UK, however, was a different ball game. To acclimatize pilots to British weather, the complex problems of navigation, and flying advanced machines, the RAF Advanced Flying Units provided an intermediate stage to operational training.

Bob Stanford had logged 203 hours when he came back across the Atlantic in the *Queen Elizabeth* and stepped into the front cockpit of a Master II at 7 AFU Peterborough. The weather was moist on that early spring morning, with cloud beginning to break up, poor visibility, and here and there patches of mist. His instructor, Sgt. Hedley, had cast an inquisitive eye at the cloud conditions but said nothing. The excitement of dual instruction in a new machine and resuming his flying was all that mattered to him.

The fen country below them, to the east of Peterborough, was a myriad of dykes, rivers, roads and little villages across a flat landscape. He was naturally preoccupied with flying the aircraft, and after carrying out steep turns, stalls and forced-landing practice, he had no idea where he was. It was a comforting thought to have Sgt. Hedley in the back seat, but when they entered the circuit in low cloud and drizzle they lost the airfield on the downwind leg!

Map-reading and cross-countries (some at low level) as a passenger in an Anson helped the navigation process, but night flying in black-out conditions was a trifle hairy! It made him realize how fortunate he had been to be able to learn to fly in wide, open spaces with splendid visibility. Over there, getting lost was no problem—all one had to do was dive down and read the location on the grain elevators! After 33 hours flying Master Is and IIs, he found himself in Scotland sitting in the cockpit of a Hurricane—and that moment was worth all the training and the hard slog at ground school.

A relatively small number of BFTS graduates were sent to a USAAF Flying Instructor School, and then proceeded to do a tour of instruction in the USA teaching RAF and American cadets. This was good public relations for both sides. One such cadet was Gordon Davies, who graduated at No. 4 BFTS Falcon Field, Mesa, Arizona. Davies became a regular officer, attaining the rank of Group Captain. He hosted most members of the Royal Family, and flew machines ranging from helicopters to supersonic jets. The following extracts from his article in *The Falcon* magazine of April 1986 bring to life the atmosphere and style of the times. (Not all RAF instructors were commissioned—there were a few sergeant pilots!)

San Antonio, Texas:
The first practical officer experience was obtained by 'overkill' the first day at Kelly field, as salutes by the hundred were returned to enthusiastic young American aviation cadets and flight mechanics. To this day my wife claims that I am the only RAF officer who, throughout a Service career, 'threw away' every salute, American fashion.

Mesa, near Phoenix, Arizona:
The whole of 1943 was a year of wondrous and unimaginable experiences, as into the vastness of the USAAF Flying Instructors' Academy there poured scores of 1st and 2nd Lieutenants, all to undertake the intensive three-week pilot instructor's course.

The spacious single-room suites in the BOQ [Batchelor Officer Quarters] had been adapted to accommodate four; here and there at random the fourth bed was occupied by an alien creature—an RAF officer, soon named a 'Tally-ho boy'! My companions came from Oklahoma, New Jersey, and South Carolina; none had ever met an Englishman before, and all set about showing me how life should be lived and introducing me to the 'stateside' culture of the future!

Everyone seemed to have an automobile. Most were roadsters of brilliant hue, from '35 Chevvies to '42 Buicks. There were variations and refinements to the genteel social style of the British in Phoenix. Downtown, most headed for the Gunter Hotel, to reserve a room for Saturday; subsequent free time seemed to be devoted to a selection process to determine which elegant blonde, ravishing redhead or beautiful brunette could be persuaded to appreciate its decor on 'the night'.

I found myself the true greenhorn, being used, because of my distinctive RAF uniform and my quaint accent, as bait, ever ready to defend my honour with the mythical baseball bat...

Into the hotch-pot of the Flying Instructors' School were scattered a few other RAF Pilot Officers, culled, in the Falcon manner, from other obscure and lesser-known BFTSs, such as Clewiston Florida, Tulsa Oklahoma, and Terrell Texas. Fourteen of us altogether, we were told that we would form about ten per cent of the instructional staff, spread through eight Flights, of a new USAAF Basic Pilot Training School just opening at Greenville, 60 miles east of Dallas, Texas, called Majors Field.

Measured Management
America was truly getting its military machine into overdrive—and it was adopting modern management techniques in the process of selecting the training of thousands of aspiring young American pilots. The hurdles were precise—40 per cent would be failed at Primary, 18 per cent at Basic and 2 per cent at Advanced. 'We'll have our crashes and casualties here in Texas, and not in the Pacific', came in one order of the day from the Major-General; it set the scene for the demanding standards which would be required of us.

Majors Field, Greenville, soon became a hive of intense activity. Courses arrived, some 70 strong each week, one to each of the eight Flights for an eight-week course. Divided into sixes by alphabetical roll between instructors (I once had a sextet of Millers or Millars, known only by their initials!), there were only 15 days before one had to be suspended. A degree of flexibility was granted if one instructor had two weak students and another six good ones; it was brutal but effective!

Flying and ground instruction seemed to go on around the clock, with 180 aircraft constantly in use and a daily average schedule of five-and-a-half hours per instructor in the back seat of the Vultee Valiant (or 'Vibrator' as the faithful BT-13A was known). The monthly 'skedule' for each of us was 105 hours; however, to retain our pilot category and rating we had to carry out some ten hours of additional instrument flying, cross-countries including night returns, and check rides with flight and squadron commanders.

It was hardly surprising that we few RAF officers were regarded with curiosity by many, and with distrust by a few. It was rare to find a Texan or a USAAF cadet who had ever met a 'Brit' before; xenophobia and a suspicion of anything 'foreign' resulted in occasional problems but, in the main, we were welcomed, and our more patient instructional technique appreciated. To make us more 'acceptable' we RAF officers were authorized to wear USAAF summer uniform and their flying badge, as well as our own 'wings'; then we were distinguishable only by Pilot or Flying Officer braid on our shoulders, a black tie and RAF hat.

Hard Work
It is probably true that I worked harder during the year I was on loan to the USAAF than I ever did in the next 43; equally, I never enjoyed the total experience of work more. One remarkable benefit of extra effort was that, if all five or six students could be brought three hours ahead of the course schedule, any instructor could have the freedom to use an aircraft for his own travel without any cost for fuel, landing fees or servicing: up to 300 miles for one day, 500 miles for an overnight stay, or a 1,000-mile radius for a long weekend.

Back to the UK
All good things must come to an end sometime. In November 1943 the experiment was drawn to a close, and all RAF instructors loaned to the USAAF were returned to the UK. With some 1,200 hours as captain on single-engined aircraft, I was immediately earmarked for Tempests or Typhoons. I stood out for heavies—Lancasters—and was designated "headless" for my pains.

Group Captain Gordon Davies' personal recollections are particularly interesting because he quotes the elimination formula imposed by the Americans in very precise terms. He describes this process as brutal but effective. During the first year of the BFTS operation the wastage factor was reported to be as low as 25 per cent, but as time went on this varied according to the demand situation. Towards the end of the war it rose to around 50 per cent.

The vast majority of cadets, British or American, had the fear of being washed out always at the back of their minds. Fear of failing to achieve a prime ambition in life is both a stimulant and a discipline in itself. That was one reason why British cadets resented the harsh discipline of the West Point system—there was no need for it because everybody was mad keen to get their wings. However, while the BFTS scheme operated a more relaxed disciplinary system, there was always a fear of being eliminated at any time.

The Towers Scheme

This scheme was the brain-child of Vice-Admiral John H. Towers, an early pioneer of US naval aviation. Towers approached President Roosevelt in early 1941, pointing out that the USN could assist Britain by training RAF cadets. Roosevelt agreed in principle, and Towers approached the RAF in June of that year. The fact that the Battle of Britain had staved off a German invasion, and that the Empire Air Training Scheme was a reality, had undoubtedly convinced the Americans that Britain was going to stay in business!

The original idea was to train 1,200 RAF cadets per year, but this was extended to include Fleet Air Arm pupils and trainee RAF observers, wireless operators and flight engineers. In addition, some 30 flying-boat crews would be trained in the USA up to operational standard. The RAF and RN acted with remarkable speed, and the first course left England on 6 July 1941—less than four weeks after negotiations had begun! Meanwhile, on 22 June Germany had invaded the Soviet Union, and the RAF were on the offensive over Northern Europe.

Naval cadet Norman Hanson, an 'old man' of 27 who was destined to become a fighter pilot, was on the second course heading for US Naval Air Station Pensacola, in Florida. In company with 29 other naval cadets, and lots of RAF types, he boarded the *Stratheden*, a liner converted into a troopship, sailing from Gourock. Having shown the RAF types how to sling a hammock, he said, 'In the Stygian darkness of a hold abreast of H deck, we eventually found ourselves a corner where we could make ourselves reasonably comfortable. Few young men in the civilized world today would dream for one moment of accepting conditions such as those for 11 days and nights. I don't suppose we enjoyed it, but we accepted it without demur—there was a war on!'

After landing at Halifax they entrained for Toronto for documentation, then headed south to Pensacola. This large US Navy station on the Gulf of Mexico housed 16,000 men, with many families in married quarters. Known in US naval circles as 'the Annapolis of the air', the site included churches, shops, bowling alleys, a superb auditorium capable of holding 2,000 people, and facilities for sport of every kind. Quarters were luxurious, by British standards, sleeping eight to a room in spacious, well-equipped dormitories. The dining rooms were spotlessly clean, airy and light, with black stewards on duty. The entire set-up was highly organized, generating an atmosphere in which one had to be 'on the ball, all the time'.

Integrated into classes of US Naval and Marine cadets, Hanson and his associates spent the first six weeks attending ground school, working the peacetime curriculum—navigation, celestial navigation, meteorology, theory of flight, fuel, oil and hydraulic systems. Lectures, instructional films, a compulsory period of two hours' physical training, and written tests on all school subjects every Friday afternoon made up the routine.

Hanson, a first-class writer with a great sense of humour, recorded his experiences in his book, *Carrier Pilot* (published by PSL). He said:

Most of us had seen only a matter of weeks in the service of the Royal Navy. Nevertheless, a month or two with the US Navy showed us some of the wide disparities between the two. There was no doubt that "on parade" to the RN officer demanded considerably more from us than did similar situations in the US Navy. On the other hand, matters which, where the RN was concerned, seemed to be treated superficially and with good-natured indifference and humour were looked upon with the utmost severity and beetling eyebrows by the young men from Annapolis.

Our living quarters at Pensacola were in Block 624, a spacious, good-looking, two-storey building of great length. At each end of both floors was a desk and a wooden armchair at which sat a Mate of the Deck, a duty we all fulfilled in rotation, standing a two-hour watch. The Mates of the Deck were distinguished from their fellows by the wearing of a khaki webbing belt.

The drill for taking over the watch was laid down explicitly in standing orders issued to us through the almighty duplicator, without which, it seemed, their Navy could never have functioned. At the appointed hour for change of watch, the new incumbent was obliged to approach the desk and stand to attention before his predecessor, announcing loud and clear:

'Sir, you are relieved.'

At this, the outgoing Mate would leap to attention and reply:

'Sir, you have the watch,' at the same time unbuckling and handing over the belt of office.

This drill was rigorously adhered to by the American cadets, whether or not an officer was present. Not without good cause, either, for America was still at peace. Pensacola was the prerogative of the best of Yale and Harvard; competition was fierce, and cadets could be fired at the drop of a hat. Naturally, they were appalled at the slap-happy change-over performed by the British.

Five to ten minutes late, the oncoming Mate would saunter along the passage towards the desk. The man to be relieved would hail him at a range of 20 yards:

'And where the f---- hell have you been, you lazy sod? Had your bloody head down, have you?'

The response was equally officer-like and gentlemanly:

'Go and get stuffed, you moaning bastard! Give me the sodding belt and stop bitching!'

Thus was the take-over satisfactorily achieved, although not without a fair amount of eyebrow-raising from any Americans who happened to be passing.

In all other respects Hanson admitted that the RN cadets showed up well. The saluting of American officers was a model of correctness, and so was the marching around the station. 'Not for one moment', he said, 'would one of us have let down Petty Officer Oliver and his beloved Whale Island!' There was also the small point that nobody wanted to get slung off the course for misdemeanours.

The use of strict discipline and hard physical training as a method of toughening up pupils and getting them sorted out was not confined to the American system. German pupils had to undergo 6–12 months of Regimental training. They learned to goose-step, fire rifles and suffer indignities on the parade ground while being continually shouted at by Prussian instructors.

Having completed six weeks' ground school (the equivalent of our ITW), the Towers cadets were sent to Saufley, a Primary Flying Training School about ten miles inland from Pensacola. There the basic trainer was the N3N Canary, an uncluttered, dual-controlled biplane built by the US Navy, with fixed undercarriage and no flaps. Hanson's comments on his first reactions to flying speak for themselves:

You either love it or you don't—there are no half measures. And if you don't fall in love with it at the very outset, you are wasting your time and everybody else's in trying to get used to the idea. The only sensible thing to do is to walk away from it and take up embroidery or flower-arranging. You will be much happier, and you won't kill either yourself or anyone else.

Hanson's point is well made. Anybody involved in the flying business should enjoy it, not only to get the best out of it but to be able to relax. This is vital during basic training when man and machine get acquainted. One has to learn to relax during the early stages of flying training, and the overseas scheme provided the best possible conditions—a peacetime environment, no enemy interference, good climate, regular trips, simpler navigation, and big, uncluttered air spaces. All this combined to give any pupil a perfect scenario in which to train, and represented one of the greatest advantages of overseas training.

One's first solo is an experience which few pilots ever forget, even surpassing the emotion of one's first flight. Hanson is no exception except that, unlike many of us, he can describe his emotions in a few words and he had an American instructor, Charlie Culp.

'OK. Let's go. Start her up; fly down the lane [this was a corridor marked by high wooden pylons leading from the airfield into the outlying country], then we'll talk some more.'

I was then put through my paces, rounding off with one or two landings and take-offs on a quiet satellite grass field. When I landed back at Saufley and taxied to the apron, we descended to the tarmac.

'I've only one question,' Charlie said. 'Can you get this thing off the ground and put it back again without killing anyone? You're entitled to kill yourself but'—this with a smile—'killing anybody else is against the rules. Can you?'

'Yes, sir. I think so.'

'Don't think, I want to know.'

'Then I can. Yes, sir.'

'OK. There ain't more than a dozen good reasons why you shouldn't. Good luck!'

He was gone.

Next morning, for the first time, my name stood alone against an aircraft number. I climbed into my N3N—and there was a yawning gap in the front seat where Charlie should have been sitting. (There was also a yawning gap, for the first time, where my intestines should have been. It was probably just as well I didn't know it that morning, but the gap was going to reappear time after time over the next few years!). I rumbled out to take off, flew out to a small field and landed and took off until the end of the period: round and round, and round and round again. Then I came back to Saufley Field and made it. And no one was killed.

The author also found his first solo a somewhat harrowing experience, not because of the flying but more from the emotional build-up. The aerodrome was Kingstown, Carlisle, and the machine was a Magister, a low-wing monoplane with a Gipsy engine. Pupils had to go solo before being transported to Canada for basic training. If a pupil hadn't soloed after some 15 hours' dual instruction, he was eliminated.

After some 14 hours of dual instruction from the patient Sgt. Harrop, and still not having been allowed to go it alone, the dreaded business of becoming a drop-out was more than worrying. Others had made it after seven or eight hours and were cock-a-hoop about the whole thing, which made one feel inferior. Harrop had explained that the problem was basically one of being too tensed-up in the air. After a series of take-offs, powered approaches and landings, the Flight Commander, Flt. Lt. Geoffrey Howard, replaced Sgt. Harrop, and instinctively one knew that the exercise would be make or break.

The day was bright and sharpish with 6/10ths cloud and shafts of sunlight. After a couple of circuits and bumps, Howard got out and carefully fastened the straps in his cockpit. He smiled, gave a thumbs-up and waved me off. I felt excited and began talking to myself as I taxied out, gave the engine a burst, and turned into wind for take-off.

I shall never forget that moment—slowly opening the throttle and forcing myself to relax—knowing that, if I didn't, then I would undoubtedly kill myself. So I talked my way around the circuit, explaining every movement of the controls, the situation regarding the airfield, and coming in on the approach under power. Getting close to terra firma and looking ahead and to one side until I could see the blades of grass, I remember saying, 'Easy, easy, gently does it, gently back on the stick, back, back, cut the throttle. You're down. You clever sod. You've made it!'

Unlike Hanson, I wasn't allowed to go round and round—just one circuit and bump, which had been a sweet three-point job. I had gone solo, and that was all the RAF required me to do. But rather like

Hanson, who sometimes had a yawning gap where his intestines should have been on later hairy occasions, I talked my way out of my terrors!

Flying courses don't differ much, except when they are shortened for some reason or another. And when they have to be shortened there is usually a vastly increased accident rate. The RAF system of basic training prevailed throughout the Empire and Commonwealth and, although there were some differences in American training, the same exercises were carried out. Instructors, however, vary in their style, but usually retain their national characteristics. A pupil once asked his Polish instructor, for example, why they kept flying around a church upside down. 'I got girlfriend. She live in vicarage. Very nice girl,' replied the Pole.

Whatever an instructor's idiosyncrasies, he is God, having the power of life or death, and as such is to be treated with respect and due reverence. Hanson was fortunate, because Charlie Culp was apparently a very good instructor—a quiet, reserved and gentlemanly American.

In the air he was as quiet as he was on solid ground. He spoke to me only when he found it strictly necessary, and long after I had left his tender care, he explained to me why an instructor who nattered unceasingly (as some did) was of no use to anyone.

'You see, if I checked you or ticked you off the instant you started to do something wrong, you would never be given the chance to develop the mistake. You would never know what the hell you had been letting yourself in for. The only way is to let you do whatever the hell you were going to do; to let you go on, getting deeper and deeper into trouble, until it dawns on you that you have gotten yourself into something you just can't get out of. Then—and only then—I'm there to dig you out. You'll sure remember never to do that again. See?'

Charlie Culp proved the point one day when they were practising emergency landings. He circled the field and cut the throttle suddenly. Hanson reacted.

Now it was all mine. I looked back to the downward end of the field—NOW! I banked over steeply and glided down-wind, past the end of the field, then into a left-hand, 180° turn. I was far, far too high. I put the N3N into a screaming sideslip—hopeless; yet in my keenness and obstinacy I persisted. Charlie's quiet voice came through my earphones.

'If you get this one in, I'll kiss your ass in the San Carlos bar.'

Suddenly I was in a jam; and I hadn't the faintest idea how to extricate myself. Jesus!!

'OK, OK,' said Culp, 'OK, I got it.'

And he had.

The system worked because some time later Hanson's engine cut when he was inverted in a loop and his carburettor float failed to fall back into position. He got it down safely in a small field by side-slipping off the height. 'I was alive. I had pulled off my first forced-landing, and was now living it all over again, wallowing in a sea of smug complacency. "Hanson, what a bright sod you really are", I thought. "What will Charlie say about that?" Next morning Charlie Culp quietly mentioned the incident. "I hear you did OK yesterday. Let's go." And that was that.'

The Americans seem to have given a lot of thought to teaching pupils how to get down safely, because they had an exercise called circle-shooting. A white circle, 100 ft in diameter, was marked on a grass satellite field, and the idea was to cut the throttle and touch down in the circle without engine assistance. On second thoughts, however, they were training naval pilots, and an aircraft carrier had a very restricted area for plonking a machine down!

Hours of Link-trainer work, and blind flying under the hood in the rear cockpit of an SNJ (Harvard), was all part of the training. Then it was goodbye to Saufley, and off to Ellyson, just north of Pensacola, to fly more advanced machines. These consisted of the Vought O3U-1 Corsair, an old biplane reminiscent of a Swordfish, and the Vought OS2U-3 Kingfisher. The Kingfisher, a monoplane, was normally fitted with floats, but those at Ellyson of course had an undercarriage, and were used solely as advanced trainers.

At this stage pupils became acquainted with landing flaps, constant-speed propellers and more advanced exercises such as formation flying, until they graduated. They did so at about the time that the Japanese attacked Pearl Harbor, on 7 December 1941. Previously, Hanson recorded that some of the residents on the naval air station had regarded 'the Limeys' with a certain degree of tolerance, but certainly not with open arms. This was because they were convinced that Prime Minister Churchill was doing his best to persuade Roosevelt to bring the United States into the war. They were right, of course, but being catcalled and booed as the British marched around the station wasn't exactly a mark of friendship.

Most former cadets who trained in the States go out of their way to point out the warm hospitality and friendship they received from local people, and this to a large extent was true. However, Hanson was on an early course, and he recalled that, with the advent of Pearl Harbor, attitudes changed in an explosion of war fever. The British had already been fighting for two years, and that suddenly became a good enough reason for the Americans to give them the glory treatment!

Basic flying training was suddenly over, and Hanson and his naval associates were elevated to the rank of Sub-Lieutenant, wearing pilot's wings on their left sleeves. They had completed some 200 hours' flying during their 30-week course. Their RAF counterparts who had successfully completed the course stayed on at Pensacola for another six weeks under the Towers Scheme. During this time they did about 80 hours' flying in PBY Catalinas, and qualified as second pilots on the large flying boats.

The Battle of Britain motivated young men throughout the Free World to volunteer for aircrew duties.

Not Winston Churchill but John Evans, Old Arnoldian, airline captain and actor.

Training for action

The Hawker Typhoon flown by 'Sheep' Milne and Bob Stanford.

Above 'Sheep' Milne (far left, displaying his watch) and pilots of 245 Squadron.

Below Outward-bound at dusk on board *Queen Elizabeth*.

Above Rear Admiral John Henry Towers, USN, whose Towers Scheme played a major role in training British naval cadets.

Above Squadron Leader Francis Butcher CBE AFC, whose *Vital Command* provided a great deal of material for this book.

Below The German ace Adolf Galland (left) talking to General Mölders.

Left The train halted somewhere in Kansas.

Below left A Stearman PT-17 flying over 'Superstition Mountains' near Falcon Field—so called because the Apaches are reported to have buried their dead there.

Below Primary (Stearman) instructors—all American civilians with backgrounds ranging from bush pilot to flying circus.

Right North American AT-6s flown by students on the Basic and Advanced stages of a course. They differed externally from the Harvard, having HF aerials in the front coaming and longer diameter propellers.

Below right North American AT-6s on the flight line at Falcon Field.

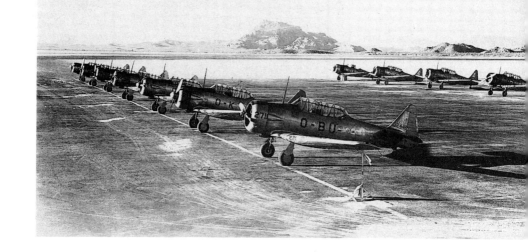

Left Cadets making a splash in the pool donated by the film company who filmed part of *Journey Together* at Falcon Field.

Opposite and this page Aftermath of a tornado. Stearman PT-17s were blown into orange groves in the course of a 30-minute tornado which broke the spell of 126 days without rain. These aircraft were picketed with chains but were facing into the wind. Chains were broken and they flew backwards about 10 ft above the ground until they got to the orange groves about 600 yd away.

Above left John Gibson—his was a long journey to graduation.

Above Captain John Gibson AFC cherishes the memories of his American experience.

Left John Evans, who was sent to Turner Field for Advanced training on the Cessna AT-17.

A Sunday morning at Turner Field, April 1942.

The Big City—Main Street, Albany, September 1942.

Travelling in style—John Evans, September 1942.

Left The plaque on the cemetery plot at Mesa, Arizona.

Below Group Captain Stuart Mills, President of the Falcon Field Association at the memorial service, Mesa, in 1983.

Above Norman Bate, originator of the Arnold Scheme Register with his daughter Nicola who is secretary, accounts and treasurer.

Below The author at 17 ITW Scarborough before training at Assiniboia and Moose Jaw, Saskatchewan, Canada.

Below 'Sheep' Milne, RCAF, training at Yorkton, Saskatchewan, Canada.

Accidents during flying training at No. 35 SFTS North Battleford, Saskatchewan, Canada. These photographs are from a very interesting collection obtained by Sqn/Ldr J. G. Millard, who was a Squadron Commander on the station. They were taken for Courts of Enquiry, Courts Martial, Investigations, etc, and were not intended for post-war archives. He found them destined for the incinerator when the station was closing down and acquired them on 'permanent loan', considering them far too valuable to be destroyed.

These Oxford aircraft were involved in a mid-air collision very shortly after the opening of the station.

Above The result of unauthorized low flying over still water (in winter this lake is frozen to a depth of about 10 ft).

Below This accident was caused by the pupil raising his flaps instead of his undercarriage on overshoot action. The aircraft fell to the ground and burst into flames (note the outline of the tailplane).

Above An accident at night caused by the pupil relaxing his concentration on the glide-path indicator during an approach for landing. The pilot was unhurt.

Below The precise cause of this accident is not clear. The pilot got into difficulties trying to land (note opposite direction of fuselage and wings). The pilot was unhurt.

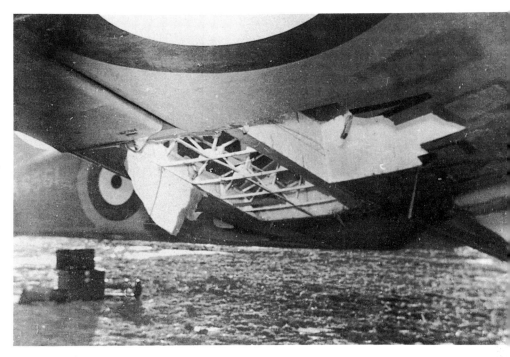

Above Partial disintegration of starboard wing surfaces whilst the aircraft was on test after a major overhaul. This was caused by an instructor diving his aircraft at a speed in excess of permitted limits.

Below A fatal accident resulting from unauthorized low flying.

Above left Derek Wilkins who trained in Southern Rhodesia.

Above Denis Stevens, the young navigator who wrote his diary of events in South Africa.

Left After graduation, a posting to Bomber Command.

Above right The Lancaster crew—Stevens is third from left.

Right Peter 'Shorty' Averill, his pilot.

Far right The author on arrival home from 32 SFTS Moose Jaw, Saskatchewan, in late 1942.

Above Flying training in the UK was often a difficult and dangerous business!

Below Harvards in the UK—pupils of No. 6 SFTS Little Rissington in July 1940. Sgt. John Studholme Bell, in the white flying suit, was later killed in a Harvard crash.

Harvards over the UK in July 1940.

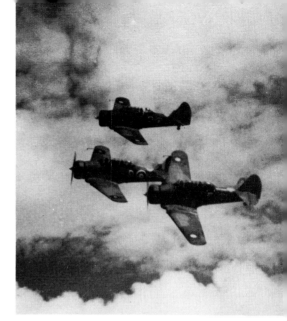

Right A tragic reminder.

TO THE MEMORY OF
SGT PILOT BRUCE HANCOCK R.A.F.V.R
WHO SACRIFICED HIS LIFE
BY RAMMING AND DESTROYING
AN ENEMY HEINKEL BOMBER
WHILE FLYING
AN UNARMED TRAINING AIRCRAFT
FROM WINDRUSH LANDING GROUND
DURING THE BATTLE OF BRITAIN
18TH AUGUST 1940

Below A DH 82C Tiger Moth (Canadian version—note the canopy).

Above The Hawker Audax Trainer.

Above The Fairey Battle Trainer.

Below An Avro Anson T.21—the last Anson built.

Above An Airspeed Oxford Mk V with Pratt & Whitney Wasp Junior engines.

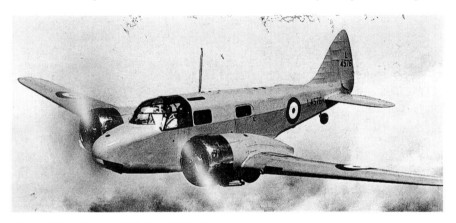

Above The Airspeed Oxford Mk 1.

Below An early Miles Magister with the original rudder.

Above A Consolidated Catalina—the only fully operational machine flown during training.

Below A Harvard Mk I with Browning 0.303s and 20-1b practice bombs.

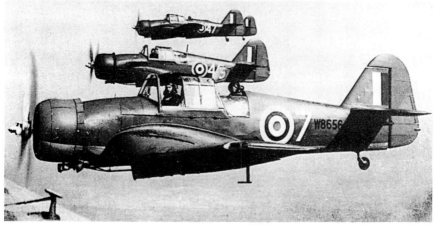

Top A Fairchild Cornell at Heany, Southern Rhodesia.

Above Miles Master Mk IIs flown by graduates returning to the UK for acclimatization courses at Advanced Flying Units.

Below Vultee Valiant BT-13As at 5 BFTS Carlstrom Field, Arcadia, USA.

Above The PT-19A Fairchild Cornell.
Below Cranking a PT-17 Boeing Stearman at 6 BFTS Ponca City, Oklahoma, USA.

During these early courses at Pensacola there was a high wastage factor, because there the grading system in the UK had not been introduced at that time. This was the course I completed at Kingstown, Carlisle, when I first went solo. It was initiated to check aptitude, air sickness and, generally speaking, the ability of a cadet to fly an aeroplane.

Having completed his basic training at Pensacola, Hanson was posted to the US Navy fighter training school at Opa Locka, Florida, some 14 miles north of Miami. During this course he flew more advanced machines and covered all aspects of fighter training, including air-to-air firing on drogues, ground strafing, camera-gun attacks and formation flying by day and night.

The first aircraft they flew was the North American Harvard, or SNJ-3 in US Navy terminology. Most pilots liked this all-metal, dual-controlled, aerobatic machine, which was fully equipped with good instrumentation, radio, retractable undercarriage, constant-speed propeller and flaps. It made for more sophisticated flying, and the 'three-point landing' was replaced by the wheeler onto a runway, dropping the tailwheel when the aircraft was fully stalled.

Having had fun with SNJs, they started the course all over again flying Brewster F2A Buffalo fighters, which the US Navy had discarded as obsolete. By this time the American instructors had handed them over to Lt.-Com. Charles Evans (later Vice-Admiral Sir Charles Evans). His job, at which he was particularly adept, was to teach them combat techniques. He bounced their formations out of the blue, and had pupils do the same while he sat up there watching points. For the first time they were learning to fly a machine 'as if it was strapped to their arse', which is an essential attribute for any fighter pilot!

Hanson's only prang came when he was flying a Buffalo at Opa Locka. He had undercarriage trouble, and finished up doing a long ground-loop, raising clouds of dust and sand. The reaction to this was typically American, and illustrates their *modus operandi*:

All I could hear was the scream of the fire tender and the ambulance. I took off my helmet and climbed down. The port undercarriage had partially retracted.

'You OK?' It was the doctor from the ambulance.

'Yes. Fine, thanks.'

'OK. Get in the wagon.'

'I'm fine, sir. I'll just walk over to my hangar there,' I said, pointing to our flight, a matter of 200 yards away.

'The hell you will! You'll get in the goddam wagon when I say! GET IN!'

So I got in. We roared off at speed, siren whining, and fetched up at the sick bay. The duty doctor gave me innumerable tests, rounding off with:

'You're OK? Feel OK? Go to the Chief Flying Instructor's Office.'

Lt.-Com. Sharp (USN) received me as a regular officer might be expected to—brisk and to the point.

'You OK? Wasn't it just great that everybody was so interested in your well-being?'

'*Yes, thank you, sir.*'

'*What happened?*'

I told him. Undercarriage indicator lights checked and rechecked. Operating lever untouched after that.

'*You sure both lights showed green?*'

'*Yessir, absolutely certain.*'

'*OK. You'll be hearing from me.*'

I was called to him two days later. With him stood an Engineer Lieutenant-Commander.

'*Sub-Lieutenant Hanson, I have to tell you that your F2A was thoroughly checked after the accident. This officer's findings are that the locking mechanism on that undercarriage leg was malfunctioning, but it allowed the indicator to show green, when in fact the lock was not engaged. You are therefore exonerated from all blame.*'

'*Thank you, sir.*' *I saluted and departed.*

After eight months in the USA Norman Hanson returned home and was trained to fly Vought F4U Corsairs—totally unlike the old biplane Corsairs. He was posted to HMS *Illustrious* and served in the South Pacific, taking part in many operations in the war against the Japanese. Promoted to Lieutenant-Commander, he was awarded the Distinguished Service Cross and was also Mentioned in Despatches. His book *Carrier Pilot* is a classic war memoir. Talking about his American experience, he said:

Eight months had passed remarkably quickly, during which we had learnt a lot about Americans and about the US Navy, who had very kindly and very efficiently taught me to fly a fighter aircraft without, as they put it so picturesquely, 'bustin' my ass'. We had met untold people and made a lot of good friends. We had enjoyed unprecedented hospitality from wonderful people who just naturally exuded generosity. I had found my way around New York, I had seen Toscanini, Duke Ellington, Arthur Fiedler, Benny Goodman, Jack Dempsey, Tommy Dorsey, Jack Benny and Betty Grable. I had emerged from Miami nightclubs as the dawn came up over Biscayne Bay, to seek bacon and eggs. I had sailed up the Mississippi in a stern-wheeler under a Christmas moon whose size I just don't believe. I had surf-boarded in the Gulf of Mexico, and flown, by night and day, over the Florida Everglades and the Mobile and Suwannee Rivers, so dear to the hearts of barber-shop quartets.

It had been fun—well, most of it.

There were many young men like Hanson who were trained for the business of war 'way down south' in the southern states. Some 4,000 British aircrew graduated out there under the Towers Scheme, and the vast majority of these were RAF and Fleet Air Arm pilots. Grading or 'elimination' courses were later introduced in the United States to cut down the wastage factor. On arrival in the States, RAF cadets were posted to the US Naval Air Station at Grosse Ile, Michigan, where they had to solo before travelling to Pensacola. This did not apply to naval cadets for some reason!

The naval authorities at Grosse imposed rigid discipline on cadets, and made life unnecessarily frustrating and difficult for them. The British resented the 'honour' system, part of the American form of discipline, because it was not a British custom to report the misdemeanours of one's colleagues or to spy on them. Some reported anti-British feeling in the establishment but, apart from that, few cadets looked forward to going on an 'elimination' course. They were allowed ten hours' dual on a Stearman, after which they had to solo for 60 minutes. If they failed the course they were washed out and sent for training, either in the USA or Canada, as wireless operator–air gunners.

There is little doubt in my mind that I would have been 'eliminated' had I been unlucky enough to have had the Grosse experience. As described earlier, it took me 14 hours' dual instruction before going solo. The atmosphere and style at 15 EFTS Kingstown, Carlisle, was one of encouragement. This degree of flexibility and patience enabled me to graduate in Canada, complete two years of operations flying Typhoons, subsequently to be trained as a flying instructor at CFS Upavon, and then to instruct at 17 SFTS Spitalgate, Grantham.

Such inflexibility was a relatively minor affair when one considers the broader issues. Nobody could have expected the Americans to change their disciplinary system to accommodate British, Empire and Commonwealth cadets. Also, the Towers Scheme was operated by the US Navy for training naval flying personnel. Its primary object was to train aircrew for service with RAF Coastal Command and the Fleet Air Arm. Naval cadets, however, received a more flexible, and in most cases longer, training than their RAF counterparts.

The deal provided highly trained aircrew for both the European and Far Eastern theatres of war at a time when they were most needed. Coastal Command was not able to absorb all graduates from the Scheme, so some served with Bomber Command, others took part in anti-shipping strikes flying Beaufighters and Mosquitoes, and some went to Transport Command. Their standard of training had been high, and their presence in the United States was a valuable public relations exercise for Britain.

Today, the Pensacola Veterans Association is still active as a by-product of those memorable times, when cadets were entertained lavishly by the local populace and made lifelong friends. In recent years British holidaymakers have invaded Florida and those parts which Norman Hanson and his associates covered daily in their Brewster Buffaloes.

An American cadet

The reactions of some British cadets to the American system of training, and their flying experiences, have already been highlighted. However, the percentage of those washed out or eliminated during pilot training in the USA was about the same for both British and American cadets. Every American obviously 'had his problems', and it is interesting to see how these relate to those experienced by our own chaps.

Donald S. Lopez had flying experience before joining the US Army Air Force. As a freshman at the University of Tampa, Florida, he had participated in the Civilian Pilot Training Program and logged 35 hours on Piper J-3 Cubs, having gone solo after eight hours' dual instruction. 'My instructor, Bill Chancey', he said, 'was a good instructor who was at ease in the air. His pleasant and relaxed manner, unlike many instructors whose inner panic is often manifest by raging and screaming at the student, made learning to fly easier than it otherwise might have been.'

He admitted that the Battle of Britain had given him the urge to become a fighter pilot, and a desire to fly a Spitfire. When the Japanese invaded Pearl Harbor, he could wait no longer and enrolled in the Army Air Force's aviation cadet program. The fight was on for places, and he had to wait six months for his notice to report to active duty. Meanwhile he continued flying, renting Cubs at his own expense: 'I practised spins, loops and an occasional extra landing, and finally amassed the 40 hours needed for my civilian license.'

Lopez's first taste of Army flying was at Primary Flying School, Union City, Tennessee—a civilian-run contract school, as were all primary schools. One could reasonably have assumed that, with his University background and flying experience, primary school would have presented few problems. The aircraft was the Fairchild PT-19 (RAF name Cornell), heavier and more powerful than the Piper Cub but easy to handle.

Sid Bennett, his instructor, let him take off and do the initial climb, and Lopez thought he was doing well until Bennett started screaming at him through the Gosport tubes. 'I soon learned that he was afflicted with some kind of 'alti-chronophobia.' The higher we climbed and the longer we flew, the madder he became. I use the word mad in lieu of angry, advisedly. He ranted and raved throughout the flight, occasionally quietening down to demonstrate a technique or manoeuvre.

'Strangely enough, when we met to discuss the day's flying, both before and after, he was soft-spoken and pleasant, and explained the good and bad points quite rationally. We dreaded flying with him, especially as the last student of the day, when his freakiness peaked.'

Lopez soloed on schedule after eight hours' dual, relieved to fly occasionally with another instructor. Bennett, however, continued to go berserk at the slightest provocation: 'Once when we were returning to the main field to land at the end of the flight, he said he would demonstrate a full-flaps landing. We normally landed with half flaps. On the final approach he called for full flaps, and I moved the manual control handle into the full-flap detent. About ten seconds later the cable snapped, the flaps came to full up, and we plunged toward the ground.

'Instead of correcting the airplane's attitude, he changed his own attitude from normal angry to furious. He turned round in his seat and almost stood while screaming at me. Since I could see the ground rushing up, I gave serious thought to screaming, too. I was just about to grab the stick when he turned round, levelled out, and landed as though nothing had happened. After we parked, and the crew chief told him that the cable had broken, he made no comment and never mentioned the incident again. I imagine that if I had touched the stick, he would have killed me or, even worse, tried to wash me out.'

Lopez was lucky, because Sid Bennett suddenly received his long-awaited commission in the Ferry Command, but not before he had washed out two cadets from his group of five. Having survived Bennett, Lopez was fortunate to have Ronald E. Boen—the complete antithesis of his predecessor. 'I was the first to fly with him, and he told me later that Bennett had given me a backhanded compliment by saying that I would be the least likely of the students to kill him.

'After I had flown for most of the period, shooting landings and practising other maneuvers under his direction, he asked if I minded if he took the controls as he had never flown a Fairchild; his previous training had been in Stearmans. He and I got on famously, and I looked forward to flying with him. Sometimes, on the very coldest days in January, we took off and, instead of going to the practice flying area, we flew on the deck directly to his airport at Milan, landed and taxied into his hangar to be met by his sister with hot chocolate and homemade cookies, a real treat after the mess-hall chow.

'Warmed and refreshed, we took off, completed our mission, and returned to Union City. Mr Boen suggested that if we were reported, I should say with my innocent demeanour that he was demonstrating strange field landings.'

The luck of the draw, one might say. But flying instructors, although gods to pupils, vary in temperament, attitude, style and technique. Bennett was one whose nervous system couldn't accommodate novice pupils with varying abilities, and there were others like him. But the fact remained that about 40 per cent of Lopez's intake was washed out at Primary school!

Lopez passed all his flight checks at Primary without difficulty, 'including the dreaded final check with the Army check pilot. Incidentally, this was my first flight with a military pilot, which made me feel more a part of the Army Air Forces and a step closer to my goal. Our class 43E, having completed Primary, was transferred to Newport, Arkansas, a new Basic Flying School.'

There he flew the Vultee BT-13 Valiant—the well-liked 'Vultee Vibrator'. He regarded it as an easy aircraft to fly, with no bad habits, and talked of his instructor, Lt. Davidson, a small, wiry Texan, as both a fine pilot and a fine instructor, which, he said, was not always the case. Apparently he accepted the Army discipline, which British cadets found irksome and frustrating, because he only mentions in a casual way that he and his associates occasionally bent the rules! The mess hall at Basic he described as an aesthetic and gastronomic disaster, appropriately known to the cadets as 'Chez Barf'. At Primary, he said, they had been served at tables by waitresses, but at Basic they had to carry metal trays along a GI chow line, and were served by prisoners from the stockade, who had little use for cadets and made no secret of it!

Everything went smoothly for Lopez at Basic, and the elimination factor on his course dropped dramatically to about 5 per cent. He was about to realize his dream of becoming a fighter pilot, as he was posted for single-engined advanced training to Craig Army Air Field, Selma, Alabama. With only two months to go to graduation, he and his fellow cadets were very wary about committing misdemeanours:

'We travelled to Selma by train via Memphis, where we were given four hours' leave between trains. This was our first time off base in more than two months. Only the certainty of punishment, and the prospect of being commissioned in the near future, restrained my more exuberant classmates from running amok. As a non-drinker, it fell to me to help many of the heavier drinkers back to the train, establishing me as a 19-year-old father figure.'

The general rule for enlisted men in the streets of Memphis was 'to salute everything in sight'. 'Obviously there hadn't been many cadets in Memphis, because, as he walked through town, we received many quizzical glances and hesitant salutes from enlisted men who, due to the close resemblance of cadets' and officers' uniforms, weren't sure what we were, but who weren't taking any chances.'

They had heard that it was almost impossible to get washed out at Advanced, because so much had already been invested in their training. Like most rumours, some cadets found that this was not completely accurate. Lopez started the course flying the North American AT-6 Texan (British name Harvard), which he said was a joy to fly, and seemed to him to be almost a fighter. His instructor was PO Richard Harry of the RAF:

'He was one of a large contingent of British cadets who had been trained at Craig, and one of the few who had been retained as instructors. He was fair, clean-cut, and looked even younger to me at 19. In fact, he looked like the young RFC pilot who was killed in every First World War aviation movie. Sad to say, he was later to be killed in combat over Europe. He was a fine pilot and a good and patient instructor, who was very well liked by all his students.'

This was a fine testimonial indeed from Lopez, and Harry, probably without knowing it, did a fine public relations job for the RAF. These words were written in 1986, when Lopez was deputy director of the Smithsonian's National Air and Space Museum in Washington. As an ex-combat pilot, he graduated from the Air Force Test Pilot School, and spent almost six years testing fighters. After a degree in Aeronautical Engineering, he spent five years teaching aeronautics at the US Air Force Academy, before becoming an engineer on the Apollo and Skylab space programmes.

The dreaded question of possible elimination was to rear its ugly head some three weeks before graduation, when the final fittings were being made on their officer's uniforms. Three instructors from another squadron would walk in and select three cadets at random for a formation check ride. Invariably, Lopez said, one, and often two, of the three would be washed out.

'Panic and rumour swept through the class. We heard that the operational units were dissatisfied with the flying ability of the graduated cadets, and had asked the advanced schools to toughen their requirements [this was true] and that 50 per cent of the class would be washed out [this was not true]. The three-instructor groups were immediately nicknamed the Gestapo, and cadets went to any extreme to avoid them.'

Many years later, Lopez met the former commander of the training squadron at Craig, who told him that the selection of cadets was not random at all. Only those cadets rated by their instructors as marginal were washed out. In my opinion, this final combing-out was simply applying the yardstick of regimented flying in the pursuit of excellence. But the effectiveness of flying training was no substitute for operational experience.

I left my Hurricane OTU with 'needs more practice in formation flying' in my pilot's assessment, being rather slow to react, and lacking in confidence when flying at close quarters. This was remedied on my first Squadron, where loose finger-four formation, unlike tight vic, was standard practice. I soon gained in confidence, but I have no doubts that by American standards I would have been categorized as 'marginal' at graduation stage.

By comparison, Don Lopez had a high rating, because he was one of the few cadets who were selected to fly Curtiss P-40 fighters before graduation. This was a big deal for a chap who hadn't yet got his wings! His description of the event will remind pilots of their first flight in a Hurricane or Spitfire:

'I will never forget the mixture of elation, awe and apprehension I felt as I climbed into this cockpit for the first time. The P-40 was twice as fast, had about twice the horse-power, and seemed, although it wasn't, twice as big as the AT-6. The nose extended so far in front of the cockpit and loomed so high that you could see nothing ahead.

'I remember having a vague hope that the engine would fail to start, but it caught on the first quarter of the prop, so there was no turning back. I taxied to the end of the runway, checked the mags, and got tower clearance for take-off. I advanced the throttle all the way and started down the runway. It was fortunate that the runway was very wide or I would have run off both sides of it. First the powerful torque turned me to the left, then I overcorrected and swerved to the right. I was finally getting it straightened out when I lifted off.'

Some 30 years later Lopez, as Chairman of the Aeronautics Department of the great National Air and Space Museum, gathered statistical material on the American Second World War flying training programme which is quite revealing. The Army Air Forces graduated 193,440 pilots between 1 July 1939 and 31 August 1945; during that same period more than 124,000 pilot trainees failed to complete their course!

One could not find a more authoritative source, but a wastage factor of about 40 per cent was high enough to suggest that it was a deliberate part of the system. It is understandable that the RAF should have been particularly concerned, especially at the number of pupils being eliminated for disciplinary offences. However, one cannot argue about the American system when one considers that over 13,000 of our pilots graduated there.

A British cadet

Don Lopez's story is an interesting one, because he reflects the attitudes of a young American dedicated to the system, who was later to become a test pilot and a leading authority on aviation matters. The case of Victor Hewes, a British cadet who trained under the Arnold Scheme, has many similarities and offers a fascinating comparison.

Like Lopez, Hewes had flying experience before commencing his training in the USA. On 15 July 1935 his father took him up in a DH Moth when the new Leicester aerodrome was first opened. He then proceeded to have dual instruction, and on his 18th birthday volunteered for the RAF, but he was not called up until the middle of 1941. While awaiting call-up he was befriended by two American Ferry Pilots, and employed by the Air Transport Auxiliary (ATA) cadet/section officer:

'This involved working in the control tower and flying as safety copilot on various aircraft, including Whitleys. There were two of us, and in Ansons we had to raise and lower the landing gear—120 turns each way! We also managed to pick up some time in Rapides, Oxfords and Blenheims.'

His experience of private flying and with the ATA helped him considerably when he started primary training at EFTS Cliffe Pypard, near Swindon. He had a fine instructor in Sgt. Addy, and flew solo after five hours' dual, which was a fine achievement. After having been given his EFTS proficiency check near the end of his course, however, he was told that they were being posted overseas to complete their training. At this stage they had only lost one or two pupils, due to air sickness or not being able to go solo.

'I do remember somebody, somewhere, asking us where we would like to go: South Africa, Canada, or America. Most of us picked this order since we thought that if we went to Africa we would be near the desert fighting. Being keen and eager, our objective was to get on "ops" as soon as we could. Little did we realize then what a big country Africa was, and how far South Africa was from the war. Canada was acceptable, but nobody wanted to go to America. In true RAF fashion we finished up by being sent to our last choice.'

After leaving Moncton, New Brunswick, they spent two days in a train heading south, and finally pulled in to a siding at Turner Field, Albany, Georgia. The sight of Beech AT-7s, twin-engined training machines, flying around uplifted them, as they expected to go straight to an SFTS and then home. Not so. They found themselves back at ITW, and had to face doing their training all over again.

Being treated as officer cadets, and the splendid food after English wartime fare, was encouraging—plenty of meat, ice-cream, and orange juice served cafeteria-style. Good living quarters, although the toilets were all lined up in a row and not in stalls as at home, and not having to wash their own eating irons or do cook-house duty also made life more amenable.

The programme at Turner was designed to acclimatize them to the American way of life. 'Looking back, I now realize that this was necessary, and that they did a pretty good job despite our opposition. We were all fairly "anti" at having to leave England, where most of us had experienced some of the horrors of war. The USA, however, had been at war for less than two months, and was still operating on a peacetime basis. Consequently, we were on different wavelengths.'

Naturally the British were itching to get up and fly, and felt they were wasting time at Turner: standing on guard duty at the sewage farm all night, shooting skeet and doing PT during the day, and taking part in the American retreat, which Hewes described as 'a big parade every night to lower the flag. Along with American cadets, and led by the band, we marched to the flagpole, where to lots of "Sound Offs", "Reports" and much bugle blowing, the flag was lowered for the night. On the way the band usually played Sousa marches, and the American cadets marched calling out their "Hup, Two, Three, Four". We marched along singing the RAF versions of Sousa, such as "Be kind to your web-footed friends, for a duck may be somebody's mother". This drove the American officers crazy. They did not know that British forces always sing when they march.'

Unquestionably it was a shock for British cadets to have to start life again at an American ITW, especially after almost completing their EFTS course. But nobody could have expected the Americans to have integrated them into their Basic and Advanced flying courses without first doing Primary. Furthermore, their sojourn at Turner did much to acclimatize them to American style and custom.

On 20 February 1942 they arrived at Carlstrom Field near Arcadia, a very nice small town in central Florida. 'The setting was like a country club, with palm trees and a swimming pool. The buildings were all white stucco, and the cadet living quarters were as good as any motel. Here once again there were only four to a room, this time with our own bathroom "en suite". Again the food was top-grade. One thing I still remember was the bacon-and-egg sandwiches sold in the little PX. We would sit and eat them while listening to the latest Glen Miller records on the juke box. What was to spoil it? The American West Point class system.'

Victor Hewes's resentment of the West Point honour code and the upper and lower class system was reflected by most British cadets who trained in the States. This form of discipline was foreign to British national character, but an ingredient of the American package deal—an invaluable contribution to Britain's war in the air.

Victor Hewes commenced his American flying experience in PT-17s, larger than a Tiger Moth and with a more powerful engine, but having brakes and a tailwheel which made them easier to ground-loop. Furthermore, there was no airspeed indicator, which meant that cadets were taught to fly 'by the seat of their pants'.

Both Don Lopez and Victor Hewes had a deal of flying experience when they started training under the American military system. Like Lopez, Hewes had problems with his first instructor: 'I could not get along with him or the American method of instruction,' Hewes said. 'I had to unlearn what I had been taught in ATA and by the RAF at EFTS. My instructor did not want to send me solo, even though, in my opinion, my flying was safe and more than satisfactory. I pointed out that I already had a lot of solo time, and please get me a new instructor. I was very lucky not to get washed out for having the wrong attitude. My new instructor, James Godette, sent me solo right away, and I never looked back, completing the course on 29 April 1942 with an "above average" rating.'

Hewes, like Lopez, was lucky not to have been eliminated by his first instructor. Getting through Primary—which had by far the biggest elimination factor—seemed to depend largely on the luck of the draw with instructors, and the ability to cope with the disciplinary system. Hewes sums it up as follows:

'Our instructors, both ground and flight, were civilians, with one or two military check pilots. Many RAF cadets, even though they had gone solo in England, were washed out for no good reason except a personality conflict with the instructor or some minor infraction of the regulations.

'The Americans thought they were still training career staff officers up to peacetime standards, instead of NCO pilots who would be in deadly operations over Germany in a few months. Chandelles, lazy eights and pylon eights were standard American manoeuvres that you had to fly. However, the instructors failed to tell you what you were trying to accomplish. For example: they would show you a pylon eight, but never tell you that its purpose was to reveal your knowledge of the wind effect on your turns.'

In fairness to the American system it should be pointed out that the purpose of flying training was to enable the pupil to handle his aircraft in all conditions of flight, including aerobatics and spins. The fact that the US curriculum included chandelles, lazy and pylon eights, was all part of their pattern—a pupil had to be able to fly these manoeuvres accurately.

Hewes was impatient—he wanted to get through his training as quickly as possible, go home, and then fly on operations, as did most of his colleagues. The USA had only been at war for a couple of months and, with a population of well over four times that of the UK, she had a huge reservoir of young talent queueing up to fly. Her peacetime curriculum, which generated problems for British cadets, had been designed to accommodate a wide range of nationalities entering the schools from small towns and cities throughout her vast territory.

It is undeniably to her great credit that her flying schools continued to absorb British cadets throughout, and there is little doubt that this Anglo/American co-operation had spin-offs for both sides. Life wasn't all 'nose to the grindstone' for a British cadet, as Victor Hewes recalls:

'Things that I still remember are flying over the orange groves and smelling the orange blossoms, even up at 1,000 ft. Also, our days off at Carlstrom were most enjoyable. Five of us, Percy Matthews, Ian Harvey, Alan Huckle, Herron and I, would rent a car in Arcadia for one dollar an hour, and drive to Miami and West Palm Beach. The roads were straight, and we drove like a bat out of hell. It is a wonder that we survived those trips, the flying was easy, but the driving was dangerous! We also went by bus to Sarasota, where the local population met us and took us to their homes for the night. We were not only wined and dined, but taken to the Ringling Brothers, Barnum & Bailey's circus, the John Ringling North Museum, and given the run of the Yacht Club.'

Like Don Lopez, Hewes left Primary with an 'above average' rating, and went on to fly the Vultee BT-13 (Vibrator) for Basic training at Gunter Field, Montgomery, Alabama. He described his monoplane as a dream to fly, with twice the power of the Stearman, a full instrument panel, and the characteristics of a military aircraft. Both Lopez and Hewes commented that, when they got to Basic, they at last felt that they were back in the air force again.

'For the first few hours', Hewes said, 'my instructor was an American 1st Lieutenant, who sent me off solo after five hours. After this he was alternated with two RAF POs, Somer and Cain, and half-way through this course Sgt. Bill Gatehouse took over up to graduation. All of these instructors were first-class, and head and shoulders above the Carlstrom civilians.'

Things had gone smoothly for Hewes at Gunter, and he had not been bothered by the 'upper class' system. Unfortunately, two of his classmates were killed during the course, having been caught out by an unexpected line squall on a night cross-country. Leaving Gunter, he returned to Turner airfield for a multi-engined Advanced course, flying Cessna AT-17s (known as the bamboo bomber) and Curtiss AT-9s. He remembers that:

'Very little had changed at Turner. We still used the same barracks and still had to march to the flagpole every night, but now the end was in sight. We flew a lot of cross-country day and night, and formation flying. Instead of flying solo, we flew with another cadet, which could be quite hairy at times. The Curtiss was a hot little twin-engined plane which could be quite a handful at times, especially if one bounced on landing. After the first bounce the bounces got bigger until you pranged. I still think that if you could fly that little plane, you could fly anything.' (It was deliberately designed that way.)

Half-way through the course, Hewes was commissioned and given American silver wings and a graduation certificate. He had mixed emotions: while looking forward to going home and getting on ops, he was happy to get a commission and a chance to build up a few more hours before going to OTU. Those receiving commissions were told that they were to go to Toronto, Canada, for uniforms, and then to return to the States to be trained as instructors.

'On arrival at No. 1 Manning Depot, in the old Toronto Exhibition Grounds, the first thing we did was to go downtown to Eton's Department store to be measured for our officer's uniform. They were ready the next day, and we put them on in the store, wrapping up our old uniform to take back to the depot. When we walked out of the store with those RAF wings on our Pilot Officer's blue uniform, we felt on top of the world. I will never forget that day.'

It is hardly surprising that Wings Day (RAF-style) should have been an unforgettable moment in Hewes's life. Most aircrews' cups were brimming when they received their flying badges, because the emblem signified the achievement of an ambition, and identified them as flying men. The rank and pay that went with graduation was, for the majority, a very secondary consideration.

On 17 September 1942, together with a selected few from his course, Hewes returned to Maxwell Field, Montgomery, for instructor's school. His experience there is interesting because, to some extent, it reveals the basic differences between the RAF and US Army Air Force systems of instruction. He said: 'US instructors' school was nothing compared to the RAF FIS course. All we did was fly around in the back seat of the twins. At no time were we ever told how to instruct, or even how to explain the manoeuvres we were doing. They had nothing similar to the RAF patter system. We just had to demonstrate out ability to fly the various manoeuvres from the instructor's seat.'

Life as an instructor had its advantages, however. He was given an increase in pay, equivalent to that of a US 2nd Lt., and was free to go into town during time off. He logged at least 100 flying hours a month, and had no administrative duties. The social life was tremendous, for the local populace invited them to their homes, country clubs and local activities.

Victor Hewes had had little choice about going back to the States to become a flying instructor. They wanted him to do a tour of instruction, during which he could build up his flying hours, gain more experience, and be away from the black-out and rationing in the UK. The opportunity gave him an extension of life, because there was a very high casualty rate amongst multi-engine pilots in the European theatre. Who was he to object? He knew that he would eventually be on ops. And so he was, flying Mosquitoes attacking air-to-ground targets, but in the Far East.

Don Lopez made the point that, however much flying experience one gained, it was no substitute for combat experience when one became operational. An experienced instructor, for example, would have the advantage of being able to fly any aircraft with confidence and precision. But flying in combat is a different game, involving split-second reflexes and, above all, experience in that particular type of warfare. My own Squadron, for example, was in Normandy, moving up the line, and was engaged in attacking Panzer armour, troop concentrations and other heavily defended targets holding up the Allied advance. Casualties were high, and replacement pilots were hurriedly being sent out from Warmwell.

These chaps had only five or six hours' flying experience converting on to Typhoons, although some of them had well over 1,000 hours in their log books. Being suddenly pitchforked into the line, with no Squadron experience, after only a few hours flying the combat machine, was reminiscent of the First World War—they were plumb unlucky, because of the demand and supply situation at that particular time. The net result was that a small band of experienced combat pilots survived, while many of the inexperienced replacements did not.

Many of those who were retained for instructional duties overseas might have faced similar situations when they finished their tour of instruction, or when their particular Scheme was closed. Victor Hewes was lucky on both counts. He enjoyed his sojourn in the States, and survived his operational tour. While in the USA he instructed only one class of RAF cadets, and after that all of his students were Army Air Force cadets. Similarly, other RAF instructors trained American cadets, and this undoubtedly helped to reduce the elimination rate from the Arnold schools, as well as providing a cross-fertilization of ideas and style in the training programme.

The Arnold Scheme

General Henry 'Hap' Arnold, Chief of Staff of the US Army Air Corps (later Army Air Force), visited Britain regularly and had many high-level contacts here. Talks were going on at this time about the possibility of training RAF pilots in the United States. This had to be by agreement with Congress and, of course, with President Roosevelt himself. As we have seen, the deal was a big one, involving the setting up of British Flying Training Schools and the training of RAF cadet pilots in US Army Air Corps schools. The agreement hinged on the Lend-Lease Bill which was cleared by Congress on 5 March 1941. This largely took care of the funding arrangement, although the Air Corps offered to pay for board and lodging and aviation fuel costs.

But the USA was a neutral country, and arrangements had to be made to circumvent the Taft Act, which was a sensitive issue as far as Congress was concerned. Lawyers suggested that it was legally possible for the United States to train British civilian pilots without contravening the act, adding that visas could be issued in Canada. They stipulated that cadets would have to be dressed in civilian clothes for entry into the US.

Why not? The Germans had circumvented the Air Clauses of the Versailles Treaty in building the Luftwaffe. When reviewing the progress of the Luftwaffe between the wars it was stated that German pilots posed as South Tyrolean soldiers and secretly crossed the border into Italy to train with the Regia Aeronautica. It was just history repeating itself for British cadets to obtain their visas in Toronto, Canada, cross the border into the USA in grey flannel suits, then wear an American KD uniform on the station, just as the Germans had worn Italian Air Force uniforms! The Germans had been accepted as students in Italy; the British cadets were officially civilians off-station, but came under Air Corps disciplinary rules and regulations at all times.

RAF cadets in their early stages of training found the discipline imposed upon them by the Army Air Corps to be frustrating and crude in the extreme. It took the form of a system known as 'hazing'—a very strange word! The only dictionary interpretation comes from the word 'haze', meaning 'to punish with unnecessary work'.

Freshmen were initiated into a number of strange cadet rules, including eating 'by the square rule'. Just imagine approaching the breakfast table laden with bottles of chocolate or strawberry milk, pancakes and maple syrup, bacon, eggs, toast and coffee, and then having to sit at attention on only two inches of board and move only one arm, first vertically and then horizontally, in order to pick up a spoon and move it mechanically to one's mouth, making sure that no part of one's body suffered any contractions! This robot-like exercise led to the cliché 'square meal'. There was no talking at mealtimes except when addressed by the Senior Classman, and cadets had to keep their eyes firmly fixed on their plate.

Misdemeanours resulted in demerits, and a number of them entailed marching up and down with shouldered arms at weekends under the glowing orb of the sun, which was very hot in Georgia! The old cliché 'When in Rome, do as the Romans do' applies, of course, but this was a trifle hard on chaps who had come over primarily to learn to fly—all of them volunteers and most of them in the RAF only for the duration of hostilities! However, their counterparts in Germany had to endure 6-12 months of regimental training.

The USA is an accumulation of many different nationalities and dialects, and civilian flying instructors were no exception. During the initial stages of the Arnold Scheme, the USA was a neutral country, and there were some instructors who weren't exactly thrilled to be involved in training RAF cadet pilots. Also, some British ears had difficulty picking up the Southern drawl instantly. Furthermore, the flying training instruction was not as standardized as it was in the RAF, and these factors, combined with the rigid disciplinary system, resulted in a high elimination rate—in some cases 40 per cent or more!

In retrospect, one has to take into account that there was also a high wastage factor among American cadets. Standards were high, the country was not engaged in warfare, and 'washing out' a number of students was accepted by the hierarchy as 'par for the course'. How-

ever, when the United States came into the war, a pro-British attitude became something to shout about, but as far as training was
concerned the exceptionally high wastage rate continued.

This elimination rate caused concern throughout. It was far higher
than by RAF standards, expensive in terms of money and manpower,
and posed problems of reclassification of rejected pupils. Also, a high
wastage factor at Primary schools reduced the intake to Basic and
Advanced schools, and made it difficult to fill places. Consequently, the
intake at Primary schools had to be considerably increased to balance
the system.

It was felt that a major cause of the elimination problem with RAF
cadets was one of acclimatization. In late 1941 the US Army instituted
replacement centres to provide acclimatization courses for new arrivals
(roughly the equivalent of our ITW courses). This was a five-week
course consisting of drill, physical training, US Army customs, American history, geography and flying terminology. Discipline throughout
was based on the code of the West Point military academy. I can find
no evidence that these courses improved the wash-out rate but, at least,
the US Army was trying hard!

But the Americans themselves had a similar problem, because
during the Second World War their elimination rate for pilot training
was just under 40 per cent. It would appear that knocking hell out of
a chap doesn't necessarily improve his aptitude in the air! However, the
Americans point out that their cadets were primarily being trained for
commissioned rank, and flying was only an ancillary part of their
training.

Primary training was conducted at five schools located in Florida and
Georgia and these were all civilian-operated. The basic machine used
was the Stearman PT-17A, and cadets did about 60 hours' flying. This
was the equivalent course to our EFTS and much the same length. The
remainder of the course was in two parts: Basic and Advanced flying.
This was done from military airfields in Georgia and Alabama. The
strict military discipline was maintained until a pilot got his wings,
having completed about 200 hours of flying.

John Evans—an 'Arnold' man

John Evans is a tallish man, well set up, with a powerful voice and
character. Today he is an actor whose primary role is his impersonation
of former Prime Minister Sir Winston Churchill, to whom he bears a
remarkable resemblance, both physically and vocally. But flying has
been the mainspring in his life, and he was an airline captain for many
years, before turning to the stage and TV to keep himself occupied.

'I cannot remember when I first became interested in flying,' he said,
'because I was born to it.' His first interest was the Royal Flying Corps,
and still is. As a young boy he had four three-and-sixpenny flips in an
Avro 504, and had a voracious appetite for flying magazines donated
by an elder brother. 'I was one of those precocious little bastards', he

admitted, 'who at the age of 12 knew the order of battle on the Western Front.'

Evans, a Warwickshire lad, volunteered for pilot/navigator training in October 1940. 'The Battle of Britain inspired me,' he said, 'and I only wished that I had been two or three years older, and could have joined them.' John has a very definite air about him, and a somewhat cynical approach to life. Looking back, he pointed out that 'with my love and knowledge of aviation, I was perfect material to be slotted into the war machine'. The RAF duly obliged and, after grading school at Perth, Evans found himself and five associates packed into a single cabin like eggs in a box, on board a steamship crossing the Atlantic. The ship was part of an empty American convoy which had ferried GIs to Northern Ireland, and by good fortune it docked in New York instead of Halifax.

Three or four days' leave in New York was a bemusing experience, and he recalled the staggering amount of food, the informality of officers at Fort Hamilton, Brooklyn, being fêted on Broadway and never being allowed to buy a drink, and the impact of the Battle of Britain on the American public. 'In our airman's blues, and with our cadets' white flashes, the Yanks thought we were B of B pilots', he said, 'and we did nothing to disabuse them.' After the party in New York some 500 British cadets entrained for Turner Field, near Albany, Georgia—the reception centre for the Arnold scheme.

Evans soon discovered that the American system was vastly different from the RAF. Moving everywhere at the double, calling senior cadets 'Sir', no talking at mealtimes, losing merit points for petty offences, and being treated like a delinquent youth, was not exactly his style, and he found it schoolboyish and unnecessary. In those days, Evans thought, British cadets were considerably more mature than their American counterparts, many of whom were high-school graduates. Also, British youth had more inherent discipline from their educational and family background. However, the US early training process was designed to break a man down and rebuild him the way the US Army Air Corps wanted him. Most cadets found this acclimatization stage extremely frustrating, and being confined to camp didn't help matters.

Getting down to the business of flying at Tuscaloosa, Alabama, in a Stearman provided the first challenge, and Evans was lucky. He had a civilian flying instructor with some 400 hours' flying experience who was a very nice man. The Stearman looked a big bastard after the Tiger Moth at Perth, and was twice as powerful with its seven-cylinder radial engine developing some 220 hp. Perhaps it was overpowered, for pupils could have been trained with half the poke, which made it expensive operationally—rather like a big Chevrolet as opposed to a Ford Prefect! Evans found the lap straps, instead of the full shoulder harness, made him feel a bit vulnerable when inverted.

'It was a beautiful aeroplane,' he said; 'for aerobatics it's as strong as could be. Like all other cadets, we started aerobatics before we were cleared to do so.' An interesting aspect of American Primary training was that their Stearmans had no airspeed indicators. This was an excellent way of training, flying straight and level by the rpm, listening to the noise in the wires, and flying by the seat of one's pants. Asked how he felt about his instructor at this stage, Evans commented, 'He's God, you don't think he can make a mistake. You are so hungry for knowledge that you soak it up like a sponge.'

The US *Gunter Field Review* records the end of Primary training for cadets in these words:

> ... *Then suddenly after weeks of Primary training, he gazes upon a new world. A world he dared not even dream of heretofore—the world of Basic Flying School.*
>
> *He is no longer a 'dodo'. He is rapidly developing into an Army Air Force pilot. If he ever had a sinking sensation upon looking at an aeroplane he probably has lost it by now, and even when anyone asks him if he can fly, he can answer 'Yes, sir' in a low, reserved tone—but with one eye cocked towards days to come.*

Young Evans finished his primary school training at Tuscaloosa. This was a civilian school, as was the Marshall School at Cambridge, England. Thus the two air forces had adopted similar systems, but with their own particular style of operation. The Arnold system in the United States made no concessions to British cadets, and carried on a peacetime formula, washing out about 50 per cent of cadets.

John Evans said: 'We had to do it the American way. We were paid $10 a week, and when we did get out of camp, which was not often, we had to scratch. Naturally we had to hitch-hike, and we had to accept hospitality which was overwhelming, but we were very frustrated. The chaps in Arizona were under RAF jurisdiction, and those lucky bastards could get out of camp at the end of each day.'

To be fair to the Americans, they had no reason to adapt their training to suit British cadets. Their country was making a vital contribution to the RAF aircrew problem in setting up the British Flying Training Schools and opening the gates of their own to British entrants. There were bound to be hiccups, but most of these were dealt with without becoming issues. RAF cadets, for example, were later obliged to conform to neither the 'honors system' (informing on each other) nor the 'square meal' disciplinary form of eating, which was standard procedure for some US Army Air Force cadets. As explained, these entrants were primarily trained to become US officers, and flying was only part of the curriculum! There was an RAF Commissioning Board in the USA which offered commissions to those selected to become flying instructors. After qualifying, these chaps stayed behind in the States to instruct. This was vital because the system had to feed itself.

However, the rate of failure was considerably higher than at RAF or RCAF EFTSs. Investigators found that a number of those who were 'failed' had been 'washed out' for being unable to adapt to the American disciplinary system. These were sent for retesting to Trenton in Canada, and many of them passed out from this EFTS and carried on at SFTS to graduate. This was a practical solution, because a great deal of money had been invested in these men and recycling recouped this investment in most cases. Also, invaluable time was saved, and the process was good for morale, for such cadets were only too grateful to be offered a second chance.

Evans flew Vultee Vibrators during Basic training. These machines were twice as powerful as the Stearmans, but less powerful than a Harvard, with a fixed undercarriage and a two-pitch propeller. Civilian instructors were left behind: Evans' course had a mixture of RAF and American instructors. By this time (mid-1942) RAF instructors were appearing on the scene, as the system began feeding itself. Night flying was included in the syllabus, and at the end of Basic, with some 130 hours' flying under his belt, John Evans really began to feel his feet. His training had been extremely thorough, although standardized, due to perfect weather conditions and the system itself. He had learned to fly with a variety of instructors, both civilian and Service, and he had set his sights on becoming a fighter pilot. Flying a Spitfire had been his primary objective. But those who passed Basic on John's Course were arbitrarily divided into two, and his half were sent to Turner Field for Advanced training on multi-engined aircraft.

The aircraft for Advanced training were the Curtiss AT-9 and the Cessna AT-17 Bobcat, two totally different twin-engined machines. While the Curtiss had a gliding angle like a brick, the Cessna AT-17 was more a gentleman's aircraft, made of steel tube, wood and fabric, with the air and gentility of a more advanced Anson. The different flying characteristics of the two aircraft certainly made pilots more adaptable, which was a considerable asset. Asymmetric flying, general handling, instrument, formation and night flying, plus ten days at another school for ground and aerial gunnery practice, made up the course.

Within one hour of being presented with his American wings and being handed his Diploma by an American General, Evans and his associates were on the train going home. 'That was the ransom that they held us to,' he said. 'Once we had got our wings we were liable to be normal. We could have set fire to the bloody camp.' So John Evans graduated as a Sergeant Pilot, and bought his RAF wings in a shop at Moncton, New Brunswick.

After ten months' intensive training from February to November 1942, he had some 300 hours' flying in his log book—one-third more than his counterparts training in Canada. The fact that he and his colleagues had graduated in such a hard disciplinary system put them in the top bracket of trained aircrew, and was a reflection on their strength of character. Ironically, RAF airmen who had been Halton apprentices, or 'Halton Brats' as they were called, would have been at home in the United States!

John Evans had no difficulty recalling his experiences of 50 years previously when he was training to be an 'Arnold' man, which shows the impact that the Scheme made on young cadets. It was certainly a rugged life, and an achievement for those who 'stayed the course' and graduated. John is an outgoing, resiliant individual with a competitive spirit, which undoubtedly helped him during his sojourn in the States!

Back in Britain, he became a flying instructor before flying Stirlings operationally. He survived to become an airline captain for many years, living in Marlow, Bucks. The strong characters that he later portrayed as an actor perhaps reflect his own personality.

A change of course

A BFTS cadet's ambition was to win his wings and become a fighter pilot. All his training had been on single-engined machines, and with luck he would be posted to a UK Advanced Flying Unit, flying Masters, and then proceed to an Operational Training Unit before joining a fighter squadron. This conjured up wondrous visions of flying Hurricanes, Spitfires, Typhoons or Tempests.

Many of those who gained their wings in the summer of 1944 were hoping that the war would last long enough for them to 'have a go' in Europe—the only other alternative being the Far East! Waiting for a posting at the Majestic Hotel, Harrogate, was frustrating—the Allies were advancing swiftly through Belgium into Holland, and events were moving fast.

Meanwhile, some 10,000 paratroopers, including glider pilots, had 'hit the deck' at Arnhem, and only about 2,000 came out. Consequently, the Army became desperately short of glider pilots—so much so that Brigadier George Chatterton (a pre-war RAF pilot) talked to his chums in high places at the Air Ministry and succeeded in 'borrowing' 1,500 RAF pilots for conversion on to gliders.

This was an amazingly large number of highly trained men by any standard, to have available 'at the drop of a hat'. It demonstrated that the reservoir of talent created by overseas flying training proved invaluable in unforeseen circumstances, and war is riddled with them! However, it must have been frustrating for those potential fighter pilots 'champing at the bit' in the Majestic when top brass from the Army suddenly appeared to give them the glad tidings.

The message was loud and clear: 'Well, chaps, we're running out of war! It's nearly over—there's just a matter of getting the Army across the Rhine in gliders, and you are the boys to do it. It will take us less time to train you to be soldiers than it will take to teach our people to fly.' Herbert Buckle was one of 200 graduates from Falcon Field who took part in the operation. He recalled:

'Within weeks we found ourselves on an infantry training course, where Army corporals had great fun in teaching us the rudiments of soldiery, with our newly acquired 'Wings' and badges of rank disguised under Army denims. We treated the training in rather a cavalier fashion, and were exhorted to 'adopt a look of grim determination' when engaged in bayonet drill. It didn't seem so amusing when we were promised that we would be in action within a few weeks. Infantry training was followed by battle training.

'Soon we were introduced to flying Horsa gliders at the end of 150 ft of rope, towed by either Dakotas, Albemarles, or the four-engined Stirling bomber. I recall that being towed behind Albemarles at night was a little hair-raising, as the stalling speed of the aircraft bore a remarkable similarity to its take-off speed when encumbered by a loaded Horsa!'

The newly-trained RAF glider pilots were then split into two groups: about half of them were posted to UK airfields for the Rhine crossing, and the remainder earmarked for India to take part in airborne operations in South-East Asia. During the Rhine crossing 101 glider pilots were killed, of whom 61 were RAF pilots.

Life after the Scheme

BFTS courses were either shortened or lengthened according to the supply and demand situation as the war progressed, and to correlate with the corresponding intakes into the USAAF programme. When the war in Europe entered its final phase, during the winter of 1944–5, some 3,000 cadets graduated under the BFTS scheme alone. By March 1944 courses had been extended by three weeks because of the backlog of pilots at UK reception centres; the need for glider pilots obviously eased the congestion in this respect. Likewise, cadets were having to wait three months or more to be sent across the Atlantic for flying training in Canada and the USA.

When the war finished in Europe on 8 May 1945 the Americans ceased all USAAF pilot training at civilian-operated schools, and wanted to close the BFTSs. Following discussions, however, it was agreed to keep the schools open until 20 August to allow the RAF to re-establish UK training. These plans did not quite reach fulfilment because on 15 August 1945 the Japanese surrendered, and Lend-Lease terminated after Course No. 25 graduated on 25 August. Thereafter, all courses were returned to the UK, and some pupils were integrated into the UK programme under special conditions.

One cadet, John Gibson, was returned home with his course before he had completed his Primary training at No. 4 BFTS, because the bomb had dropped on Hiroshima and Falcon Field was shut down. He was a young man of strong character, obsessed with flying, and so he signed on, determined to get his wings somehow. Looking back over his long and frustrating journey to graduation, followed by a lifetime of flying, he never forgot his experience at Falcon Field, and in 1991 he found himself reliving those days:

'Sometime in 1988,' he said, 'I received a DHSS communication including a letter from the Secretary of the Falcon Field Association asking me if I was the John Gibson on 27 Course at Falcon Field and, if so, would I provide some details. After all these years I still cherish the memories of my American experience, because it became a milestone in my life, and so I gave him a brief resumé of my flying career. They then passed me on to a chap collecting data who was on 27 Course, and that was how it all started.'

Months later, Gibson attended a mini reunion of 27 Course in Birmingham, organized by the same fellow cadet who had had the same instructor as he had, and about 25 of them turned up, some with their wives. Gibson explained this nostalgia by saying that somebody once told him that a young man looks forwards and an old man backwards! 'Meeting up after 43 years was quite an experience,' he said. 'Slide shows and chit-chat brought the old Falcon atmosphere back to life, and a mini reunion focuses on a particular group of people who all knew one another.'

Gibson had wanted to be a pilot from the age of 13. He had never flown, but he had this ambition because he was addicted to aeroplanes. Some of his seniors at school before the war entered the RAF through the RAF College at Cranwell, but when he was old enough to apply, the College had closed because of the war, and became just another flying training school. During this period Gibson had an additional incentive to get in and fly, because his parents had been caught by the Germans in the occupation of the Channel Islands.

In August 1943, at the age of $17\frac{1}{2}$, he volunteered and was accepted for aircrew training. Seven months later, in March 1944, the RAF sent him to the University of St Andrews to do a three-month course equivalent to ITW training. He wore a battledress with shoulder flashes: 'St Andrews University Air Squadron'. Everything was paid for except pocket money! Called up on 30 October 1944, he was posted to ACRC Torquay, and then spent a considerable time misemployed as an ACH GD at an operational bomber station in Lincolnshire whilst awaiting a flying course. He found himself working on the salvage wagon, in the cookhouse, bomb dump, and in the intelligence section (which he found most interesting, attending raid briefings and debriefings).

He commenced flying Tiger Moths at Grading School, Burton-on-Trent, in April 1945 and soloed after $9\frac{1}{2}$ hours' dual. Finally, he found himself at Heaton Park, and was sent off on embarkation leave, during which the war in Europe ended. It was difficult for him to reconcile his emotions at this stage, because his parents and sister were languishing in internment camps in Bavaria, while he was about to cross the Atlantic to fulfill his ambition.

In company with some 450 cadets he sailed in the *Aquitania* for New York, without being concerned about U-boats—although full blackout was observed, cadets guarded doors, and guns were still mounted because of a possible submarine threat. A three-week stint at Camp Kilmer, an American Personnel Disposal Camp in New Jersey, and, at last, they were off to the southern states for flying training, having been kitted out with US Army issue KDs and brown shoes, to be worn with an RAF forage cap and black tie.

During the three-day journey to Mesa, Arizona, the train split in Kansas. Some cadets went to No. 1 BFTS Terrell, Texas, others to

No. 3 at Miami, Oklahoma, others to No. 5 Clewiston, Florida, and the rest to No. 4 Falcon Field, at Mesa.

The graduation course commenced on 21 June 1945 and was scheduled to last for six months, with two months for each phase: Primary, Basic and Advanced. After completing each phase, cadets were sent on a week's leave. The Primary course went smoothly until a tornado blew away most of the aeroplanes and they had to wait a week before replacements arrived. This time was made up by extending flying hours beyond 3.30 pm. The weather in those parts became very bumpy at that time and flying instruction normally ceased. Gibson, however, was unlucky because he picked up an eye infection just after the tornado, which gave him a boil under his eye and a week in hospital.

This meant he had lost two Course weeks. Although he had passed his ground exams, he was 19 hours short of flying time, which resulted in his being recoursed to No. 28 Course. This was frustrating for him, but there was nothing he could do about it. At least he had the advantage of additional experience in the air and at ground school, and being a meticulous person, he had planned his forthcoming leaves well ahead, according to schedule. Suddenly on 6 August 1945, the atomic bomb wiped out Hiroshima, and three days later a second dropped on Nagasaki. Japan surrendered on 15 August and, as already explained, the Lend-Lease scheme was rapidly brought to an end. Courses in progress were returned to the UK, and some cadets were given the opportunity of completing their training at home.

On 10 September 1945 John Gibson found himself at Fort Hamilton, an American Personnel Despatch centre, where on arrival they were sent on a week's leave as there was no accommodation available. Having spent most of their liquidity on presents to take home, leave in New York presented financial problems.

Gibson had only $13, but there were a few opportunities available to servicemen which helped to cut the cost of living: a bed in the YMCA cost 50 c. per night, and the United Services Club offered free tickets to shows, and afternoon tea in a proper pot with cream cakes served by American ladies. Gibson found that he could get an evening meal from an automat for about a dollar, and go up the Empire State Building for nothing but, nevertheless, he had to supplement his income somehow. This he was able to do via a professional blood bank on Lexington Avenue which enabled him to increase his equity by 30 per cent by selling a pint of his blood (not an armful) for $5 and a tot of whisky!

He said that a couple of the less-affluent chaps nipped into Coney Island and managed to get jobs by virtue of their English accents. He was wandering around there with a chum and heard an English voice calling out to them, 'I say, you chaps, how about a ride on this jolly old thing?'—it was the parachute jump!

Back in the UK in October 1945, with 51 hours on Stearmans and having passed his Primary ground school examinations twice, Gibson was posted to an Aircrew Holding Unit at Bircham Newton in Norfolk with some 4,000 other u/t aircrew of all descriptions who had returned to the UK from the States, Canada, Rhodesia and South Africa. The RAF had no alternative other than to absorb them as ACH GDs and give them menial tasks, with a proviso that some of them might get further aircrew training at some time in the future. For the vast majority it was a question of sweating it out until they were demobbed.

So the curtain came down on the big show. In retrospect, some aviation historians reviewed it as an undertaking of great magnitude, outstanding in its concept but, if anything, possibly too successful! In fact, they found it hard to level any serious criticism. And so they should. Who could have foreseen that the Japanese war would have ended so suddenly? It might have dragged on for two or three more years, sucking in aircrew like Bomber Command! Had that happened, the mass-production of aircrew would have continued, perhaps in a modified form. As it was, the RAF was confronted with a large surplus of fully or partially trained aircrew, and had no idea what size or type of force would be needed to meet peacetime requirements.

The vast majority of cadets under training overseas decided to opt out and return to civilian life as soon as possible. They had volunteered to serve as aircrew during the national emergency, and the RAF could not possibly have absorbed them. AC2/Aircrew Cadet John Gibson, however, was amongst those determined to become pilots and stay on in the RAF until they achieved their ambition. What happened to him makes an interesting story, because his journey to graduation was a long and often frustrating process—from flying Stearmans in the States in June 1945, until he got his wings flying Harvards at Ternhill, England, in April 1948!

In October 1945, five months after the cessation of hostilities in Europe, 4,000 'bolshie' aircrew cadets was more than RAF Bircham Newton could handle. However, the RAF was in the process of running down through demobilization, and many stations were short of ACH GDs. So these cadets were posted all over the country in batches of 50 and 100 to fill these vacancies.

Gibson was posted 'just down the road' to Great Massingham, a satellite of West Raynham, initially having a daily chore of stoking the Nissen hut boiler and cleaning the wash-house and the latrines. This was not exactly a stimulating occupation, but, once he and his chum had completed the exercise, they were free to go anywhere they liked. Later, while carrying out other menial tasks, including manning a fire tender, Gibson was told that there were opportunities for a selected few to carry on their training, but when they got their wings they would have to sign on for a period of three years. In order to apply they had to sign a piece of paper to that effect. Also, the applicants were told they would have to face a selection board. It transpired that so few applied that they all got taken on without any selection board.

The UK flying training system had still carried on and there were cadets being trained, which meant that Gibson and his associates had to wait until the system could absorb them. Meanwhile they had to carry on their odd-job tasks. Unfortunately, Gibson hadn't even completed his Primary training, which put him at the end of the line, and when interviewed he was told that he would have to do a refresher Grading School course before being posted to an EFTS. So he had to start his flying training all over again, despite the fact that he had logged over 60 hours! He commenced flying at No. 7 EFTS Desford, near Leicester, on 24 October 1946—a little over a year after leaving the USA, during which he had been shunted around as a part-time handyman.

Having completed his refresher, Gibson started his EFTS course on Tiger Moths, in the same place with the same instructor. Some six months later, due to a very bad winter in 1946, he still hadn't completed the flying course, Desford was closed down, and he was sent to 15 EFTS at Kingstown, Carlisle, for a month to finish off. Then it was back to an Aircrew Holding Unit at North Coates, near Grimsby, for eight weeks, where he planted cabbages and potatoes during the lovely summer of 1947. The RAF really didn't know what to do with these chaps, so they were given leave at the drop of a hat.

Having done no flying during this time, he was then posted to Booker, near High Wycombe, for a refresher course during August 1947, comprising 20 hours on Tiger Moths. By this time Gibson reckoned that he must have been really proficient at flying biplanes, having logged 152.35 hours, two-thirds of them on Tiger Moths. Basic training at SFTS finally emerged, and he was posted to No. 6 FTS Ternhill, Shropshire, to fly Harvards. He finally graduated on 12 April 1948.

John Gibson's uphill struggle to become a pilot had taken him about four years. At the end of it he had gained his precious wings, and was designated a Pilot 4—a ranking project which only survived a few years, although 'Master Pilot' (the old WO rank) was retained. When shipped out to the Middle East as a Pilot 4, he had to use the airmen's mess, his rank equating to corporal! He flew Tempests and Vampires in the desert, then was commissioned in 1951 after doing his OCTU at Spitalgate. Gaining an 'exceptional' rating for his air-to-ground gunnery and rocketry, he went on to log over 1,000 hours on Meteors. After completing ETPS at Farnborough, Gibson became involved in testing V-bombers at Boscombe Down, and he was awarded an AFC when a Flight Lieutenant.

He resigned his commission in 1964 to become an airline pilot, flying Tridents for several years before he retired as a British Airways captain. Thus, flying has been the mainspring of his life. His determination to become a pilot and his strength of character enabled him to stay the course on his long journey to graduation. His BFTS course obviously made a deep impression upon him:

'The instructors', he said, 'were all American civilians with a couple of RAF officers as check pilots, and a Wing Commander CO. My instructor had taught himself to night-fly with the aid of car headlights. He was an ex-bush pilot in his 40s, had flown all sorts of light aircraft including floatplanes, and had over 10,000 hours under his belt (I don't think any of them had less than 5,000 hours). After we had all our aircraft blown away by the tornado, and the half-hour of torrential rain which flooded the field about a foot deep, he said to me, "Gibson—it don't rain much in Arizona, but when it does, it's just like a cow pissing on a flat rock."

'I remember at Falcon, crickets used to invade the barrack rooms at night, but were all gone by morning. There were hundreds of them lined about ten deep all along the walls. After lights-out the odd one started to make the usual cricket noise, keeping us awake. After a while someone wouldn't be able to stand it anymore—you'd hear him getting off his bed, a torch would go on and he'd move along the line of crickets looking for the one that was rubbing its legs together. Then there would be a slap, and the cricket and some surrounding mates were hit with a shoe—then silence would reign once more and there would be a patter of feet as the irate cadet walked back to his bed.'

Gibson also talked about flying in an environment inhabited by scorpions, black widows, crickets and rattlers: 'We were advised not to jump into the cockpit in the morning before having a look inside. Rattlers had a habit of crawling into the open-cockpit Stearmans and curling up around the control column. I never saw one and don't know anyone else who did, but we took the advice, nevertheless.'

After a lifetime of flying all kinds of aircraft, Gibson gave his BFTS Stearman a high rating: 'It was twice the size of a Tiger, with twice as powerful an engine—a lot more stable in the air, and a delight to fly. Having brakes and a tailwheel made it easily manoeuvrable on the ground, and an ideal machine for converting on to Harvards. I logged 50 hours on Stearmans, and 100 on Tigers. Of the two I preferred the Stearman, although I think the Tiger required a better pilot to fly it well.'

7. Wireless operators/air gunners

BOMB AIMERS, WIRELESS operators and air gunners also played a key role during the war in the air. Over 60,000 of them were trained overseas as part of the Commonwealth Air Training Plan. They were originally volunteer tradesmen who earned an extra sixpence a day flying pay, and an extra one shilling and sixpence when engaged in flying over such hostile territory as the North-West Frontier in India. This could be a highly dangerous business if confronted by illiterate tribesmen armed with sharp knives. Aircrew all carried pieces of paper guaranteeing a reward of gold if they were returned 'balls intacto'— hence these were known as 'ghooli-chits'!

There was no recognized promotion for these flying tradesmen except through advancement in their particular trade. Their amateur status, from the time when the observer/bomb aimer/air gunner of the First World War clutched a Lewis gun on a Scarff-ring mounting, had continued virtually until the outbreak of the Second World War. It was not until January 1939 that the Air Ministry began to look into the question of aircrew status. Hitherto the pilot had been the only recognized professional whose duties were regarded as a full-time occupation.

The advent of new guns such as the Browning and the VGO (Vickers Gas-Operated), combined with reflector sights and, above all, the emergence of the power-operated turret, which segregated the gunner, forced the issue. Incredibly, the war had been going for several weeks before the Central Gunnery School was formed! Air gunnery at last became a full-time occupation, but air gunners had also to double-up as wireless operators—they were given their well-known AG brevet and the rank of sergeant. However, it was not until 1942, following the emergence in 1940 of the four-engined bomber, that these two duties were segregated.

Arthur J. Gurr, a Londoner, served throughout the European war as a WOP/AG owing to a 'cock-up' on the admin front at the outset. When he was called up, on 10 September 1940, he applied for an extension to take his accountancy examinations and was given one month to the day. He had gone with an accountancy colleague who had volunteered to be a WOP/AG while Gurr wanted to become an accounts officer.

In the event, he was posted to Signals school at Blackpool. They told him that he was in the wrong place, and should have been sent to Uxbridge, and 'that's how I joined aircrew', he said. 'I had gone through the motions, there was nothing I could do about the situation, so I accepted it.'

Young Gurr relinquished 'double-entry' book-keeping, credit and debit balances, and found himself being drilled up and down Blackpool roads by an Irish flight sergeant every morning, and having Morse instruction in the Winter Gardens every afternoon. Then he was posted to No. 1 Signals School at Cranwell, where he had further Morse and signals classwork, including the 'Harwell Box' flight simulator. There he commenced flying, but there was little dialogue with the pilots, because they were all Polish and couldn't speak English! However, there was lots of sport, during which he played rugby for Cranwell against the Army!

Then followed the usual routine of wireless school and flying at Yatesbury, Wiltshire, where Gurr found it easy to hitch-hike up to London every weekend. He recalled an amusing incident while on duty as Orderly Sergeant, going round with the Orderly Officer. They were asked by one lad how a condom happened to get into his rice pudding? (No explanation was given.)

Finally, gunnery school at Dumfries, Scotland, where the weather was so bad that their four-week course had to be extended to three months. During air-to-air firing, Gurr and his pilot encountered a 'spoof' Hudson (captured by the Germans), which, he said, 'was well peppered'. Apart from getting his sergeant's stripes and AG brevet, Gurr was found to have bad teeth, and 19 were promptly extracted, along with most of his bottom gum. This was Christmas 1941, and it had taken him some 14 months to qualify as a WOP/AG.

In January 1942 Arthur Gurr and associates sailed out of Liverpool on the troopship *Dominion Monarch*, with no clear idea where they were going or for what purpose. Rumour had it that they were heading for the Middle East, but in the event they docked in Cape Town and were sent to Polsmoor Camp (where Nelson Mandela was later to be kept). They spent a month in this holding camp, during which Gurr and his friend Chris were adopted by a Scottish-speaking couple, the husband being the General Manager of the largest car sales establishment. The couple entertained them and took them all over the surrounding area, including Muizenberg which has a beautiful beach some five miles long.

Looking back, Gurr remembers a high-spirited party of Australians who had got their hands on several horse-drawn brewer's drays, and organized a series of chariot races up and down Adderley Street, a main street of Cape Town, much to the concern of surrounding traffic! He also remembers an enormous Great Dane called Able Seaman Nuisance who was on the payroll of the naval base at Simonstown. He would travel up and down on the local electric train, collecting all sailors 'under the influence' and dragging them on to the trains. He didn't seem to bother with any of the other Services, despite the fact that most of the lads were in khaki!

During dental inspection they found that Gurr had virtually no teeth, and told him that he should not have been abroad as he wasn't properly 'kitted out'. Overnight they made him a complete set of teeth, so that he could join the others on parade, just as they marched off to join the troopship.

It was to be a further eight months before Gurr and company returned to the UK. Their postings took them north to Suez, south to Kenya and back to Durban, for no real purpose. Consequently, when they got home they had to be retrained. Even today Gurr has no idea why they were sent out in the first place. Perhaps there was nothing to occupy them in the UK, as there was a shortage of multi-engined aircraft. Maybe the planners wanted to build reserves in Africa, because they couldn't be certain which way the war was going to develop out there, and the chaps were trained wireless operators and gunners. Gurr pointed out that there were several thousand of them in the camps, so there had to be a specific reason to have such a large crowd 'in limbo'. But many curious things happened during the war, and this must have been one of them.

Arthur Gurr, having completed his Advanced training and been 'crewed up', at last joined No. 9 Squadron in July 1943, on Lancasters. During his 13th trip, his pilot became unconscious while flying over the Baltic on their way to Hanover. The bomb aimer and flight engineer managed to get the aircraft home, and the pilot recovered sufficiently to be able to land it. They found out later that the pilot had suffered severe sinus trouble.

The crew were then posted to 44 (Rhodesia) Squadron, flying Lancasters from Dunholme Lodge. His new pilot was Flt. Lt. Pat Dorhill, a highly decorated pilot and a nephew of the Governor of Southern Rhodesia (later Lord Huggins). Because of the new pilot's vast experience, they were given special jobs: Arthur Gurr as WOP/AG had to broadcast the weather forecast to all aircraft over Europe during operations; they were one of six Lancasters selected to carry out a low-level bombing operation on an aircraft-assembly factory outside Lourdes; because their 13th trip had been aborted, they were sent to Danzig Bay to block up the entrance of the harbour leading to a submarine school. 'They fired at us,' Gurr said, 'bursting at about 10,000 ft while we were flying at almost 30,000 ft, so they actually showed us the way out.'

Arthur Gurr was awarded the DFM and was later commissioned. Finally he completed his RAF service as an Accounts Officer (at last) before being demobilized in April 1946.

8. The Joint Air Training Plan in South Africa

THE UNION OF South Africa, as it was in 1939, was still very much a part of the British Empire, but its mixed government of British and Boer populations meant that entry into the war on the side of the Allies could by no means be guaranteed.

Great pressure was naturally exerted by the British Government, and it was paradoxically the respect that Churchill and Field Marshal Smuts, then Prime Minister of South Africa, had for each other—old enemies as they had been—that tipped the scales. The South African Government in Pretoria voted to enter the war by the slimmest of margins, but even then with certain important reservations. It was a damn close-run thing, with a great deal at stake for the Allies, as was soon realized when the war progressed to North Africa, and the Mediterranean was almost closed to Allied shipping.

It was vital that the Cape remained open, and the great naval base of Simonstown was secured. Thus, the only route to the Western Desert was the long haul via the Cape—a life-line indeed! Many British and Allied troops will remember the warmth with which they were welcomed when they disembarked for a few days at Cape Town, before proceeding to more serious matters in the north of the continent.

Political problems having been resolved, the Air Ministry started negotiations with the Union of South Africa for the training of pilots and observers of both countries. The financial arrangements for carrying out the Air Training Memorandum of 1 June 1940 were not concluded at the time of its signature. It was at that time the intention to devise a scheme of capitation rates, payable by the United Kingdom Government on the number of UK pupils under training.

A new situation arose, however, involving an important expansion of the original scheme and a revision of the administrative arrangements. It became desirable that certain air training units in the UK should be moved to South Africa *en bloc* to enable their training to be carried on with the minimum of disturbance. Thus, with the approval of the Union Government three such units were transferred.

This was a very hectic and often traumatic period for the RAF, whose flying training schools were being transported all over the globe. At this time FTSs were going to Canada, six BFTSs were being set up in the USA, the Rhodesian scheme was under way, and back-up was needed in Australia and New Zealand. Francis Butcher, then a senior Flight Lieutenant commanding two Flights at 12 SFTS Grantham (there was an acute shortage of experienced Flight commanders), remembers:

'We thought that we were destined for Moose Jaw in Canada, but we didn't go. They decided to send bits of us to South Africa. On arrival, I found myself Second-in-Command to a South African Air Force Captain of only two years' commissioned service. Then, to add to my chagrin, I found that four of the Hawker Hart Trainers available to me were those I had gladly got rid of months before in England, in the belief that they were to be scrapped.'

The final agreement with South Africa provided for seven EFTSs, seven SFTSs, six combined Observer, Navigation and Air Gunnery Schools, two RAF Observer Navigation Schools, the General Reconnaissance School (being the third of the three training schools from the UK), the Central Flying School, and the proposed Assembly Station for the assembly and testing of aircraft for training and operational needs.

The financial implications for the scheme were complex, but fair. In general, the Union Government agreed to equip and maintain all stations necessary up to the standards agreed between the Union Defence Department and the Air Minstry mission. The UK agreed to provide all aircraft and spares and other miscellaneous equipment, although the Union Government contributed an initial £250,000 towards such costs, together with the heavy burden of supplying all fuel and oil during the duration of the scheme. Each Government agreed to pay their own personnel, together with various other emoluments and the cost of transport. There were additional conditions contained in the scheme, which provided considerable flexibility, but the main principle enshrined in the Memorandum was that training should be for both the South African Air Force and the Royal Air Force.

One of the reasons why South Africa decided not to join in with the Empire Air Training Scheme was that she had ongoing and expanding schemes of her own. A five-year programme started in 1934 had by early 1939 exceeded its objective of nine squadrons, each of 25 machines. Five were for training, two were fighter-bombers, one was reconnaissance and one troop-carrying. In 1937 a scheme involving Volunteer Reserves was instituted to train 1,000 pilots over six years, and by 1939 was far ahead of programme.

South Africa had limited aircraft production resources. There was a de Havilland Factory outside Johannesburg manufacturing Tiger Moths, and a Government factory making Hawker Hartbees (a form of Hart) but importing the Rolls-Royce Kestrel engines. Service aircraft included DH.9s, Westland Wapitis, Hawker Hartbees and Hawker Furies. Most pre-war Service machines had been purchased in England with the proviso that, if war broke out, South Africa could buy the latest types for first-line defence (she bought some Blenheims early in the war). Like other Dominion Air Forces, the SAAF was given non-military tasks during peacetime, and the link between civil and military aviation was very strong indeed. All 18 Junkers Ju 86 aircraft of the SA Airways fleet were converted into bombers, and a number of Ju 52s were also converted for military requirements.

The original joint training scheme was to provide at least 136 pilots and 60 observers a month, but as time went on, and the requirements from squadrons built up, these figures were increased considerably. This increase also applied to South Africa because of the war in the Western Desert. The Government's commitment to hostilities limited it to the defence of the Union alone. However, servicemen were permitted to volunteer to fight anywhere in Africa, which embraced the Western Desert.

South African squadrons manned by volunteers, of which there were many, had to be supplied by the Training Schools, thus demanding a greater quota of South African aircrew. These volunteers, both aircrew and ground staff, were distinguished by the wearing of a red 'tab' on each epaulette, indicating 'Anywhere in Africa'. This aroused some quite unjustifiable hostility between the British and South Africans, particularly amongst the other ranks. A number of British ground crew appeared with A.B.W. pencilled on their shoulder tabs, indicating 'Any Bloody Where', and this had to be stamped out by Commanding Officers and should never have happened.

There were of course many South Africans who flew with the RAF. In early 1940 there were about 400 South Africans in the Royal Air Force, wearing RAF uniform, and this number increased as the war progressed. Group Captain 'Sailor' Malan was one of the most famous fighter aces of the war, and there were many other South Africans who served with the RAF with great distinction. Bob Stanford, who related his experiences in Canada, subsequently flew with a Typhoon Wing whose Wing Leader, Charles Green DSO, DFC, was a South African farmer. When Stanford's squadron suffered heavy casualties in Normandy, amongst the replacements were three South Africans, Lieutenants Cook, Cluelow and Gale.

The RAF personnel who ran the flying training scheme in South Africa enjoyed a comfortable life in idyllic surroundings. It was so far removed from the conditions of wartime Britain that many who had left their wives and families behind could not avoid a feeling of guilt at being away from it all. This was not helped by the intransigence of the Air Ministry, who had originally agreed to wives and children joining their husbands. Many wives, who had been told to be prepared to leave at a moment's notice and had lived out of suitcases for months, were not informed that the scheme had been cancelled until long afterwards. There was of course justification for this in the number of convoys being sunk, but there was no justification for not informing the anxiously waiting families.

Francis Butcher, who had to leave his wife and family behind, recalled that one extremely popular Group Captain did not immediately increase his popularity by getting his wife to join him by a devious route. He had been the Air Attaché in Lisbon, and a flight was contrived from there to Lourenço Marques, then Portuguese and neutral. He was such a good commander that he was soon forgiven by all, but his wife, equally delightful, was inevitably dubbed 'The diplomatic bag'.

Compared with Canada, the distance from home seemed immense. A few days crossing the Atlantic was nothing compared to a five-week stint to Cape Town. The vast continent of Africa, Nazi-occupied Europe and the English Channel lay implacably between. Sea voyages between the UK and South Africa, often resulting in losses of shipping with valuable cargoes, not least aircrew, were a vital matter to be taken into account, and most ships were taken in convoy. Convoy deals between Britain and all other countries involved in the the mass-production of aircrew made a great contribution to the success of overseas training. For example, one navy would take over from another to mother convoys, and countries would also provide air cover and support on a co-operative basis.

A young cadet by the name of Denis Stevens trained in South Africa and graduated as a navigator. He returned home, and later joined 196 Squadron, of Bomber Command, equipped with Lancasters. From the time he embarked in the troopship *Stirling Castle* on 26 October 1942, until he graduated in June 1943, he kept a meticulous daily diary of the voyage and training period. He died a few years ago, but his little black book mirrors a cadet's reaction to the South African adventure. Written at that time, it makes a unique document.

In common with most of his associates, this was his first trip out of Britain, and he wrote about the initial difficulties of sleeping in hammocks on board an overcrowded vessel. 'If you try to turn round you either fall out or start the whole thing rocking. When you start to swing, you knock against six others—so you can guess how pleased the occupants are ...'

Cadets were paid 2/6d per day, and were given various tasks to carry out, such as washing up, cleaning up their quarters etc, and frequent boat drills. They joined a convoy and found that 'those who came straight from ITW could read messages in Morse from accompanying destroyers about weather, position of U-boats and where to pick up convoy.'

The food was plentiful but water was scarce, and they had to wash in warm sea water. Time was passed in reading, playing cards and attending lectures—the start of their courses.

'Friday 13 November: DROs today say we are arriving in a Brazilian port on Sunday—probably first English convoy to do so. I hope we can go ashore .... Saw a Catalina in distance, so we can't be far from land'.

'Sunday 15 November: ... had my shower and a walk round the deck to catch my first glimpse of a foreign country. It seemed very nice from five miles out, with dark-green wooded slopes and long stretches of white sand. After a while we came to a headland on which stood a several-storied white building, maybe a lighthouse. Behind this opened out a wide bay or estuary into which we turned in "column of route" and docked or moored out in the Bay.'

'The view was beautiful—everything was such a definite shade, no colours mingling into each other but each contrasting to the other. Real golden sands, vivid green trees and palms, an entirely different shade of green water, white buildings of skyscraper design and red-roofed houses, and in the harbour itself a brilliantly painted Swedish ship—painted to be obvious to U-boats, I suppose...'

'I discovered that the port was called Bahia which I believe is the second port of Brazil. The locals came out in well-built skiffs with runners on seats. It was quite amusing to watch their pantomime gestures to endeavour to make us understand what they were saying. Later several bum boats came around the ship with bananas. Although it is forbidden, several chaps managed to get some before a warrant officer threw them overboard (the fruit I mean).'

They were allowed ashore in the morning: '... some of the lads bought English whisky for a shilling a bottle, others bought undistilled spirit or cheap port. In the afternoon more troops went out but many came back tight. About 200 of the troops on board failed to return to the ship, and she eventually sailed without them.'

'Thursday 19 November: Still out in the bay... We had a navigation exam (*sic*) in the morning. It consisted of a few simple questions which even I could answer... We weighed anchor at 4 o'clock and away we went, obviously going eastward now.'

'Monday 23 November: ... FFI [a medical] and navigation. We had our papers back and to my great surprise I had 95 percent—and this without any previous swotting, not that the type of paper needed it...'

Nearing the coast they entered dangerous waters. 'Monday 30 November: ... Our escort destroyer in front turned back and, as she passed us our loudspeakers told her that there were two men in the water on their port bow. I looked but I could not see anything at all. The destroyer however turned broadside on, and I could see something black against her hull which must have been them because we started to move again. This caused any number of rumours, from the sinking of a large troopship to the drifting of fishermen from the shore...'

'We also picked up several fast destroyers, who were continually circling us. During the day we have had a lot of Hudsons flying around us. Also in the afternoon we sighted Table Mountain. I was very surprised, because I thought we were quite a long way past it... In the evening apparently a lot of wreckage was seen floating by, and another three men were picked up off a raft.'

'Tuesday 1 December: Well, I woke up still in my hammock, so evidently the danger of sinking is not so bad as we thought it to be last night.'

They start to unload the hold baggage which had been stored during the voyage. 'I managed to find mine easily, so that up to the moment

I have my full kit, which is a strange thing in this "den of thieves"....
Land is still in sight, a very reassuring factor in a dangerous area.'

They finally left the ship at Durban at about 1800 hours and went straight into a train for a journey lasting two days, which they found very luxurious after five weeks at sea. Their camp was at East London, a very pleasant town on the coast about 400 miles south-west of Durban facing the Indian Ocean. The camp was encircled with barbed wire and the guards were armed with rifles, but the cadets enjoyed a lot of freedom. The course was soon under way, but there was plenty of time for swimming, sunbathing on the sands and enjoying local hospitality.

Stevens was fortunate to find himself in such lovely surroundings with freedom to enjoy himself—a vastly different experience from those cadets training under the American system and others in places totally isolated, or enduring the Canadian winter! His diary at this stage reveals something of his character and ability.

Obviously he was a highly intelligent young man, and examinations presented few problems. He had to do very little preparatory work, and occupied his spare time learning to play bridge with the Godfrey family, who were endlessly kind and welcoming for the whole of his stay at the camp. The middle Godfrey daughter Maisie became his first girlfriend, and he took dancing lessons to cut a dash at the usual Saturday night fling—a more entertaining and socially acceptable life compared to that of other cadets in the USA who, for a loose shoelace or a misdemeanour, found themselves trudging round the square in full pack to work off demerit points!

'Monday 1 March 1943: Well, the blow has come and I am posted to Queenstown and am going sometime today together with Chaplin Stewart [his friend]. Why Queenstown, when my first choice was Collondale and my second Port Elizabeth? I straight away rang up Maisie and told her we were going in the evening .... The rest of the day I moped and packed alternately—mostly moping.'

'I tried to swop postings with a chap, but they weren't having any—very dim, because what bother is there in changing names, but Red Tape you know ... 9.00 at Station, all of family there and Wagners also, very touching half-an-hour's talk and sentimental chatter, and then away. It is like leaving home, in fact when your own home is so far away I think it is worse ... I will miss Maisie's company more than I have missed any previous pal's. She makes a jolly good friend altogether.'

'Tuesday 2 March: Woke up at 6.30 and we were nearing Queenstown—7.00 arrive and what a deadly-looking place it seems. Certainly not as big as Farnham [Surrey], surrounded by big mountains, all of which are covered in mist and hardly a soul in sight and you have Queenstown, Cape Province (and you can keep it).'

Denis had a few days before his course began and spent his time swimming, playing table-tennis, and writing to Maisie. Then he started flying in Oxfords.

'Friday 12 March: Woken up at 5.45 (what an unearthly hour to rise).

Early breakfast and away to 'drome. We did not help bomb up after all but stayed on tarmac—it is just as well, because it is a dangerous job anyway. Ready in parachute room 12.10 and away to "ops" room. Nice chap as first navigator and good pilot. Airborne 12.26 and away. Hangclip Mountain looks pretty good from above and I am determined to get up it one day when I feel energetic.'

'The countryside seems to be all one range of hills, and dozens of them with salt pans and pools dotted in between. I tried to map-read but roads on map marked with thick red lines look like cart tracks, rivers turned out to be dried-up beds and railways hardly distinguishable. It was quite enjoyable for three-quarters of way. After that I became sick and was glad when we turned for home and missed bombing, as pilot thought it was too bumpy—I certainly agreed with him. Went for a swim later on.'

Like most cadets, he found long lectures boring. 'All afternoon spent on armaments, so I was "cheesed", fed-up or otherwise uninterested. I scrounged off early and managed to get a shirt from stores and a haircut before going out for a swim. Grill in Santa's Canteen while it rained— a jolly good thunderstorm. I received an airgraph from Mum which only took 3 weeks—bags of up-to-date news.'

His air sickness concerned him and he wrote on:

'Friday 26 March: Flying this afternoon down as far as Port Alfred and this time I did not feel at all sick—until I came down, when I at once felt faint and empty. Still, I pulled together at the thought of a weekend in East London, and seeing Maisie and the rest of the family again.'

For the first time he writes about the seriousness of what he is doing:

'Our train did not leave until 9.30, so we had plenty of time to get ready and stroll into town. We found our reservations were first class so travelled in grand style—this is the way to live, if only there were not such a very serious background behind it all—not that it worries me an awful lot—I am not worried overmuch at it—except for the thought of leaving South Africa and all it means to me.'

'Monday 29 March: Flying in afternoon. Quite an interesting trip, 10/10 cloud half-way, so we turned round and came home. I brought the plane home on an air plot and after two or three changes of course hit Queenstown fair and square.'

'Tuesday 30 March: Fed up with lectures—they want to squeeze too much in, and the main part becomes useless.'

'Thursday 1 April: Parade in morning to celebrate 25th Anniversary of RAF. It made a break and there was very little bullshit. All afternoon firing on range—waste of time, and we had to fill up magazines afterwards.'

'Friday 2 April: Afternoon spent in DR trainer—very interesting. Sat in cubicle dimly lighted and flew on "dry swim". All courses I gave my pilot are converted into a track by previously arranged wind. I did not know my actual track but pilot did. It was jolly good practice and clock was speeded up, so we had to work fast. I missed target so we got home on a series of fixes .... Back to camp and more binding, this time seriously. Instruments exam tomorrow. I am not very sure of the stuff though.'

'Wednesday 7 April: Flying in morning—quite a nice trip and I was up with Jim Chaplin. It became so thick that we returned after two hours. I nearly lost them and we came home on a QDM.'

'Thursday 8 April: Another quiet day—all lectures finished early. . . I took a few Astro shots—enthusiasm awakening at last?'

'Saturday 10 April: Flying twice today with Jim and second time with Jarvis but twice seems too much.'

'Monday 12 April: Flying in afternoon, DR trainer in morning. Quite an interesting flip—ended up only eight miles out.'

'Thursday 15 April: Whole day spent in DR trainer—quite interesting but lousy for a whole day. The red light and darkness is very trying.'

'Friday 16 April: DR Plotting exam for intermediate marking. I am afraid that I have not done too well. I could not get started and it is a suspension exam so I may have had it. I hope not—though I don't really want to finish the course I certainly don't want to go out at this stage. Analysis of Photo in afternoon quite interesting.'

'Tuesday 20 April: Flying—nice trip today. Square search at end of first leg—went for a burton though. I gave the pilot the ground speed and told him to fly to it. A radius of action came out nicely though, right on ETA.'

'Wednesday 28 April: Up fairly early, read a bit about photography— bags of panic. Fairly easy day—not a bad photography exam. I think I have managed it OK even with very little work I have so far put into it. I don't expect to get a very high mark, though—just a pass is good enough, although I would like some good marks to help on my aim for an instructor's billet. I certainly don't want to go home just yet.'

The weather was approaching South African winter by now and it was getting steadily colder, with rain turning to snow in some places. Denis's somewhat 'laissez-faire' attitude towards the course and his immediate future prospects at this stage is revealing. He vacillated between doing just enough cramming to pass his exams, and then putting in more work at short notice to get good marks in the hope of becoming an instructor in order to stay on in South Africa.

He was enjoying the social life, especially the swimming, table-tennis at the YMCA, his evenings out with a local family, and going to the grill in town for an occasional evening meal. A highly intelligent young man who was never without a book at bedtime, Denis lacked drive and ambition, but at the same time did not want to fail the course.

This attitude applied to his attachment to his girlfriend Maisie, with whom he corresponded regularly. On Monday 3 May he wrote:

'Recco exam—I feel doubtful about this result—I have done no swotting and in any case it is a subject to be picked up and not learned by binding away at it—it seems such an unnecessary subject. Funny letter from Maisie—she thought I had shown signs of being more fond of her than just friendship, and as she had fallen for a SAAF Air Gunner and did not want me to continue on that line and maybe feel hurt in the end she was wanting to tell me.'

'It was certainly nice of her writing this way, and it took me all the evening getting out a reply. As if I could stop her or want to anyway. I had to sound as if I did not care a bit. Not quite right of course but not a long way off the truth. I certainly think of her as a jolly good pal, but how could I go further—penniless, prospectless airman that I am?'

'Wednesday 5 May: Bullsh[it] parade—for our Wings Parade—counting chickens all night. Two chaps recalled from Aliwal North and have been taken off course. I bet its my turn next—rumours that I was mentioned—so much for my enthusiasm. I must pull up my socks—I rather want to go out now—if it is not too late. Out to Dickensons in evening—roast duck and very pleasant evening.'

The course continued and he found he had passed the photography exam with 79%, Instruments with 72% and had maps and charts 'in the bag'. On 11 May the cadets packed for their rail trip to Aliwal North, where they were to do their night flying.

'On the train I met Tom Murphy—my pal in Manchester—they have finished their course and were on their way back to Durban—and maybe home. I had a long talk with him—I felt quite envious of his nav wing and stripes.'

'Monday 17 May: Easy day follows easy day—long lay-in in morning, easy afternoon. Interesting flip in evening. I went up to Kimberley—nice long trip, 178 miles each way, and I hit it first time without altering course at all, good going. It is good flying at night.'

Back at East London to complete the course, he did well in his radio nav and astro nav exams. He coped well with anything to do with navigation, but found subjects like armaments and recco unnecessary and took little interest in them. His attitude to armaments went deeper: '. . .We seem to have less armaments instructors than anything else, and what we do have seems to be insufficient—of course I am prejudiced against a subject of this nature.'

In June 1943 Denis Stevens graduated as a navigator and was awarded his stripes. In early 1944 he joined 196 Squadron flying Lancasters, and his aircraft was shot down over Holland during the Arnhem airborne operation. He never kept another diary, which undoubtedly had something to do with his inner feelings about his occupation.

His diary covering his experiences in South Africa is a unique document. It is exceptionally well written for a young man of his age, with good word choice and grammatical composition. Above all, it is a sincere and honest reflection of his thoughts and attitudes while training to be a navigator. He emerges as a highly intelligent, cool and totally reliable chap—essential qualities for a man whose job was to navigate an aircraft in difficult and dangerous circumstances.

It is quite remarkable that a young cadet should have kept up a diary during those times. It reveals how naïve we were—Stevens perhaps more than others, because he came from the small country town of Farnham in Surrey. He fluffed pilot training at Grading School, lacking aptitude, but there is no mention at all of it in his diary so he had no regrets. He was prone to air sickness, which must have had something to do with it.

* * * * *

Len Cullingford was another navigator who, like Denis Stevens, trained at Queenstown, but he began his training in South Africa two years earlier, in 1941. The accommodation then was very different from the comfortable huts enjoyed by Stevens and his associates:

'We were under canvas, three in each Bell tent, on standard iron beds. Washing was in the open air, very cold first thing (no such comfort as hot water) as we were at about 5,000 ft and it was their winter! Sometimes the water was frozen and, when it was, we washed properly and shaved in the middle of the day. The toilet arrangements were primitive—four buckets close together with seats over, so one sat almost cheek to cheek. Very matey and chatty though. They were cleared each evening by natives who emptied the contents into a horse-drawn cart which we called 'the tumbril'. One thing we did not have to cope with was rain. It was a really lovely climate, sunny but not hot. We wore blue uniforms, not tropical kit. Battledress had not yet been adopted by the RAF, so we still had brass buttons to polish.'

He described his flying as trouble-free, and the Anson as '. . .a friendly aircraft to fly in, it plodded on at no great speed, like a flying cucumber frame. No toilet arrangements except a small tin funnel from which a rubber tube led through the frame and outside the aircraft.' And he had this to say about the Course, during which he did 19 flights totalling 48 hours of practical navigation:

'It was a "pass or fail' Course. We all passed, which is not surprising as, despite the social life, we all worked hard and were all dead keen. The sad thing is that it was an unlucky Course, as very few of the 60 or so on it, many of them my companions for months, survived the war. For many of that happy band of young men, less than two years of life remained—for some far less.'

After Queenstown, Len was off to Youngsfield—a South African Air Force airfield—for his bombing and gunnery course.

'The aircraft we were to fly were Wapitis [which had been the aircraft on the NW frontier of India during the late '20s and the '30s, used for controlling the tribesmen], Audaxes and Hinds [front-line aircraft in the mid '30s, well-known at Hendon Air Displays before the war]. All these aircraft were single-engine biplanes with two cockpits, the front one for the pilot and the one behind for the observer, and were merely extrapolations of First World War aircraft. The Wapiti took off almost like a lift, a slow, ponderous aircraft, steady as a rock. We did preliminary bombing exercises on them, but they were used mainly for drogue towing for our air gunnery exercises.'

'The Audaxes were used for gunnery and the Hinds for bombing.

Classes consisted of all aspects of guns and gunnery, bombs and bombsight. My months in the Station Armoury at Leuchars paid dividends. The gun we used was the Lewis, a product of the First World War but still being used in the Second. In fact, Audaxes and Hinds had been used on operations against the Italians in Eritrea during the campaign there in 1940.'

'The classes were dull, but the flying was fun. I have always looked back on the flying I did then in open cockpits as the only real flying. Floating between the sky above as one looked up, and the Earth below as one looked down, was a marvellous feeling. One clambered up and into the rear cockpit and attached oneself to what was called the 'Monkey Chain'. The pilot was strapped in, but not the observer—just a chain bolted at one end to the aircraft and fastened at the other with a quick-release catch to the rear of one's parachute harness.

'Communication between pilot and observer was via a speaking tube—surprisingly efficient. One sat down back to the pilot for take-off, then if it was a bombing exercise (for which we used 4-lb practice bombs), as soon as we reached the bombing range, down flat on one's tum on the floor of the aircraft, set the bombsight (Mk IX) and, peering along its wires and the hole in the floor of the aircraft, direct the pilot left, left, right, right, steady, on to the target and then at the right moment, press the tit and down goes the bomb. This was a very pleasant, quite leisurely and most enjoyable occupation.

'So was gunnery in the Audax, but in a much more exciting way. Before take-off, there was the business of setting the Lewis gun on the Scarff ring, which enabled one very easily, as one leaned back on the ring which encircled the cockpit, to swing the gun from side to side seemingly regardless of pressure caused by the 100-mph airflow. The real fun started after the last firing pass when we would fly over the sea looking for sharks and take pot-shots at them, then stall turns and loops on the way back to Youngsfield. We completed the fun by diving on the airfield and sweeping up in "Prince of Wales feathers" formation, which was very exciting.'

'In all, I spent seven months in South Africa—a wonderful country, particularly Cape Province with its superb climate, with much sun and a definite rainy season. Flying at Youngsfield, despite the serious underlying purpose, was an experience I am very fortunate to have had.'

Organizing the Joint Training Scheme had been an immense task for South Africa. Airfields had to be selected, plans drawn and approved, contracts awarded for buildings, site earthworks completed, camps and technical areas constructed, drainage, water and lighting provided, and hardstandings for aircraft constructed. Some existing airfields were used, such as Port Elizabeth and Port Alfred, but the vast majority were entirely new. The various schools were grouped geographically, allowing EFTSs and SFTSs to operate in pairs. These were situated where weather conditions were ideal, hence the Transvaal and Orange Free State were obvious choices. The construction and operation of these schools had a phenomenal impact on small towns such as Witbank,

Kroonstad and Queenstown, boosting their economies and changing attitudes.

Up to late 1941 training in South Africa had concentrated on bringing existing and planned SAAF operational units up to strength. Having achieved this objective, courses began to absorb intakes of RAF pupil pilots, Tiger Moths being used for Primary training, and Masters and Oxfords for Service training. However, by the end of December 1941 the Miles Masters were creating severe problems, with engine failures, corrosion, cylinder wear and plugs oiling up. Nos. 24 and 25 AS had only about one-third of their aircraft serviceable, and this caused blockage in EFTS output. These technical problems, however, were gradually resolved and eventually Masters were replaced by Harvards.

During 1941, when the Joint Training Scheme was being established, 970 RAF pupils graduated, comprising 341 pilots and 629 navigators. Despite the availability of aircraft, spares and serviceability problems, 4,240 RAF cadets graduated in 1942, of which 1,529 were pilots, 2,541 navigators and 170 air bombers. In 1943, however, training peaked, reaching a total figure of 6,477 graduates.

9. Australia

AUSTRALIA'S CONTRIBUTION TO the Empire Air Training Scheme was quite remarkable when one considers her pre-war situation. The Royal Australian Air Force had failed to meet expansion targets during 1938, due to delays in getting final approval for the preparation of sites and buildings to house new units, and the inability to obtain deliveries of new aircraft from the UK remotely according to schedule. This stifled a planned intake of personnel, and in November 1938 the total complement of the RAAF was only 228 officers and 2,530 NCOs and airmen. In early 1939 the Prime Minister, Mr Lyons, stated that plans were being formulated to enlist 900 men during each of the next three years.

A few months later, in October 1939, an Australian delegation was in Ottawa, Canada, listening to Lord Riverdale's original proposals for Australian participation in the Empire Scheme. Basically, these included the supply of recruits at the rate of 1,164 every four weeks, to consist of pilots, navigators and air gunners. Only Elementary Flying Training of pilots was to take place in Australia. Service Flying Training would be undertaken in Canada, and Australia would provide pupils and contribute towards the training.

The Australians were naturally astonished, and to a certain extent annoyed, by these proposals. No prior consultation had taken place to understand the Australian point of view, and Riverdale had 'dropped a blockbuster'. From where, they asked, were the Canadian dollars to come for such an expensive operation? There were additional doubts as to how Australia was to find the proposed number of pupils. Fairburn, the Australian delegate, added that it was too much to expect a small community of 7,000,000 people to provide 26,000 aircrew of high standard over the period envisaged. Furthermore, was it not absurd that Service Training Schools already in operation in Australia should not be used? They pointed out that cadets would be far happier to complete their training at home, and they asked why Australia should have to pay Canada for training which she could undertake for herself.

Both Australia and New Zealand insisted that the majority of training of their own men should take place in their respective countries, and they had an undeniable case. As we have already seen, at this juncture, in late November 1939, the Riverdale mission was facing considerable opposition to some of its proposals from Canadian Ministers, and there was a danger that the entire Empire Air Training Scheme might collapse. It became obvious that the plan put forward by Balfour for Riverdale to execute had presumed far too much, and that too little groundwork had been done with the countries concerned.

Faced with a situation in which the Australian and New Zealand delegates temporarily withdrew their original agreements to re-examine their own positions, there wasn't much that the British could do except compromise. The war had started, and time was running out. In retrospect, the British mission was wise not to attempt to disguise the enormity of the problem, and dropping it into the laps of the countries concerned had its advantages. It presented a challenge in the race for survival, allowing the various parties to work things out for themselves while providing the professionalism of the RAF, aircraft, aviation technology and finance.

Britain has always been adept in the art of compromise, and the mission was quick to respond to Australia's doubts. The mission proposed that 50 per cent of Australia's quota of 1,164 cadets per month should continue with their training in Australia, the remainder proceeding to Canada after the completion of Elementary training. Thus the problems of dollar shortage and under-used airfields in Australia were neatly resolved. This reduction in the Service training of Australian cadets meant that Canada would be losing considerable income, and there followed days of horse-trading to adjust the situation.

Complementary to training facilities in Australia was the supply of aircraft, instructors and other personnel. Tiger Moths were to be used for *ab initio* training, whilst Avro Ansons, Harvards and converted Fairey Battles would be required for Advanced work. It was intended that the Moths would be constructed in Australia, after an initial injection of 100 Gipsy engines from the UK. The Anson fuselage would be supplied by the UK, with the wings being made in Australia. The supply of Fairey Battles would be the responsibility of Britain.

There would be no problem with the Harvards as these were being manufactured locally by the Commonwealth Aircraft Corporation under licence, and called Wirraways. These were generally identical to our Harvard two-seater trainer, being a North American design with Pratt & Whitney Wasp engine and retractable undercarriage. It was thought that these would be available in sufficient quantities, but purchases from the USA would make up any deficiency.

In retrospect, the Empire Air Training Scheme was to have a great impact on the Australian aviation industry. The de Havilland Aircraft Company, for example, had established their first overseas subsidiary at Melbourne on 7 March 1927 to support the de Havilland aircraft already in service with Australian airlines. The company's first premises were a semi-derelict, 6,000-sq-ft warehouse, where about a dozen Moths were assembled and towed with their wings folded to the aerodrome at Essendon seven miles away. The following year the company began to grow, when the Cirrus Moth was adopted as a Primary trainer for the RAAF and the first Gipsy Moths arrived for civil customers.

In 1930 a new hangar and offices were built at Mascot Aerodrome, Sydney, in order to manufacture components instead of importing them from the UK. In 1935/36 the Australian company completed their first three wooden Moths for private owners. These were followed by orders from the Australian Government, not for aircraft but for propellers. Then in 1938 came an initial contract for 20 Tiger Moths, the metal fuselage framework being imported.

Against this background, wartime production of Tiger Moths made wholly in Australia finally totalled 1,085, several hundred of which went to South Africa and Rhodesia for the Empire Air Training Scheme. Apart from other aircraft, the de Havilland Company in Australia also manufactured 218 Mosquitoes—far more complicated aircraft—for use by the RAAF in the war against Japan.

More than half the Fairey Battles built were shipped to Australia and Canada for work under the Empire Scheme. Starting with the delivery of four which reached No. 1 Aircraft Park at Geelong, near Melbourne, at the end of April 1940, over 360 more were assembled in Australia. Thus the Empire Air Training Scheme galvanized the aviation industry in Australia, as it did in other participating countries, at a time when the industry itself was in its infancy. This was coupled with the construction of a network of aerodromes and outbuildings, of which 22 were required for the operation of the Scheme.

The provision of flying instructors and maintenance personnel was not expected to pose any difficulties, but the RAF agreed to augment such staff if necessary on loan. In a note from the Australian mission to the UK mission it was proposed that the following organization be set up in Australia: four Initial Training Schools, ten Service Flying Training Schools, and five Air Observer Schools, three Wireless Operator Air Gunner Schools, three Bombing and Gunnery Schools and one Air Navigation School. This was to be established and set up as soon as possible to service the following flying training programme: 336 pilots (Elementary Flying Training); 280 pilots (Advanced Flying Training); 184 observers; and 320 wireless operator/air gunners (these figures based on a monthly output).

It was also agreed that Australia should provide pupils to feed training schools in Canada as follows: pilots (Advanced Flying Training)—2 schools (80 pupils each four weeks); observers (32 pupils each four weeks)—1 school; WOP/AGs (72 pupils each four weeks)—1 school. The initial training for all these cadets would have been completed in Australia.

The above represented a mammoth task for Australia, and Fairburn pointed out that, despite the colossal work and sacrifice involved, Australia was prepared to accept it. Much to Riverdale's relief, a final agreement was signed. The RAF had an agreement with the RAAF and accepted a small quota of trained cadets annually for further training and service with the RAF. During these years Australia and New Zealand were considered too remote for Royal Air Force training. To a large extent Commonwealth and Dominion air forces, small as they were in the 1930s, were based on RAF format and practice, especially with regard to training and servicing procedure. Such liaison and co-operative practical experience provided the basis for the overseas training scheme, and the expansion of overseas air forces.

The RAAF was well represented in the Battle of Britain, providing 21 pilots who participated. Fourteen of those were killed: Sgt. K. G. Holland, POs C. C. Bennett, F. W. Cale, J. D. Crossman, B. M. McDonough, R. F. G. Miller and W. H. Millington, FO R. L. Glyde, Flt. Lts. F. W. Flood, P. C. Hughes, J. C. Kennedy, R. C. Reynell, S. C. Walch and L. C. Withall. Those who survived were POs A. N. Constantine, A. L. Hamilton, FO J. R. Cock, Flt. Lts. R. W. Bungey, C. G. C. Olive, R. M. Power and D. F. B. Sheen.

In 1940 a total of 153 aircrew were trained in Australia, compared to Canada's 520. This was no mean achievement when one considers that the Scheme was still under construction. Also, a large input of trained aircrew into the UK at this stage would have been difficult to absorb and surplus to requirements. Australia's output increased to 3,334 in 1941, 6,668 in 1942, 9,369 in 1943 and then decreased to 3,708 in 1944, when it became apparent that the war was reaching its final stage.

10. New Zealand

THIRTEEN DAYS AFTER Britain declared war on Germany, Prime Minister Chamberlain received a cable from the High Commissioner in New Zealand stating that: 'New Zealand as a nation is indissolubly bound up with the United Kingdom and other units of the Commonwealth. We stand or fall together in war or peace, defeat or victory. Defeat might mean the collapse of the British Commonwealth and domination of our land and people by foreign power. Ruthless treatment of Czechoslovakia and Austria conveys a warning. The distance from operations should not engender a false sense of security. Let there be no mistake. The future of New Zealand is at stake equally with that of Great Britain.'

The agreement of flying training was yet to come, and it was on this basis of total commitment that the New Zealand delegates approached the Riverdale mission in Canada in late 1939. The many problems arising in Canada have already been described. However, New Zealand's contribution towards pupils training in Canada was originally estimated at 28.5 million Canadian dollars, representing 8.8 per cent of the total budget—a very large amount for a small country!

The United Kingdom agreed to provide (a) 50 per cent of engines for all Moths required for initial equipment and immediate reserves; (b) all the Anson aircraft required for initial equipment, immediate reserve and wastage. New Zealand to pay half both cost and freight of Anson wings because Canada and Australia were manufacturing wings at their own expense; (c) spares for Moth engines and Anson engines and airframes; (d) the first 67 Harvard airframes and 84 Wasp engines; (e) packing and transportation charges to New Zealand of everything in (a), (b), (c) and (d), except for Anson wings which were at half cost; (f) the pay, allowances, non-effective benefits (which included pensions) and the transportation costs from New Zealand of pilots who completed their training in New Zealand, pay allowances and non-effective benefits being at RAF rates.

These concessions by the UK were the result of hard bargaining in Ottawa in order to achieve a signed agreement to enable the Empire Air

Training Scheme to get under way. Both Australia and New Zealand had insisted that some Service and Advanced training be carried out in their respective countries. Almost all pupils were New Zealanders, as the long sea journey prohibited the transfer of trainees from other sources.

The output of pilots in 1940 was 318, rising to 1,300 in 1941, with a total of 3,890 by the end of 1944. However, these figures reflect only those trained up to Operational Training Unit requirements in New Zealand itself. There were a great many others who, after Elementary Training, passed on to Canada for Service flying training and were included in Canada's figures.

New Zealand's war record stands on its own. The contribution made by the Navy, Army and Air Force was incalculable, but in no way overshadowed the immense value of its air training programme.

Postscript—bridging the gulf

THE RECENT WAR in the Gulf was the biggest explosion of high technology that the world has ever encountered. Thousands of sorties were flown around the clock by aircraft each costing as much as whole squadrons of their Second World War predecessors. Command of the air coupled with the ability to deliver precision weapons precisely on targets were vital factors in the conflict, during which the United States Air Force and the RAF operated alongside each other as they have done before.

The Gulf War happened to coincide with the 50th anniversary of American involvement in the training of British aircrews during the Second World War, as covered in the preceding chapters. It is particularly appropirate, therefore, that many veterans who trained under the Arnold Scheme visited air bases in the south-eastern states of America at that particular time. In true American fashion, those families who hosted them all those years ago, and veterans who helped in their training, joined in a series of reunions and other social events to mark the occasion.

This nostalgic trip is symbolic of the special relationship which exists between these two countries. It also represents the culmination of five years' work by an enterprising Arnoldonian, Norman Bate, who was on Course SE.42-F. His flying days began in 1941 and ended in 1982, after he sustained severe damage to his spine caused on the ejector seat ramp at Wymeswold airfield when acting as Auxiliary Adjutant/Meteor Pilot in 504 County of Nottingham Squadron, Royal Auxiliary Air Force. This injury also forced him to take early retirement from his job as Group Planning Officer for the Hosiery Division of Courtaulds.

So Bate, although to some extent incapacitated, had time on his hands. He had previously met Dr Gilbert S. Guinn of South Carolina, an American Professor of History who had contacted several hundred former RAF and American cadets while researching flying training. Guinn was able to trace Bate's host family connections from Georgia. Long ago Bate had promised to make sure that the story of their tremendous hospitality to a very large number of RAF cadets would eventually be told. Having renewed his contact with them, he decided to do what he could to keep that promise.

Delving into the Arnold Scheme soon presented Bate with a challenge. He discovered that over 7,800 cadets had entered the Scheme for pilot training and 1,200 for observer training. Also, there were no records of what had happened to these men following their induction, either in the United States or in the UK. The idea of gradually building a register of all those who had entered or were related to the Arnold Scheme motivated him, and in 1986, working from his home in Leicester, he officially announced the formation of The Arnold Scheme Register.

His commercial experience, particularly in marketing, enabled him to get his project off the ground. He began building class lists and tracing personal histories and soon found that most Arnoldians were keen to find former colleagues, donate material and spread the gospel. Material of both official and personal historical importance is being catalogued and preserved for future placement in Service archives.

Having lit the fuse on what initially had seemed an almost impossible task, Norman Bate found his attic office, known as 'The Eagle's Nest', overflowing with paperwork and historical treasures including photos, letters, documents and log books. The Register soon gave birth to a society of former cadets, with subscribing members receiving regular issues of *The Arnold News*, which provided detailed information concerning the growing list of contacts, happenings to former friends and reunions.

Within five years the Register had listed over half the 7,800 cadets who entered the Scheme, and the project developed substantially to combine the objectives of the Register with the interests of its membership. This is astonishing endorsement of the fact that Norman Bate and his associates are answering the need of graduates, those who were eliminated, and those who lost a husband, son, brother, father or friend.

Conducting research work and presenting it to members in reasonable format is funded by subscriptions. The service includes directing enquiries from men trained in the six British Flying Training Schools, the Towers Scheme and the Pan American Airways' Observer School. There is also a growing membership of Americans, all eager to be part of a project that is not simply a veterans' organization, and to establish their own trace-histories. Albany, Georgia, opened up its own project in 1991 based on the Register.

Appendix A: Contact addresses for Veterans' Associations

The Arnold Scheme Register
Norman Bates, 51 Henley Rd, Leicester LE3 9RD

The British Pensacola Veterans Association
Leon Armstrong, 47 Rutland Road, Wanstead,
London E11 2DY

No. 36. SFTS Penhold Association (Canada)
Jim Colburn, 53 Twelve Acre Crescent, Farnborough, Hants GU14 9PP

British Flying Training Schools:

No. 1 BFTS Terrell, Texas
Bert Allam, 5 Thornton Crescent, Old Coulsdon, Surrey CR5 1LJ

No. 2 BFTS Lancaster, California
Ken Clarkson, 2 Ribble Rd, Blackpool, Lancs FY1 4AA

No. 3 BFTS Miami, Oklahoma
Group Captain Deryk Maddox (RAF Ret'd), Cedar Lodge,
Sedgeford Rd, Docking, Kings Lynn, Norfolk PE31 3UT

No. 4 BFTS Mesa, Arizona
Captain Bill McCash AFM, 349b Dereham Rd, Norwich, Norfolk
NR2 3UT

No. 5 BFTS Clewiston, Florida
Ray Searle, 16 Marineside, East Drive, Bracklesham Bay, Sussex
PO20 8JJ

No. 6 BFTS Ponca City, Oklahoma
Tel: Norman Dear, 0775 820494

Appendix B: Bibliography

The Right of the Line by John Terraine (Hodder and Stoughton)

Carrier Pilot by Norman Hanson (Patrick Stephens)

Into the Teeth of the Tiger by Donald Lopez (Bantam Books)

By the Seat of Your Pants by Hugh Morgan (Newton)

The German Air Force by Asher Lee (Duckworth)

The Luftwaffe by John Killen (Frederick Muller)

Appendix C: Facts and statistics

N.B. All columns in Tables 1–9 show January figures unless indicated otherwise.

1. Training Schools in the UK, 1935-44

Type of School	1935	1936	1937	1938	1939	August 1939	1940	1941	1942	1943	1944
Central Flying School	1	1	1	1	1	1	1	2	2	1	1
Flying Instructor School								2	3	5	5
Initial Training Wing								9	15	16+1P	15+1P
EFTS	4	12	13	18	31	46(a)	20	20	23+1P	16+1P	15+1P
SFTS (b)	3	7	10	10	10	14	14	13+1P	11+1P	18+1P	18+1P
Navigation:											
Air Navigation School		1	1	1	1	1	1	1(c)	1	1	1
Air Observer School		1	1	1	2(d)	4	1		7	3	2
Air Observer Navigation School					4	9	8	4	1		
Armament:											
Air Armament School	1	1	1	2	2	2	2	1	1	1	1
Air Training School (or Camps)	3	2	4	7	9(e)	7	4				
Bombing & Gunnery School							7	7			
Central Gunnery School							1	1	1	1	1
Air Gunners School									7	7	10
(P) Advanced Flying Unit										12	14
(O) Advanced Flying Unit										5	8

Continued overleaf

1. Training Schools in the UK, 1935-44—continued

Type of School	1935	1936	1937	1938	1939	August 1939	1940	1941	1942	1943	1944
OTU:											
Coastal								3	6	10	10
Bomber (g)								11	16	22	23
Fighter								4	11	13	14
Army Co-operation									2	3	
AEAF											1
Transport											1
HCU:											
Coastal											1
Bomber										10	15
AEAF											1
Flying Training (Glider)										1	1
Signals:											
Electrical & Wireless Schools	1	1	1	1	2	2	2				
Signals School											
Radio School								4	9	10	13
Technical:											
Technical Training School	2	2	2	2	4	6	7	13	14	13 + 1P	13 + 1P

P = Polish

Notes:
(a) Five opened only in July and four in August.
(b) All figures are exclusive of No. 4 SFTS and up to 1939 inclusive are exclusive of RAF College, Cranwell. From 1940 onwards all figures are inclusive of Cranwell (No. 17 SFTS). Decrease in the number of SFTSs after 1941 is due to transfer to Canada.
(c) Half No. 1 School transferred to Canada.
(d) Includes temporary school at Acklington ex Leconfield.
(e) Includes temporary ATS at Leuchars.
(f) Converted to AOS, closed or transferred overseas.
(g) Includes No. 18 Polish.

2. Training Schools in Canada, 1941–4

Type of School	EATS				RAF Transferred				Canadian SUMMARY
	1941	1942	1943	1944	1941	1942	1943	1944	
Initial Training School	2	7	7	7	—	—	—	—	The Empire Air Training Scheme was renamed the British Commonwealth Air Training Plan on 3 June 1942. To produce well over 100,000 trained aircrew it required the following:
EFTS	16	22	15*	16	—	2	5	5	32 Elementary Flying Training Schools; 29 Service Flying Training Schools; 11 Air Observer Schools; 1 Central Nav School; 5 Air Nav Schools; 11 Bombing and Gunnery Schools; 1 Central Flying School; 3 Flying Instructor Schools; 1 Instrument Flying School; 1 Naval Gunnery School; 2 General Reconnaissance Schools; 10 Operational Training Units; 4 Wireless Schools
SFTS	8	16	16	19	3	8	10	10	
Air Observer School	4	10	9	8	1	—	—	—	
Air Navigation School	—	1	—	—	—	3	2	2	
Bombing and Gunnery School	3	9	9	11**	—	1	1	1	
General Reconnaissance School	—	—	1	1	—	1	1	1	
Wireless School	2	4	4	4	—	—	—	—	
OTU	—	—	1	2	—	2	4	4	
Central Flying School	1	1	1	1	—	—	—	—	
Flying Instructor School	—	—	3	3	—	—	—	—	
General Navigation School	1	1	1	1	—	—	—	—	

* The reduction in the number of EFTS from 22 to 15 during 1942 was brought about by the conversion of a number of half-size schools to full size.

** Includes a Naval Air Gunners School.

3. **Training Schools in South Africa, 1941–4**

Type of School	JATP				RAF Transferred				South African			
	1941	1942	1943	1944	1941	1942	1943	1944	1941	1942	1943	1944
Initial Training School	—	—	—	—	—	—	—	—	1	1	1	1
Elementary Air Observer School	—	—	1	1	—	—	—	—	—	—	—	—
EFTS	2	7	7	7	—	—	—	—	—	—	—	—
SFTS	1	5	7	7	—	—	—	—	—	—	—	—
Combined Air Observer Navigation and Gunnery School	1	5	7	7	2	—	—	—	1	—	—	—
General Reconnaissance School	—	1	1	1	1	—	—	—	1	—	—	—
Signals School	—	1	1	1	—	—	—	—	1	—	—	—
OTU	—	—	—	2	—	—	—	—	—	—	—	—
Central Flying School	—	1	1	1	—	—	—	—	1	—	—	—

4. Training Schools in Australia, 1941–4

Type of School	EATS				Australia			
	1941	1942	1943	1944	1941	1942	1943	1944
Initial Training School	5	5	5	6	–	–	–	–
EFTS	7	11	6*	7	1	1	1	–
SFTS	2	7	5*	6	1	1	1	–
Air Observer School	1	2	2	} 7**	–	–	–	–
Air Navigation School	1	2	2		–	–	–	–
Bombing and Gunnery School	1	2	3		–	–	–	–
General Reconnaissance School	–	–	–	–	1	1	1	1
Wireless Air Gunner School	1	3	3	3	–	–	–	–
OTU	–	–	–	–	–	–	5	6
Central Flying School	–	–	–	–	1	1	1	1

Remarks

* The reduction in the number of EFTSs from 11 to 6 and of SFTS from 7 to 5 during 1942 was due to a merging of schools and did not involve reduction in overall capacity.

** These 7 schools were re-organized in December 1943, and converted into 3 Combined Air Observer, Navigation and Gunnery Schools and 1 Air Gunnery School.

5. Training Schools in New Zealand, 1941–4

Type of School	EATS				New Zealand			
	1941	1942	1943	1944	1941	1942	1943	1944
Initial Training School	1	1	1	1	–	–	–	–
EFTS	3	4	3*	3	–	–	–	–
SFTS	3	3	2*	2	–	–	–	–
General Reconnaissance School	–	–	–	–	1	1	1	1
OTU	–	–	–	–	–	2	2	2
Central Flying School	–	–	–	–	–	1	1	1

Remarks

* The reduction in the number of EFTS from 4 to 3 and of SFTS from 3 to 2 during 1942 was due to a merging of schools and did not involve reduction in overall capacity.

6. Training Schools in Southern Rhodesia, 1941–4

Type of School	EATS			
	1941	1942	1943	1944
Initial Training School	1	1	1	1
EFTS	2	4	4	4
SFTS	2	4	4	4
Bombing, Gunnery and Navigation School	–	1	1	1
Central Flying School	–	1	1	1

7. Training Schools in Kenya, 1941–4

Type of School	No. of Units			
	1941	1942	1943	1944
Training Flights	1	–	–	–
OTU's	–	1	3	–

Remarks

It was originally intended that this training flight of the Kenya AAU should be replaced by an EFTS at Eastleigh and that an SFTS should be formed at Nakuru. These two schools were, however, formed in South Africa instead of Kenya.

8. Training Schools in India, 1941–4

Type of School	No. of Units			
	1941	1942	1943	1944
EFTS	2	2	2	2
SFTS	1	1	1	1
OTU	–	–	2	2
Air Navigation School	–	–	1	–
Wireless School	–	–	1	–
Air Observer School	–	–	1	–
Air Gunners School	–	–	1	1
Flying Instructors Flight	–	–	1	1
General Reconnaissance and Air Navigation School	–	–	–	1
Air Fighting Training Unit	–	–	–	1
Heavy Bomber Conversion Flight	–	–	–	–
Refresher Flying Unit	–	–	–	1

Remarks

Training at these schools was mainly for the Indian Air Force.

India: Not covered in this book—details for general information only.

9. Training Schools for RAF personnel in the USA, 1941–4

Type of School	Number of Schools			
	1941	1942	1943	1944
British Flying Training Schools (All-through Training Scheme)	—	6(a)	6	5
US Army Air Corps Schools (Arnold Scheme)	—	(b) { 5 (Primary) / 2 (Basic Flying) / 3 (Advanced Flying)	4 (Advanced Flying) (f)	—
US Naval Air Service Schools (Towers Scheme)	—	(c) { 1 (Pilots) / 1 (WOP/AG) (Pilots & W/Ops.) (AGs Advanced)	1 (Pilots) (g) / 1 (Pilots Advanced)	1 (Pilots) / 1 (Pilots Advanced)
Refresher Schools	—	3(d)	—	—
Pan-American Airways School, Miami	—	1(e)	—	—

Notes

(a) Civilian-operated schools under British contract providing a 9-weeks' elementary and 18-weeks' advanced course of instruction for RAF pupils. Pupils trained to a standard equivalent to that attained at the end of the normal SFTS course.

(b) Schools allotted for the flying training of RAF pupils. 9-weeks' course at each type of school. Pupils trained to a standard equivalent to that attained at the end of the normal SFTS course plus the equivalent of the conversion-to-type portion of RAF OTU stage.

(c) Schools allotted for the training of RAF pilots and WOP/AGs and FAA pilots. Complete course of approximately 6 months' duration both for pilots and WOP/AGs.

(d) Provided refresher training for American nationals recruited for service in the RAF.

(e) Provided a 15-week course of *ab initio* training of observers.

(f) These 4 schools closed in February 1943, following the closure of the Primary and Basic Flying Schools in October and December 1942 respectively.

(g) WOP/AG training ceased in October 1942.

10. Output of pilots and other aircrew—Dominion sources

Type and year of output	Canada	Australia	New Zealand	South Africa	Southern Rhodesia	Total
1940						
Pilots	240	60	318	–	110	728
Navigators	112	39	–	–	–	151
WOP/AGs and AGs	168	54	–	–	–	222
Total	520	153	318	–	110	1,101
1941						
Pilots	9,637	1,367	1,292	341	1,284	13,921
Navigators	2,884	681	–	629	23	4,217
WOP/AGs and AGs	4,132	1,296	–	–	110	5,538
Total	16,653	3,344	1,292	970	1,417	23,676
1942						
Pilots	14,135	3,033	943	1,529	1,666	21,306
Navigators	7,404	1,375	–	2,541	237	11,557
Air Bombers	1,742	–	–	170	–	1,912
WOP/AGs and AGs	6,896	2,280	–	–	387	9,563
Total	30,177	6,688	943	4,240	2,290	44,338
1943						
Pilots	15,894	3,869	836	2,309	2,083	24,991
Navigators	8,144	1,662	–	3,250	239	13,295
Air Bombers	6,445	–	–	918	–	7,363
WOP/AGs and AGs	8,695	3,838	–	–	419	12,952
Total	39,178	9,369	836	6,477	2,741	58,601

Continued overleaf

10. Output of pilots and other aircrew-Dominion sources—*continued*

Type and year of output	Canada	Australia	New Zealand	South Africa	Southern Rhodesia	Total
1944 (to 30 September)						
Pilots	8,807	1,684	502	2,025	1,188	14,206
Navigators	7,953	696	–	2,403	180	11,232
Air Bombers	5,131	–	–	742	–	5,873
WOP/AGs and AGs	7,998	1,328	–	–	309	9,635
Total	29,889	3,708	502	5,170	1,677	40,946
TOTAL	116,417	23,262	3,891	16,857	8,235	168,662

Summary

Pilots	75,152
Navigators	40,452
Air Bombers	15,148
WOP/AGs	37,910
GRAND TOTAL	168,662 to 30 September 1944

Remarks

1. The country is that in which the training was carried out and does not indicate the trainees' nationality.
2. The figures are those for outputs from the SFTS or its equivalent, i.e. an Australian trainee who did his EFTS training in Australia and his SFTS in Canada would be shown under Canada.
3. The figures include trainees retained to meet the Dominions' own local requirements.

Appendix D:
Training aircraft used under the Scheme

De Havilland Tiger Moth

THIS TWO-SEAT elementary trainer constructed in composite wood and metal with fabric covering became one of the world's most famous training aircraft. Over 4,000 were built for the RAF, including 3,433 built by Morris Motors at Cowley, and a further 2,949 in Canada, New Zealand and Australia for the Commonwealth Air Training Scheme. Wartime production in Australia alone totalled 1,085, and several hundred of these were sent to South Africa and Rhodesia for the Empire Air Training Scheme.

This light little biplane was developed from the Gipsy Moth DH60, which had captured the imagination of the public at large throughout the world by making long-distance flights, including those by Amy Johnson. A number of DH60T Moths had been supplied to overseas air forces, and there were over 150 of them employed by the RAF for training purposes during the late 1920s. By 1931 the RAF was forced to replace the ageing Avro 504, and the Moth successfully competed against the Avro Tutor and the Hawker Tomtit for the contract. The modified DH60T—it differed in having staggered and swept-back wings (the latter to allow ease of exit by parachute from the front cockpit)— was reclassified as the DH82. The Mark II version of this trainer, powered by a Gipsy Major 130-hp engine, became the DH82a, the machine in which so many young cadets learned to fly during the Second World War. The Canadian version, built by de Havilland Aircraft of Canada and designated DH82C, had a sliding plastic canopy for weather conditions.

It was difficult not to have a love affair with a Tiger Moth, particularly if one savoured the thrill of flying a light, fully aerobatic, sensitive machine. She demanded perfect co-ordination and a gentle touch when making the sky a playground, or settling down to earth on three points. But she could cope with the ham-fisted and allowed the uninitiated a great deal of licence. It is fair to say that most people should have been able to fly a Tiger Moth, but few could fly it accurately.

The maximum speed of the Tiger Moth Mk II was 109.5 mph at sea level, and she had a service ceiling of 13,600 ft, with an initial rate of climb of 637 ft/min.

Hawker Hart Trainer

The genius of Sydney Camm, Chief Designer of Hawker Aircraft Ltd, became apparent with the emergence of the Hawker Hart light day bomber and a wide range of Hart variants in the late 1920s. The Hart became standard equipment for the RAF, and in 1932 the Service was looking for a training version for future pilots of Hart variants. Camm responded by utilizing an early Audax, and converting it into a dual-controlled advanced trainer. Except for the removal of the gunner's Scarff ring on the rear cockpit and the installation of dual controls, it differed little from the day bomber.

By 1933 the Hart Trainer had assumed its role and began superseding other trainers, including the Atlas Trainer and the Siskin. A number were shipped overseas for service with the RAF and caught the eye of Empire air forces, while others were supplied to squadrons of the Auxiliary Air Force. At this time the RAF was rapidly expanding its pilot training programme, and Hart Trainers were given to University Air Squadrons and to Reserve Flying Training Schools of the RAFVR. During the late thirties, many RAF pilots who participated in the first phase of the Second World War had graduated on Hart Trainers.

The Hart Trainer and its variants (Hinds and Audaxes) were used in South Africa under the Joint Air Training Plan, but were eventually replaced by Masters and Harvards. This beautiful biplane, which made aerobatics a delight, inspired Sydney Camm to create the famous Hawker family of aircraft, which bore similar appearances in outline from the Hurricane to the Tornado. The Hart family was powered by 16 versions of the famous Rolls-Royce Kestrel engine, each designed for the particular requirement. Such co-ordination between aircraft designer and engine manufacturer was a remarkable achievement in those days!

The Hart (Variants) training aircraft used in South Africa were powered by a 510–640 hp Rolls-Royce Kestrel 1B engine giving a maximum speed of 165 mph at 3,000 ft. Its service ceiling was 22,800 ft, with an initial climb rate of 1,500 ft/min.

Fairey Battle

The prototype Fairey Battle first flew in March 1936 and during the late thirties, when the RAF expansion programme was well under way, it emerged as a front-line light bomber. This rugged and attractive machine respresented a major advance over the Hawker Hart and Hind open-cockpit biplanes, and was scheduled for mass production. Unfortunately, her operational career was curtailed because she was underpowered and vulnerable to German fighters. A Hurricane pilot flying one for the first time said it was 'like flying a football pitch around the sky'.

A cynical remark, perhaps, bearing in mind that the Battle was the first RAF machine to shoot down a German aircraft in the Second World War, and that the first VCs won by the RAF were awarded to Battle crews for their suicidal attack on the Maastricht bridges on 12 May 1940. Following the German occupation of Northern Europe, the Fairey Battle was withdrawn from front-line operational service and seconded for training duties.

Two hundred Battle Trainers were built which required fairly extensive changes to the fuselage structure to accommodate two pilot cockpits. The first appeared in 1940, and instructors found it rather strange to be sitting so far from the front of the aircraft, but they described it as a fine aircraft to fly. Its variable-pitch propeller, retractable undercarriage, flaps and Sperry instruments provided a fine platform for instructing those going on to more advanced machines. Thereafter, the Battle and its variants played a valuable role in training aircrew of all categories. About 800 were shipped to Canada under the Commonwealth Air Training Plan and another 400 to Australia. Some 266 Battles were built as target towers, and total production reached over 2,400 (many of which were built by Austin Motors).

Avro Anson

A well-mannered and forgiving old lady, nicknamed 'Faithful Annie' by the RAF, she became the work-horse of the air for air forces during the Second World War and for several years after. Her duties included general reconnaissance, communications, ambulance, training of all types of aircrew, transport, and three-and-a-half years' service with coastal squadrons. On 5 September 1939 an Anson of No. 500 Squadron, flying from Dettling, made the first RAF attack of the war on a German U-boat. Later, in June 1940, three Ansons were attacked over the English Channel by a swarm of Bf 109s. The engagement was no hatchet job for the Germans, because the Ansons shot down two 109s and damaged another!

The Anson came from a famous stable, A. V. Roe Ltd, whose offspring included the 504K and Lancaster, and later the Shackleton, Lincoln, York and Vulcan 'V' bomber. In 1935 the RAF was looking for a general reconnaissance aircraft and became interested in the Avro 652, capable of carrying six passengers, which had gone into service with Imperial Airways. Responding to the RAF's requirements, Avro developed the 652A which became known as the Anson. The RAF ordered 170 of them for GR duties and in 1936 converted a number of them for pilot training.

The Anson Trainer, fitted with flaps and a modified windscreen, did not go into production until 1939, when 1,500 were ordered. Meanwhile, many GR Anson Is had been fitted with turrets and were serving with Air Gunnery Schools. On 18 December 1939, when the vast Empire Flying Training Plan was inaugurated, the Anson was selected as one of the standard trainers for schools in Canada. Two hundred and twenty-three British-built Anson Mks III and IV, fitted with Jacobs or Wright radial engines, were shipped across the Atlantic. Subsequently, over 2,800 were built in Canada, over 700 saw service in South Africa during the Joint Air Training Plan, and it was used extensively by the South African Air force for GR duties and aircrew training. Southern Rhodesia also used Ansons, including the post-war Anson T.20 with new metal wings and tailplane and a transparent nose for bomb-aiming.

Over 11,000 Ansons were built during 17 years of continuous production in the UK and Canada. There were several variants and many modifications with regard to specific requirements. Hydraulically operated flaps and undercarriages, for example, proved a great blessing—especially after having to wind the undercarriage up and down by hand in the early Mk Is!

The Avro 652A, Anson Mk I, employed two 350-hp Armstrong Siddeley Cheetah IX engines giving a maximum speed of 173 mph at 7,000 ft. Its service ceiling was 19,500 ft, with an initial rate of climb of 750 ft/min.

Airspeed Oxford

The Airspeed Oxford was the RAF's first twin-engined monoplane advanced trainer, and was affectionately known as the 'Ox-box'. Airspeed Ltd, who designed and constructed the machine, was founded in 1934 and based at Portsmouth. The company, working in partnership with shipbuilders Swan Hunter and Wigham Richardson, had previously built the civilian Airspeed Envoy, an eight-passenger, twin-engined development of the Airspeed Courier.

In 1935 the Air Ministry was looking for an advanced twin-engine trainer and expressed interest in the Envoy. Airspeed submitted a tender to meet Specification T. 23/36 and was granted an initial order of 136 aircraft. This machine became the Oxford Mk I, powered by two Armstrong Siddeley Cheetax X engines, and the prototype first flew on 19 June 1937.

The Central Flying School took delivery of the first production Oxfords in November 1937, marking the beginning of a long and successful career for the 'Ox-box'. Between 1937 and 1945 8,751 of them were built by Airspeed and sub-contractors de Havilland, Standard Motors and Percival Aircraft. The original Oxford Mk Is were used for all aspects of aircrew training, including gunnery, for which an Armstrong Whitworth dorsal turret was fitted.

The Oxford Mk II was used extensively for pilot training overseas, but the machine had problems in South Africa due to the climatic conditions deteriorating its wooden structure, and was replaced by the Avro Anson towards the end of the war. The Mk II was powered by two 370 hp Armstrong Siddeley Cheetah X engines, giving it a maximum speed of

188 mph, a climb rate of 960 ft/min, and a service ceiling of 21,000 ft. The Mk V, which was similar to the Mk II, was given extra power through the installation of two 450-hp Pratt & Whitney Wasp Junior radial engines.

Miles Magister and Master II

The Miles Aircraft Company was formed by the brothers F. G. and G. H. Miles and was formerly known as Phillips and Powis Aircraft Limited. The brothers had previously built up a reputation as designers, beginning with the Cirrus-Hawk—£395 list price—of 1932, and including the Hawk Major, Hawk Speed Six and the Hawk Trainer (working with other aircraft manufacturers). The Miles Company, based at Woodley, Reading, began manufacturing military aircraft in 1936.

The Miles Magister, known in the RAF as 'the Maggie', entered service in September 1937 when it was introduced to the Central Flying School. Based on the Hawk Trainer, and of all-wooden construction, this new elementary trainer of the low-wing monoplane type, powered by a 130-hp DH Gipsy Major I engine, partnered the Tiger Moth in giving many RAF cadet pilots their first taste of the air.

A number of cadets did their Grading Course on 'the Maggie' before being posted overseas for flying training. Faster than the Tiger Moth, it had a leisurely landing speed of only 45 mph. Fully aerobatic, it introduced fledgeling pilots to the novelty of trailing-edge split flaps at an early stage. A total of 1,293 were built between 1937 and 1941, some being exported for *ab initio* training overseas. It had a maximum speed at 1,000 ft of 145 mph and a service ceiling of 18,000 ft.

The Master II evolved from the Master I, which was based on the earlier Miles Kestrel trainer. The Kestrel, having a remarkable speed of 295 mph, aroused interest at the 1937 RAF display but failed to meet Specification T.6/36. The Air Ministry decided to adopt a modified version which became known as the Master I. This advanced trainer first flew in 1938 and was extensively used during the early years of the Second World War to convert pilots on to Spitfires and Hurricanes. Powered by a Rolls-Royce 715 hp Kestrel XXX, the total number produced reached 900.

The Master II advanced trainer first flew in November 1939, and was powered by a Bristol Mercury XX radial, giving it a maximum speed of 243 mph, a service ceiling of 28,000 ft, and an initial rate of climb of 2,000 ft/min. A number of these were sent to South Africa as part of the Joint Air Training Plan and others to the air forces of Egypt, Portugal and Turkey. It had problems in South Africa due to the climate warping the wooden structure, and was replaced by the Harvard.

Miles Masters were employed at Advanced Flying Training Units in the UK for acclimatization and further training of single-engine pilots who returned home after graduating overseas. It was also used as a glider tug, which led to the development of the Miles Martinet, designed specifically for target towing.

Consolidated PBY Catalina

The Catalina or 'Cat', as she was known in the RAF, served throughout the Second World War, carrying out many functions including those of night bomber, torpedo-carrier, long-range reconnaissance, convoy protection and anti-submarine weapon, advanced trainer, air–sea rescue, communications, and as a glider tug. She was one of the most successful flying-boats in aviation history and the most numerous. Apart from her operational and other duties with the RAF, she was employed as an advanced trainer under the Towers Scheme in America to train RAF cadets, and was the only real operational twin-engined aircraft to be flown by RAF cadet pilots during the war.

The prototype first flew in March 1935 and embodied some revolutionary features of flying-boat design which immediately improved performance. The parasol wing constructed on the basis of a cantilever wing eliminated a mass of struts and bracing wires inherent in flying-boat design (although two small struts were, in fact, mounted between wing and hull on each side). Furthermore, stabilizing floats were introduced which retracted in flight to form the wingtips. Initial trials were so successful that the US Navy immediately recognized its potential and the Catalina entered squadron service in 1937; a year later there were 14 operational squadrons!

There were many variations of the Catalina, designed for specific duties, but the PBY-5A amphibian version (flown by RAF cadet pilots) accommodated a crew of seven. Two 1,200-hp Pratt & Whitney Twin Wasp engines gave it a maximum speed of 196 mph, and it took four-and-a-half minutes to climb to 5,000 ft. Its maximum range at critical altitude was 3,100 miles and service ceiling 18,200 ft.

Consolidated merged with Vultee in March 1943, when the Consolidated Vultee Aircraft Corporation was formed, and aircraft were then designed and manufactured under the Consolidated Vultee label.

Harvard AT-6

Many ex-fighter pilots throughout the world look back on their Harvard experience with nostalgia. For those who stepped out of a Tiger Moth into the front cockpit of a Harvard for the first time, the contrast could come as a shock. Sitting up high in the roomy office, facing a mass of instruments and the big radial Pratt & Whitney, feeling the grip of the control column and the toe brakes, you were wary of touching any lever in case the undercarriage folded!

However, its qualities as an advanced training machine were such that over 20,000 Harvards were built in various countries. Fathered by North American Aviation Inc, it evolved from the fixed-undercarriage BT-9 Yale, recognized as being under-powered and difficult to handle by student pilots. Nevertheless, a number of Yales were used in Canada during the early days of the Empire Training Scheme before being superseded by the more advanced AT-7A.

North American, incorporated in Delaware in 1928, had been engaged solely in the design and manufacture of military aircraft under contract since 1934. Apart from its success with the Harvard, it became famous for its Mustang single-seater fighter, and for the Mitchell medium bomber. In 1941 a new modern production plant was established at Dallas, Texas, for the manufacture of the entire trainer series, including the series of Harvards which varied mainly in matters of equipment. The British Harvard versions, for example, were fitted with British instruments, radio, shoulder harness, etc.

The AT-6A (SNJ-3) was built in Canada under licence by Noorduyn Aviation Ltd, and was designated the Harvard IIB. Canadian-built Harvards were also delivered to the US Army as AT-16s. The AT-6A was powered by a 600-hp Pratt & Whitney R-1340-49 Wasp piston radial engine, giving it a top speed at 5,000 ft of 210 mph. It had a service ceiling of 24,000 ft and took 7.4 min to climb to 10,000 ft.

Harvards were universally employed throughout the overseas air training projects and replaced the faster Miles Master II in the Joint Air Training Plan in South Africa because of climatic conditions which affected the Master's wooden structure. They were also used in the UK for Service Flying Training (including bombing and gunnery), and immediately post-war to train students from occupied countries including Holland and Turkey.

Fairchild Cornell PT-19, PT-26

Sherman Fairchild founded his company in 1925, but it was taken over by the Aviation Corporation in 1929. Sherman left in 1931 but remained with Kreider-Reisner, a subsidiary company. This company was renamed the Fairchild Aircraft Corporation, and in 1940, when the Cornell primary trainer was being manufactured, the company was renamed the Fairchild Engine and Airplane Corporation.

The Cornell was a low-wing cantilever monoplane flown by RAF cadets in the USA, Canada and S. Rhodesia. It originated from Sherman's M-62, a low-wing trainer which had interested the USAAC. The Army purchased a large number of these open-cockpit, two-seater PT-19As, powered by a 175-hp Ranger L-440-1 inverted inline engine. Having a maximum speed of 132 mph, it took 19.4 min to reach 13,000 ft, with a service ceiling of 15,300 ft. It was equipped with hydraulic brakes, and the steerable tailwheel could be disconnected to become fully swivelling for taxiing.

The Cornell was a large machine compared with British primary trainers, and was fully aerobatic and easy to handle. The PT-26, with an enclosed cockpit, was adopted by the Canadian Government as a standard primary trainer for the Commonwealth Air Training Plan. A further 670 closed-cockpit versions, designated PT-23A, were ordered through Lend-Lease. The majority of these were built by Fleet Aircraft Ltd of Toronto, Canada.

Vultee BT-13 Valiant

The contract for the well-liked Vultee BT-13 Valiant was awarded in September 1939. Vultee Aircraft Inc, who had been created that year at Nashville, Tennessee, had designed and built their Model 54 as a private venture. The USAAC recognized its potential as a basic trainer and the Valiant emerged. This large, tandem cockpit, fixed-undercarriage monoplane became a standard basic trainer and over 11,500 were built, including several variants.

The Valiant, affectionately known as the 'Vultee Vibrator', was designed specifically as a basic trainer. The American system of pilot training included three phases: Primary, Basic and Advanced. Basic training constituted an intermediate stage between Primary and Advanced training. The BT-13A Valiant was used by the BFTSs, Arnold and Towers Schemes for this intermediate stage of training.

RAF pilot training, however, had no intermediate stage. In early 1943 the Valiant was phased out at RAF civilian-operated schools in the USA. Having completed the primary stage on Stearmans or Cornells, cadets moved directly on to the AT-6A Harvard. The Americans were not influenced by this decision, and British cadets training in the Towers and Arnold Schemes had to do Basic training as part of the American system.

In 1943 the Vultee Aircraft Company merged with Consolidated, and the basic trainer was designated the Consolidated Vultee Valiant. The Valiant, a big machine by British standards, had no bad habits and was pleasant to fly. The BT-13A was powered by a 450-hp Pratt & Whitney R-985-AN-1 Wasp Junior engine providing a maximum speed of 180 mph. It had a service ceiling of 21,650 ft and could climb to 10,000 ft in 9.2 min.

Boeing Stearman PT-13, PT-17, PT-27

When the first experimental DH 71 Tiger Moth monoplane racer made its first flight in June 1927, Lloyd Stearman had formed his company in Venice, California, and shortly afterwards moved it to Wichita, Kansas. Here, as part of the United Aircraft and Transport Corporation, the company built a number of private and commercial aircraft, including mail delivery and training aeroplanes. The US Government dismantled the UATC in 1934, and the Stearman Aircraft Company became a subsidiary of the Boeing Airplane Co.

At this time Lloyd Stearman had developed his X70, powered by a Wright 225-hp radial engine, designed to attack the USAAC market. In 1936 the Army gave him an order for 26 machines, to be powered by Lycoming R-680-5 engines. Hence the first Service training version of the Stearman Model 75—known as the PT-13—was born. This was followed by the PT-17, powered by the Continental R-670-5 piston radial engine, which became the machine used by most RAF cadets in the USA. The PT-27 was specially built for use in Canada. It had the same engine and airframe as the PT-17, but was fitted with cockpit enclosures and heating, night-flying equipment, a blind-flying hood and additional instrumentation.

The Stearman was a considerably larger and more powerful machine than the DH Tiger Moth—rather like stepping out of an MG Midget into a Buick. It required firmer and more positive handling than the Moth, and its additional power was conducive to aerobatics. Those who had done a Grading Course in the UK, either on Tiger Moths or Miles Magisters, before going overseas quickly discovered that the Stearman had toe brakes and a tailwheel—hence, cadets had to master the technique of avoiding or coping with ground loops.

The maximum speed of the Stearman PT-17 at ground level was 135 mph, and it had a service ceiling of 13,200 ft, taking 17.3 min to climb to 10,000 ft.

Cessna AT-17 Crane and UC-78 Bobcat

During the depression of the early 1930s, the Cessna Aircraft Company of Wichita, Kansas, was building gliders and racing aircraft in its struggle for survival. Despite the closure of its main factory, Cessna built the T-50, a commercial five-seater cabin monoplane. In the late thirties both the USAAF and RCAF became interested in this machine as a potential multi-engined conversion trainer.

In 1941 the T-50 was converted to Service requirements, initially for the RCAF. Designated the Crane, it was powered by two 225-hp Jacobs engines. The USAAF version was powered by two Lycoming R-680-9 engines and was known as the AT-17 (later UC-78) Bobcat. Both aircraft were used as Advanced trainers and flown by RAF cadets in the USA and Canada.

The Crane and the Bobcat were virtually identical machines—except for variations of power-plant—and were made in large numbers. They had no particular vices, and were pleasant to fly and easy to handle. The AT-17 had a maximum speed at sea level of 179 mph and an initial rate of climb of 1,525 ft/min, with a service ceiling of 15,000 ft.

Index